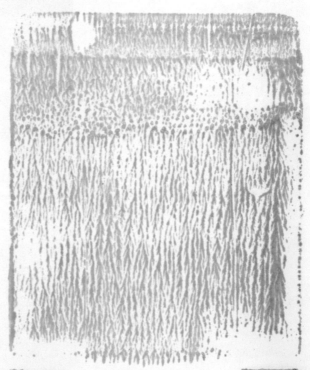

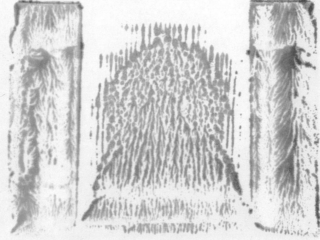

Chemistry of Solids

CHEMISTRY OF SOLIDS

An Introduction to the Chemistry
of Solids and Solid Surfaces

Andrew K. Galwey
B.Sc., Ph.D., D.I.C.

Lecturer in Physical Chemistry
The Queen's University of Belfast

London
CHAPMAN AND HALL LTD
1967

© 1967 Andrew K. Galwey
First published 1967 by
Chapman and Hall Ltd
11 New Fetter Lane, London, EC4
Printed in Great Britain by
Butler & Tanner Ltd, Frome and London

Distribution in the U.S.A.
by Barnes & Noble, Inc.

Contents

PREFACE   *page* vii

1 CLASSIFICATION OF SOLIDS   1
  1. Introduction. The Solid State   1
  2. Classification of Solids   4
    Molecular crystals   5
    Covalent crystals   9
    Ionic crystals   16
    Metals   22
    The hydrogen bond   28

2 THE CRYSTAL LATTICE   30
  1. Properties of Crystals   30
  2. Quantitative Examination of Crystals   36
  3. X-ray Examination of Crystals   50
  4. Structure of Solid Substances   58
    Ionic solids   58
    Silicates   66
    Organic polymers   74
  5. 'Semi-Solid' States of Matter   78

3 BAND THEORY OF SOLIDS: DISLOCATIONS,
  DEFECTS AND IMPURITIES IN SOLIDS   82
  1. Band Theory of Solids   82
  2. Departure of Solids from Ideal Behaviour   91
    Dislocations   91
    Defects   95
  3. Electrical Conductivity of Ionic Solids   98
  4. Impurity Systems   100
    Non-stoichiometry   101
    Foreign impurity atoms or ions   104
  5. Solid Solutions   106

4 THE CHEMISTRY OF SOLID SURFACES *page* 111
  1. Solid Surfaces 111
    Direct study of the properties of solid surfaces 113
  2. Adsorption of a Single Gas by a Solid 118
    Adsorption isotherms 121
    Physical adsorption 124
    Chemisorption 126
  3. Solid Catalysts 137
    Industrial catalysts 139
    Mechanisms of catalytic reactions 141
    Chemisorption bonds in catalysis 153
    Catalysis in liquids 154
  4. The Solid-Liquid Interface 156

5 REACTIONS OF SOLIDS 163
  1. Reactions of a Single Solid 165
    Thermal decomposition reactions 166
    Kinetic characteristics of solid phase decomposition reactions 170
    Initial deceleratory reaction 182
    Arrhenius parameters 182
    Arrhenius activation energy 183
    Photolysis of solids 184
    Self-heating and explosion 186
  2. Gas-Solid Reactions 189
    Powder reactants 193
  3. Liquid-Solid Reactions 194
  4. Solid-Solid Reactions 195

BIBLIOGRAPHY 201

INDEX 205

Preface

Some years ago it was possible for a single author to write a General Textbook of Physical Chemistry. More recently the rapid development of science, as reflected in the large volumes of new information and concepts which are becoming available with every passing year, has made the task of anyone writing such a general textbook very much more difficult. A potential author is now faced with various alternatives, which include the possibilities that either the size of such a book must increase to unmanageable proportions or a degree of specialization must be introduced into the choice of subject matter or selected topics must be treated at less advanced levels. There is, however, a different approach to the provision of student textbooks through replacement of a general survey by monographs devoted to specialist topics written by authors who have particular interest in, or who may be active in developing the particular aspect of the subject about which they are writing. The present volume is intended as a monograph of this latter type.

It has recently become fashionable to provide arguments to justify the publication of a particular volume. I consider that such a justification is not important or even particularly necessary since any rapidly developing scientific subject must reflect changing ideas through a changing literature. The ultimate success or otherwise of a particular book will be apparent, in the fullness of time, to the two parties, the author and the publisher, responsible for its conception and appearance in the market. However, the dictates of pattern are forceful so perhaps it may be reasonable to define the so-called 'gaps' which it is intended to fill. Accounts of that part of chemistry which is concerned with the properties of solids are widely scattered in the literature, some aspects being described only in advanced texts, so that it has seemed worth while to prepare a short review between a single pair of covers.

The present monograph was originally conceived as a text covering the subject matter contained in a course of five lectures entitled 'Crystal Chemistry' given by the author as part of the main B.Sc. (Pass degree) in Chemistry at the Queen's University of Belfast. No suitable textbook giving adequate coverage of the topics included in this course, and those in the subsequent honours course (these include properties of crystals and lattices, theories of the solid state, types of crystals, defects in perfect crystals, etc.) appeared to be available. It was also apparent that the kinetics of homogeneous and of chain reactions have been extensively covered in student textbooks but the different, yet often relatively simple principles which underlie the kinetic characteristics of reactions of solids have received scant attention; this topic has also been included.

The amount of mathematical knowledge required for an understanding of the arguments in this monograph has been kept to a minimum, and, throughout the book, emphasis is on the presentation of verbal explanations of the principles underlying the characteristic behaviour which is being considered. It has been assumed, however, that the reader has some knowledge of other branches of physical chemistry (chemical kinetics, elementary quantum mechanics, etc.) so that this monograph may be treated as a chapter in the study of the wider subject, chemistry.

The second half of the book provides a general introduction to the chemistry of reactions involving solids and it is hoped that this may prove useful to students intending to undertake research on solid phase or solid surface phase reactions before specializing on some particular topic. Examples quoted in the text of Chapters 4 and 5 often consider particular aspects of published research and some references to these papers have been included in the Bibliography to assist any reader who wishes to follow up some aspect of a topic mentioned, or read the argument presented by the authors themselves.

It is my very great pleasure to record my thanks to people who have helped me to prepare this book. To avoid any distinction in the warmth of my thanks I will mention them in the order in which they provided their very much appreciated assistance. Firstly I wish to express my thanks to Professors P. W. M. Jacobs and C. Kemball, F.R.S., for their parts in awakening an interest in the chemistry of solids and surfaces, and in directing and encouraging my initial attempts in original research. I also thank Messrs J. Freel and R. J. Acheson, Ph.D. students at the Queen's University of Belfast, for their helpful and constructive comments on the manuscript; my wife for her help in drawing diagrams and reading proofs; my mother for the arduous task of transforming an untidily written manuscript into a neat and orderly typescript and Dr R. G. R. Bacon for assistance with the section on 'organic polymers'. I also thank the Clarendon Press, Oxford, for permission to quote from the *Concise Oxford Dictionary*; also the Faraday Society and Professor F. C. Frank, F.R.S., for permission to reproduce the diagram given as Figure 25*b*.

I thank Mr S. J. Coey for help with proof-reading.

A. K. GALWEY

CHAPTER ONE

Classification of Solids

1. INTRODUCTION

Chemistry may be defined as that branch of science which is concerned
with the study of the formation and breaking of bonds between atoms.
While this definition cannot be regarded as covering every possible
aspect of all those fields of studies which are generally accepted as being
chemical in nature, it does focus attention on the principal object of
many researches which have been undertaken to obtain knowledge
about the ways in which atoms can group themselves to form molecules.
Chemistry may be considered, therefore, as some particular aspects of
man's study of his environment. The definition given in the first lines
is one rule by which the areas of endeavour described as chemical in
nature may be delimited, but the world around us shows many diverse
phenomena and it is only for convenience in study that we divide this
continuum into separate subjects. Furthermore, that given above is not
the only definition. The *Concise Oxford Dictionary* provides the alternative, very satisfactory, definition of chemistry as the 'Science of the
elements and their laws of combination and behaviour under various
conditions'. In making such definitions in an attempt to delimit a field
of endeavour scientists are often also concerned with drawing attention
to some particular common factors within a group of observations.
When such factors have been recognized, they may be used to establish
the principles which control or determine a particular type of behaviour.

The present monograph is concerned with the very large number of
substances which are classified as solids. For convenience in discussing
and describing the chemical properties of these substances, general
divisions within the subject are made as defined by the five main chapter headings. Division has been made here by chemical properties and
behaviour rather than by consideration of particular elements (as, for
example, is often used in systematic inorganic chemistry). The first two
chapters are concerned with the classification of known solids and a
description of the atomic arrangement in idealized crystals. The third

1

chapter considers the ways in which real crystals may deviate from the idealized models described in the first two chapters. The fourth and fifth chapters are concerned with some aspects of chemical reactions which occur on or at the surfaces of and within the lattices of crystalline solids respectively.

THE SOLID STATE

The ability of solids to withstand a shearing force, and to regain their original shape after a small deformation, are the properties which most readily distinguish them from substances in the other important states of matter, liquids and gases. Solids have been put to innumerable uses in those fields of human endeavour where hardness and strength are required. This has applied from the time that the first primitive men sheltered under raised rocks and shaped stones for use as tools in the never-ending quest for food. Originally our forebears were forced to use only those materials which nature provided, but, as time went by, man undoubtedly increased the accuracy with which he could select those solids which possessed the most suitable properties for a particular requirement. This must have led, in time, to the desire to adapt or to modify the substances which nature provided, in order to enhance some useful quality. It was this form of enquiry, based on necessity, which laid the foundations of the attitude of mind which eventually caused the development of modern technology. As result of centuries of experimentation man has now reached the position in which he is capable of preparing solids which possess particularly useful combinations of more than one desirable property. Such preparative processes may use relatively complex mixtures of natural ores and/or substances which do not occur in nature and must therefore be the product of a previous synthesis, since nature ultimately provides all the starting materials used in technology. Solids which are manufactured for use in demanding situations include aluminium alloys, used in aircraft construction, where strength coupled with low density are of greatest importance. Other examples are the alloys used as the cutting surfaces of heavy machine tools, which have been developed to give particularly hard edges which can also withstand shock. These examples have been selected from those substances prepared for uses in which hardness is one of the important qualities. However, hardness is not the only characteristic property of the solid phase and other significant properties, found only in solids, include certain types of electrical behaviour, the ability to exist over an appreciable composition range and the arrangement of atoms within the material in a regularly repeating pattern. These topics will be discussed at appropriate places later, but it should be emphasized from the outset that hardness is not the only unique physical property characteristic of the solid phase.

Before considering the chemistry of the solid state, it is useful to mention the main differences between the three main divisions, or states of matter, into which substances may be classified: gases, liquids and solids. Most, but not all, samples of known material can be placed in one of these three groups. The exceptions are those substances which, within various ranges of temperature and pressure, show properties characteristic of two of these main divisions. Therefore, the unambiguous assignment of all known substances into one or other of the above divisions is not possible. Two further states of matter, glass and liquid crystal, are described in Chapter 2; substances in both these states exhibit some properties characteristic of both the liquid and the solid states.

For use as a criterion in the classification of a given sample of a pure substance into the gaseous, liquid or solid states, we will consider the relative ease of motion of the atoms or the molecules in each of these states as follows:

Gas. Random three-dimensional motion of atoms or molecules in the gaseous state results in equal probability of particles colliding with all the walls of the bounding vessel; thus the gas completely fills the container which it occupies. Any two molecules repel each other when the random motion results in their close contact (providing that a chemical reaction does not occur) but at larger separations interaction is so weak that the motion of molecules between collisions may be considered to be largely independent of other gaseous species present. The ideal gas laws are derived on the assumption of completely random motion of particles. Deviations from these laws are attributed to the bulk of the constituent molecules and to weak, long-range, forces between these molecules.

Liquid. In contrast to gases, the molecules of a liquid tend to aggregate so that the fluid is retained in a particular region of space. Here molecules are in relatively close proximity but largely random movements can occur through the motion of adjacent particles relative to each other within the volume occupied by the liquid, which may not be the complete volume of the containing vessel.

Some local preferred orientation of the molecules relative to one another can result from the influence of the shapes and the disposition of electrical charges on neighbouring molecules, when these are closely spaced. Such tendencies towards alignment are opposed by the thermal motions of the particles and are continually changed by the diffusion of molecules within the liquid phase. There is no long range (i.e. several molecular lengths) positioning of molecules relative to one another. At the liquid surface a molecule may acquire sufficient thermal energy to escape the attractive forces of the liquid phase to gain the relative freedom of motion of the gaseous phase. Similarly a molecule in the volatile phase may dissipate excess energy at the liquid surface and enter the liquid phase.

Solid. The component particles of a solid are rigidly held at positions relative to one another as a three-dimensional network in which molecules are located at regular repetitive positions; this network is known as a *lattice.* In the perfect solid every molecule (atom or ion) is held at a constant spatial position relative to its neighbours and long-range ordering is maintained, so that molecules are located in regular positions relative to one another over distances extending to many molecular lengths, to the edges of the crystal. Each particle, or unit constituent of the lattice, can execute thermal vibrations about a mean position but it does not move from this position except in comparatively rare instances.

On heating, thermal vibrations increase until a point is reached where movement of particles relative to each other becomes possible, thus destroying the long-range order. At this point the solid melts to form the liquid phase in which random molecular motion within the bulk of the liquid is possible. Real solids show deviation from the somewhat idealized model described above, and this will be discussed in later chapters.

2. CLASSIFICATION OF SOLIDS

The above general description of solids includes a very large number of substances possessing widely different properties in other respects, so that it is convenient to subdivide solids into groups having common characteristics. As mentioned in the introduction, it is possible to use more than one set of criteria for such a classification, depending on the particular aspect of the solid state which is under consideration. For the present discussion we shall classify by consideration of the nature of the forces which bond the molecules together to form the crystal lattice of the solid. This approach emphasizes the correlations which may be found between the observed physical properties of the solid and the properties of the forces operating between the molecules, atoms or ions which constitute the lattice. Also knowledge of the nature of the bonds within solids is important when considering their chemical properties and reactivity. Four main groups of solids may be distinguished and classified according to the dominant type of chemical bond in the crystal lattice. These are:

(1) Molecular crystals.
(2) Covalent crystals.
(3) Ionic crystals.
(4) Metallic crystals, including alloys and intermetallic compounds.

Hydrogen bonding may also play a significant role in the bonding of some solids; this will be explained later.

Classes (1)–(4) comprise the main groups into which solids may be divided, but solid substances are known which exhibit properties characteristic of more than one of these groups. We must not, therefore, regard these divisions as completely exclusive and some intermediate behaviour between the main types will be observed. Such intermediate behaviour may be found either in those solids which contain two different types of bond, each characteristic of one of the above classes, or in solids which contain individual bonds which are intermediate in character between the main limiting types (1)–(4). Examples of both types of behaviour will be given in appropriate sections below. Only a brief outline of metallic bond theory is given in the present chapter; the application of this theory to a wider range of solids is deferred to later chapters, after a more complete introduction to the theory of the solid state has been given.

Molecular crystals

In substances of this class, the identity of the individual molecules, as they exist in the liquid and gaseous states, is maintained in the solid. The crystal lattice of the solid is formed by the comparatively weak van der Waals bonding between the individual molecules. The primary valence forces, often covalent in character, between the constituent atoms within each molecule are retained during formation of the solid. Physical evidence strongly indicates that these forces may be little influenced by the relatively weaker secondary bonds which hold the molecules in the fixed positions of the crystal lattice.

Van der Waals forces result in attraction between molecules in all three states of matter. Van der Waals interaction in gases is one of the factors responsible for deviations from ideal gas behaviour; in liquids such forces hold the molecules in close proximity to one another and these are the bonds which control the formation of the crystal lattice in molecular solids. The total cohesive energy derived from these forces depends on the physical properties of the particular molecules involved. In solids, three different effects are believed to contribute to the attractive forces which yield this type of bonding:

(i) Attraction between the permanent dipoles which may be present in the molecules. The charge clouds of electrons in molecules such as NH_3, H_2O, HCl are unsymmetrical, so that the mean position of the centre of the positive charge of the molecule does not coincide with the mean position of the negative charge. This causes a resultant directed electric field in the molecule which is known as a *dipole*. Attractions between such dipoles provide part of the binding energy in many molecular solids. The magnitude of such energy depends on the dipole strength; the value of this, for example, decreases rapidly in the series HCl, HBr and HI. The effective attraction between dipoles is reduced by increase in temperature, since increasing thermal vibrations counteract the tendency towards an alignment of dipoles.

(ii) Since the measured influence of temperature on cohesive forces in certain solids did not quantitatively agree with the values calculated theoretically for model (i) above, Debye introduced a further term, the *induction effect*. The induction effect considers the generation of a dipole in surrounding molecules due to the presence of the dipole on any particular molecule. The total energy resulting from this effect is smaller than (i); it depends on the magnitude of the dipole and the ease of displacement of electrons (polarizability) in the molecule in which the dipole is being induced. Molecules with large, loosely held electron clouds are more easily polarized than those having more tightly bound electron clouds.

(iii) Both of the above effects were derived on the assumption that there is a permanent dipole on the molecules being considered. The attractive forces from this source cannot be significant, however, in those molecular crystals derived from constituents for which there is no permanent dipole, for example, argon, nitrogen and those symmetrical molecules for which the influence of dipoles in individual bonds is cancelled out by the geometrical disposition of bonds as in methane or benzene.

London, therefore, postulated that all molecules possess temporary dipoles, or, as they are more usually termed, dispersion forces, which arise from the internal displacements of the charge centres during orbiting of the electrons. The electrons in non-polar molecules, when considered over an appreciable time interval, statistically constitute a symmetrical charge cloud having centre coincident with the positive charge centre. However, at any instant, the centre of negative charge may be removed from that of positive charge, so that the molecule, or atom, may then possess a temporary dipole. Interactions between such dipoles result in net attractions between neighbouring atoms or molecules. The magnitude of the binding energy of the solid due to London dispersion forces is dependent on the frequency of the zero-point vibrational motion and on the (square of) the polarizibility of the molecule.

From quantitative calculations of the magnitude of the attractive forces between molecules, it is possible to calculate the binding energy of many molecular crystals and values thus found agree fairly well with the measured heats of sublimation. The heat of sublimation is the energy required to overcome the forces binding the molecules together within the solid and remove them to relatively large separations. This agreement confirms the concept that such solids consist of relatively weak dipolar attractions between the molecules and that the strengths of the constituent bonds within individual molecules are substantially the same in the solid and gaseous states. For many molecular crystals the dispersion forces are the most important source of binding energy, and, since these are non-directional, it is found that molecules tend to solidify having a crystal lattice in which each is surrounded by a maximum number of neighbouring molecules. Such attractive forces tend to make molecules approach one another as closely as possible. The equilibrium positions within the assemblage of molecules in a crystal will be reached when these attractive forces are exactly counterbalanced by repulsions from interaction between outer electron clouds of the molecules, which overlap to some extent during thermal vibration. Each atom, or molecule, in the solid is subject to these forces which tend to locate it in a constant position relative to its neighbours and, below the melting point, thermal energy is insufficient to permit appreciable migratory movements within the solid. Thus the mean positions of neighbours relative to one another are fixed and molecules are held in a three-dimensional periodic pattern of repetitive units which extends throughout the crystal. Such an arrangement has long-range order which means that two molecules in the solid, separated by a distance many times the length of a molecule, remain in constant positions relative to one another; this contrasts with the long-range disorder characteristic of liquids.

The molecular crystal formed on condensation of the inert gas, argon, consists of the spherical single atoms arranged in a pattern which is identical with that found for the closest packing of spheres of equal size; each atom is equidistant from the centres of twelve nearest neighbours. Numerous other molecular crystals are formed by the aggregation of molecules which are not spherical and the arrangement of molecules in the lattice must differ from that observed for an inert gas crystal. Molecules in such solids are oriented in a regular manner in such directions as to allow the closest possible approach of a particular molecule to a maximum number of nearest neighbours. Benzene, for example, cannot be regarded as a spherical molecule, but, when the solid is formed, the molecules are disposed in such a manner that each unit is surrounded by twelve nearest neighbours.

When molecules are condensed to form a molecular crystal the secondary valence forces used to form the solid are weak compared with the primary valence forces directed to form the bonds within the individual molecules. Solids of this type are, therefore, relatively soft. For the same reason these solids have relatively high coefficients of expansion and low melting points since the amplitude of the thermal vibrations of molecules can increase rapidly with increase in temperature. Iodine, a molecular crystal, has the relatively large coefficient of expansion $9 \cdot 3 \times 10^{-5}$. Some examples of melting points, bond dissociation energies and heat of fusion (which is the energy necessary to overcome the bonding forces of the solid (part of the van der Waals energy is retained in the liquid phase)) for molecular crystals are given below:

Substance	Bond dissociation energy of the molecule kcal mole^{-1}	Heat of fusion kcal mole^{-1}	Melting point °C
Argon	—	0·27	−189
Chlorine	57·9	1·63	−103
Bromine	46·1	1·29	−7·2
Iodine	36·1	3·74	113·7
Methane	(C—H) 104	0·23	−184

The bond lengths within individual molecules in a crystal of this type are close to those observed for the gaseous molecules and the distance of nearest approach of atoms in different molecules is appreciably greater than the distance between atoms of the same molecule. This demonstrates that molecules retain their identity in the solid phase and that the distortion of the intramolecular bonds on solidification is relatively small. Some data for molecular crystals is as follows:

| Substance | Internuclear separation $\mathring{A}$ | | Interatomic separation of neighbours in the solid $\mathring{A}$ |
	Gas	Solid	
Chlorine	1·82	2·10	2·52
Bromine	2·27	2·28	3·30
Iodine	2·65	2·70	3·54

The infrared spectra of substances which form molecular crystals are very similar for solid, liquid and gaseous states. This shows that the frequencies of vibrations, and thus the force constants of the bonds between the constituent atoms of the molecule, undergo relatively small changes on solidification.

Substances in this class of solids do not conduct electricity. The electrons are localized in the bonds within the individual molecules and are unable to migrate from any molecule to a neighbour, on the application of an electric field across the crystal.

Summarizing the main characteristics of molecular crystals, it is seen that the structure of individual molecules (bond lengths, vibration frequencies) undergo relatively minor changes when the molecules are packed by the non-directional secondary valence forces in the lattice. The distances between atoms in different molecules are appreciably greater than the bond lengths within individual molecules. Such solids are mechanically weak, do not conduct electricity, melt at low temperatures with a low heat of fusion and have a high coefficient of expansion.

Covalent crystals

The constituent atoms of a covalent crystal are bonded to neighbouring atoms through covalent bonds; these are primary valence forces. The relative positioning of atoms in the solid results from the geometrical disposition of these strong, directed linkages, which are controlled by the spatial characteristics of the bonding orbitals of the constituent atoms. The properties of solids in this class are most readily discussed by consideration of a particular example, eg. diamond. The arrangement of atoms in the diamond crystal lattice is shown on Fig. 1, which represents a small part of the repetitive pattern which continues throughout the solid since each face of this cube forms a common face with a similar adjoining cube. At a point which does not constitute a crystal edge, we may describe this lattice as follows: The atoms which form the solid (every atom is carbon) within each unit of the lattice are arranged so that one atom is at the centre of a cube and twelve atoms

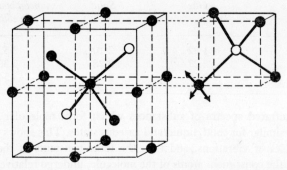

FIG. 1. The arrangement of carbon atoms in the diamond crystal lattice. The two open circles are situated at the centres of cubes comprising the rear half of the larger cube. Each atom is tetrahedrally covalently bonded to four nearest neighbours, this disposition is illustrated for two atoms, and, for clarity, the bonds around the other atoms have not been included.

are at the mid-points of the edges of that cube. In addition there are four atoms at the centres of alternate small cubes, eight of which comprise the larger cube. Two examples of the arrangements of the covalent bonds around particular atoms have been included in the diagram and other (similar) bonds omitted to clarify the representation. The atom at the centre of the small cube is covalently bonded tetrahedrally to the four atoms at the corners of it. The atom at the centre of the large cube is bonded to the four atoms at the centres of the nearest four occupied small cubes. It may be noticed that the repeating unit of the lattice may be alternatively represented as a cube in which all eight corners and the centres of all six faces are occupied by carbon atoms with, again, carbon atoms occupying alternate octants. This may be seen by consideration of Fig. 1 if one of the planes through the centre of the cube shown is taken as the outside edge of a new cube and four further octants are placed on the face opposite to the centre plane which is taken as the edge of the new cube. Diagrams of this type have found extensive use in the description of crystals, and other examples will be discussed in the next chapter.

The bond length of the tetrahedrally directed C–C linkages in diamond is 1·54 Å; this value is very close to the distance between carbon nuclei in many alkanes. Covalent bonds in paraffins, and in diamond, are derived by sp^3 hybridization of the carbon atomic orbitals. These strongly directed bonds in diamond result in a relatively open lattice structure, each atom only having four nearest neighbours. This contrasts with very many solids in which each constituent has a larger number of close neighbours, for example each argon atom in the solid was mentioned as having twelve.

Since every atom is held rigidly in its lattice position by four primary valence forces, this results in a particularly hard solid; diamond is the hardest substance known. Repeated bonding by primary valence forces between neighbouring atoms extends throughout the solid and thus the whole crystal may be regarded as a giant molecule. Since the bonding forces are strong, thermal vibrations exert little influence on the crystal dimensions with the result that the coefficient of expansion is low and the melting point is high. Localization of electrons in covalent bonds prevents their migration in an electric field, giving diamond insulating properties. Silicon carbide (carborundum, SiC) has a structure similar to that of diamond except that in this solid, alternate carbon atom positions of the diamond lattice are occupied by silicon atoms and the solid is bonded through a system of tetrahedrally directed Si–C linkages. Again this is a particularly hard crystal; this substance has been used as an abrasive. Silicon, germanium and (grey) tin all form crystals having lattices similar to that of diamond. The high bond strengths in the crystal lattices make typical solids of this type hard with high melting points; they have a high latent heat of fusion and low coefficient of expansion.

The above examples have been drawn from those solids in which covalent bonding between atoms extends in three dimensions. Other solids, which are usually included in this class, have covalent bonding between large numbers of atoms but such macromolecular units are connected with each other through bonds of a different type; these may be van der Waals, ionic or metallic. Furthermore, the latter form of bonding may be somewhat intermediate in character between the types of force listed.

(i) Van der Waals bonding

Graphite. Diamond has been mentioned as a macromolecule in which the C–C bonds result from sp^3 hybridization and are similar to those found in alkanes. The second allotrope of carbon, graphite, possesses a bond system derived from the sp^2 hybridization of carbon atomic orbitals, which is characteristic of aromatic ring systems. In the graphite crystal, carbon atoms are located in layers within which the C–C bond distance (1·42 Å) is closer to the value for benzene (1·39 Å) than to that for diamond (1·54 Å) and the alkanes.

In graphite each carbon atom is covalently bonded through directed primary valence forces to three neighbours (sp^2 hybridization) to form hexagonal rings which extend in two dimensions across each crystallite; a region of this type of lattice is shown diagrammatically in Fig. 2(a). The crystal is formed by parallel stacking of planes of this type. A representation of the double bonds has not been incorporated in the diagram since the π electrons are located in the spacings between successive planes of rings, i.e. above and below the plane of the page as shown.

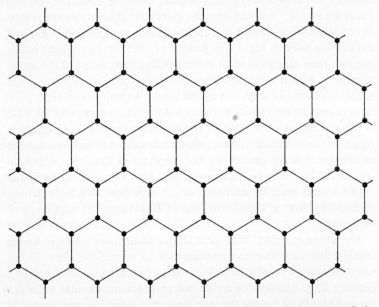

FIG. 2(a). Arrangement of carbon atoms within a single plane of the graphite crystal. The crystal is formed by the regular stacking of successive planes. Each plane of atoms may be compared to a highly condensed aromatic system.

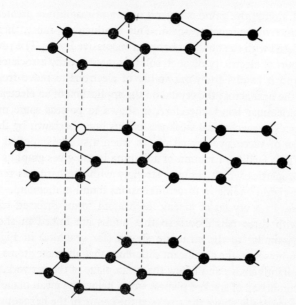

FIG. 2(*b*). Stacking of successive planes of atoms in the graphite crystal. Successive planes are stacked parallel, with displacement of the hexagons one bond length, so that every alternate atom is vertically above an atom in the plane below and below an atom in the plane above. Atoms in alternate successive planes are vertically above one another.

The crystal is stabilized through the multiplicity of structures which can contribute to the resonance energy of the network. The π electrons of each planar hexagonal ring system interact with those of the next successive planes of atoms, which in the crystal are spaced at intervals of 3·35 Å. Successive planes are stacked parallel with displacement of the hexagons one bond length so that every alternate atom in the plane is vertically above one atom in the plane below and below an atom in the plane above, as shown in Fig. 2(*b*). The remaining atoms in the plane considered are vertically above and below atoms in the 'next-but-one' planes above and below the selected plane.

The bonding between successive sheets of atoms in graphite is largely of the van der Waals type since the distance between successive planes is very much greater than that over which a normal covalent carbon bond can be formed. However, the attractive forces between successive planes are not due to dispersion forces alone, since graphite does show a slight electrical conductivity in the direction parallel to the sheets of atoms; the value is several orders of magnitude greater than the conductivity normal to them. This conductivity must, therefore, be associated with the bonding between successive layers. The property of transport of electricity through solids is more usually associated with metals and it results from the ability of electrons to move from one atom to the next across the crystal on the application of an electric field. The interlaminar bond, therefore, is shown to possess some metallic character. The mechanical weakness of this bond is shown by the ease of motion of successive crystal planes when a stress is applied to the crystal. This facility of motion of adjoining layers gives graphite lubricating properties which contrast strongly with the hardness resulting from the rigid bonding in three dimensions found in diamond.

Arsenic. In a crystal of arsenic each atom forms directed covalent bonds with three neighbours so that atoms are linked in sheets of hexagons similar to the structure shown (for graphite) in Fig. 2(*a*). There is, however, the significant difference that alternate atoms in any ring lie slightly above and below the mean plane of the network. In the crystal comprised of stacked planes, atoms below the mean plane of one sheet are vertically above the spaces at the centre of the hexagons of the next successive sheet below.

In arsenic, bonding between successive planes is largely due to dispersion forces, the distance between nearest pairs of atoms in any ring is 2·51 Å, whereas the closest approach between atoms in successive layers is 3·15 Å. Similar crystal lattices are found for antimony and bismuth. There is, however, an increase in the metallic character of the interlayer bond in the sequence arsenic, antimony, bismuth, which is accompanied by a relative decrease in the distance between successive planes, when due allowance is made for the increased size of the atoms in the series. Interatomic distances for bismuth atoms within the layer and between successive layers are 3·10 and 3·47 Å respectively.

Phosphorous. Phosphorous resembles the other Group V elements in that each atom is bonded to three neighbours but differs in that each group of four atoms forms tetrahedra rather than sheets of atoms.

Sulphur. Solid rhombic sulphur is composed of molecules in which each atom is bonded to two neighbours to form eight-membered puckered rings. However, if liquid sulphur is rapidly chilled from ~400° it forms plastic sulphur which consists of tangled chains of —S—S—S—S—S— units formed by the opening and linking of the S_8 molecules to form chains. Each chain may be regarded as being a one-dimensional polymeric molecule. Dispersion forces bond these tangled chains together and the solid is mechanically rather soft since chains, bonded by weak forces, readily move relative to one another when a stress is applied.

The 8-N rule. The substances mentioned above, with the exception of graphite, obey the 8-N rule. This rule is the application of the octet rule, of inorganic chemistry, to covalent crystals. It states that, in solids of this type, each atom has 8-N nearest neighbours to which it may be covalently linked, where N is the group of the periodic table to which the element belongs. Diamond, carbon in Group IV, consists of tetrahedral linkages to four neighbours, the Group V elements have three nearest neighbours and sulphur forms two covalent bonds. This rule can be regarded as having only limited usefulness since it is more appropriate to consider the halogens as molecular crystals than to regard them as covalent crystals in which each atom has only one nearest neighbour. Plastic sulphur, with two different types of bonding, has properties intermediate between covalent and molecular crystals, and graphite is somewhat similar.

(ii) Ionic bonding

Silicates. Many silicates are formed by the repetitive bonding of the $(SiO_4)^{4-}$ tetrahedral unit, silicon atoms being joined through an intermediate oxygen atom $\rightarrow$Si—O—Si$\leftarrow$. The four tetrahedrally directed bonds, derived from the four valence electrons of each silicon atom, result in strong directed linkages which may be regarded as covalent. It may be mentioned that, due to the electronegativity difference between the atoms involved, these bonds possess a slight dipole with a small negative charge on the oxygen. In silicates, condensation of the anion through continued linkage of the type $\rightarrow$Si—O—Si$\leftarrow$ yields fibres or sheets of silicon and oxygen atoms bearing a net negative charge, located on those oxygen atoms which are bonded to a single silicon atom. These condensed species may be regarded as covalently bonded macro-anions. In the solid such units are electrostatically attracted to cations packed between the sheets or fibres; these are ionic forces. Since each cation usually has only one or two positive charges, and these are accommodated in the solid at positions between four or six —O^- ions, the ionic bonds which control the positioning of positive and negative ions are often very much weaker than the covalent bonds within each polymeric anion. Mica, in which the macroanion consists of sheets of silicon, aluminium and oxygen atoms held together by electrostatic attraction to alkali metal ions interspersed between them, may be readily broken open along planes parallel to the anion. Silicates have been mentioned here as examples of compounds containing both covalent and ionic bonds; the structures of naturally occurring silicates will be discussed in greater detail in the latter part of Chapter 2.

(iii) Metallic forces
Examples quoted above include reference to substances for which bonding between covalent units is intermediate in character between dispersion force bonds and metallic bonds, e.g. graphite, arsenic, antimony and bismuth. A more detailed consideration of the metallic bond will be given below.

The above account shows that a small number of solids are known in which all the linkages between neighbouring units in the lattice are covalent in character; these are mechanically hard, high melting point non-conductors. Many substances are known which possess extensive covalent bonding, and, in addition, a second type of bonding. Where van der Waals forces exist in the same solid as covalently bonded polymeric species it may be possible for electrons in the solid to be transferred from one atom to a neighbour rather more easily than in molecular crystals, in which successive covalently bonded units in the lattice may be separated by somewhat greater distances. When this can happen there is the possibility of electron migration in an electric field and thus the van der Waals bond takes on a somewhat metallic character, as has been found in graphite and in bismuth. In silicates, bonding within each anion is largely covalent and such macroanions are linked to form the lattice array by electrostatic or ionic bonding through the cations.

Ionic crystals
Ionic crystals are formed from constituents for which the difference in electron-attracting power is sufficiently great to allow electrons to be transferred from one species to another on or before formation of the solid. Such crystals consist of an array of positively and negatively charged ions attracted into an assemblage by forces which are very largely electrostatic. Typical compounds in this class are substances formed from a pair of elements, one of which tends to donate electrons (e.g. alkali metals) and the other tends to accept electrons (e.g. halogens). Sodium readily donates the outer ($3s$) electron, to form a positive ion

having the neon electronic configuration, and chlorine accepts an electron to form a negative ion with the stable argon electronic structure to form sodium chloride which is a typical ionic solid. Ionic crystals are also formed from species consisting of a group of atoms which bears a positive charge as a whole, for example the $[Ni(NH_3)_6]^{++}$ ion present in nickel hexammine perchlorate and the $[Fe(CN)_6]^{3-}$ ion found in potassium ferricyanide. Halides of those elements which occupy the central region of the periodic table, for which the attainment of the stable inert gas type structure through electron transfer is more difficult, tend to form chlorides containing covalent bonds. The solid chlorides of boron, carbon and nitrogen are molecular rather than ionic crystals.

The electrostatic charge fields resulting from individual ions are not oriented in preferred directions in space. The crystal lattice, therefore, results from the closest possible packing of the constituent ions which will approach one another until repulsive overlap of the outer regions of the electron clouds of the ions reach equilibrium with the electrostatic attractive forces between those ions bearing charges of opposite sign. The shape of the component particles influences the form of crystal lattice which is adopted within the solid; this has been mentioned previously as a factor which determines the structure of molecular crystals. Covalent and ionic solids possess a point of similarity in that the bonding forces are non-directional.

The three main factors which influence the arrangement of ions in an ionic crystal are:

(i) relative numbers of ions bearing different charges, i.e. the formula of the salt A^+B^-; $A_2^+B^{2-}$; $A_3^+B^{3-}$; $A_2^{3+}B_3^{2-}$, etc.,

(ii) relative sizes of ions,

(iii) the shapes of the ions.

The influence of these factors on lattice structure will be discussed in greater detail in Chapter 2; here we are concerned with the nature of the ionic bond and the cohesive forces in such crystals.

In theoretical calculations of the ionic crystal formation energy most of the research hitherto undertaken has been on the alkali halides and, as an example to illustrate the principles involved, we shall consider the sodium chloride crystal. The first step in bond energy calculations is to establish the arrangement of ions in the crystal lattice. The experimental methods by which such structures may be established are described in Chapter 2, and for the present purpose we shall quote the results found as the lattice arrangement shown diagrammatically in

Fig. 3. Sodium and chloride ions are located at the corners of repetitive small cubic units, each of which shares faces with similar adjoining units. The ions are situated at the corners of the cubes in such positions that any one cube edge is terminated by ions of opposite charge. Two such cubes are shown in Fig. 3 in which the common face has been extended to show that the central ion, which may be either Na$^+$ or Cl$^-$, is surrounded by six equidistant nearest neighbours of opposite charge sign.

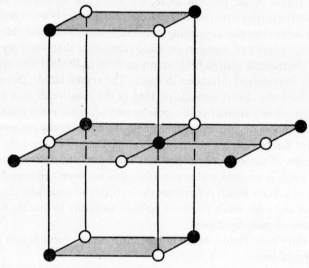

FIG. 3. The disposition of ions in the sodium chloride lattice. The central ion in the extended plane has six nearest neighbours of opposite charge. The two different types of symbol shown represent the different ions, the positions of which are interchangeable in the lattice. Although ions are here represented as being of equal size, the chloride ion has the greater diameter (see Fig. 17 also).

The total energy released on formation of this lattice from the ions results from the contributions from a number of effects, though the greater part is derived from two main sources:

(i) The greater fraction of the bonding energy results from electrostatic attraction between the oppositely charged ions. Since the charge on each ion (e) is known, and the distance between the nuclei of neighbouring ions in the solid may be measured experimentally (Chapter 2), it is possible to calculate the electrostatic attractive forces' contribution to crystal energy. Considering the arrangement of ions in Fig. 3, we see that each ion has six nearest neighbours of opposite charge at distance equal to the edge of the small cubes (a). The potential energy due to attraction is thus ($-6.e^2/a$). Inspection of the lattice shows that there are twelve further ions, having the same charge as the selected ion (not all are shown in Fig. 3) at distance $a\sqrt{2}$ which repel with total energy ($12e^2/a\sqrt{2}$). Extension of this treatment to ions at greater distances, the numbers and dispositions of which can be calculated from the geometry of the system, allows summation of interaction energy between the ion and its neighbours in the lattice at increasing interionic separation. Since every term includes (a number of ions $\times$ (distance)$^{-1} \times e^2/a$) it is possible to express the total in the form $-A.e^2/a$, where A may be found from geometrical calculations. The above example was illustrated for sodium chloride; but, in principle, a similar calculation may be made for the various regular ionic arrays which have been determined for different ionic substances. The values of A (known as the Madelung constant) found from calculations for several different crystalline lattices, are as follows:

Type of lattice	Madelung constant A	Example
Rock salt	1·748	NaCl
Caesium chloride	1·763	CsCl
Rutile	4·816	TiO_2
Fluorite	5·039	CaF_2

The arrangement of ions in these lattices will be described in Chapter 2. Thus, if A and a are known for a particular ionic solid, it is possible to calculate the total electrostatic attraction energy. The nett attractive forces contribute the greater part of the cohesive energy for sodium chloride.

(ii) The greater part of the remainder of the total bonding forces of ionic crystals is due to repulsive energy between adjoining ions, and this is derived from interaction of the charge clouds between neighbouring ions which are electrostatically attracted towards each other. The repulsive energy term which results from the close attraction between ions has the form $B \exp(-a/\rho)$ where B and ρ are constants for any particular crystal. The total energy of the solid (V) is therefore given by:

$$V = -A\frac{e^2}{a} + B \exp\left(\frac{-a}{\rho}\right). \quad (1)$$

The equilibrium value of a ($= a_0$) can be measured for any crystal and A, the Madelung constant, may be found by the calculations outlined above. Differentiating (1) and putting $a = a_0$ when $dV/da = 0$, the potential energy being a minimum when the crystal is in equilibrium, we find the crystal energy at equilibrium is

$$V_0 = -A\frac{e^2}{a_0}\left(1 - \frac{\rho}{a_0}\right). \tag{2}$$

The value of ρ/a_0 for a particular crystal can be found from measurements of the compressibility, which is related to the rate of energy change with internuclear separation (d^2V/da^2). Compressibility directly measures the energy required to reduce the distance between neighbouring ions in the crystal by forcing adjacent electron clouds to approach and overlap with one another. From the measured values of ρ and a_0 for particular crystals the V_0 value may be calculated from Eq. (2). Results obtained by this method, for the solid alkali metal halide crystals, for which the calculations have been most fully investigated, agree within about ± 6 kcal mole^{-1} with values directly measured or obtained indirectly from experimental measurements. Some calculated values for ionic salts are as follows: NaCl 184; KCl 168; RbCl 161 kcal mole^{-1}.

The greater part of the crystal lattice energy results from effects of types (i) and (ii) above, but further contributions may be derived from the following sources:

(iii) Van der Waals forces. These cannot be calculated in isolation from terms (i) and (ii), but the indications are that the energy is of the order of 2–3% of the lattice energy.

(iv) Covalent bonding. It has been assumed above that the electron transfer from the electropositive to the electronegative constituents is complete, and there is reason to believe that the field developed within the crystal lattice tends to facilitate such transfer. However, there is also evidence from X-ray scattering experiments that some slight covalent bonding may persist in the crystal. This effect is small, but allowance for such a contribution must be included in the most accurate lattice energy calculations.

(v) Ionic vibration energy. Vibration of the ions in the lattice will occur even at the absolute zero of temperature. This will make a small contribution to crystal energy, the magnitude of which can be approximately estimated and the contribution included in the total energy calculation.

The Born-Haber cycle

For some solids the calculated crystal energy found by the methods out-lined above, may be compared with a directly measured experimental value. For other substances, however, it is more convenient to deter-mine the crystal energy, V_0, by an indirect method which is known as the Born-Haber cycle. This approach enables the crystal energy to be derived from more readily determined thermochemical values through the use of a thermochemical cycle in which the crystal energy is the only unknown quantity and which, when the cycle has been completed, must result in zero total energy change. The method may be illustrated by the application to sodium chloride and values of the experimentally determined thermochemical quantities are included on the diagram below. (All units are kcal mole^{-1}.)

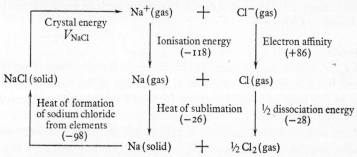

The complete cycle must result in zero energy change, hence the re-quired quantity V_{NaCl}, is given by

$$V_{\text{NaCl}} = 86 - (118 + 26 + 28 + 98) = -184 \text{ kcal mole}^{-1}.$$

Similar calculations have been made for all the alkali halides and the values found are in good agreement (usually within $\pm 3\%$) with those found by theoretical crystal energy calculations. Such agreement sup-ports the basic assumptions of the theory and from this it is concluded that the electrostatic attractions between ions of opposite charge provide the main source of cohesive energy in ionic crystals.

Physical properties of ionic crystals. The bonding force in ionic crystals is greater than that of molecular crystals, and ionic crystals differ from the strongly bonded covalent crystals in that attractive forces are non-directional. The high bonding energy of ionic crystals is reflected in the high melting points and latent heats of fusion of solids of this type; values are higher than those found for molecular but lower than those of covalent crystals.

Substance	Melting point °C	Latent heat of fusion. kcal mole^{-1}
NaCl	801	7·25
KCl	776	5·52
CaCl$_2$	772	6·03

Ionic solids are not good conductors of electricity since the electrons in the constituent particles are strongly held within the charge clouds of the ions and cannot readily migrate on the application of an electric field. Some current-carrying properties are, however, observed which are largely attributed to the presence of impurities or regions of imperfection in the solid. Discussion of this important topic in greater detail is deferred to Chapter 3.

Metals

Metallic crystals are characterized by two main features, both of which must be explained by any theoretical description of the mode of bonding in this class of solid. These are (a) in the crystal lattices observed for metals each atom has a large number (often 12) of nearest neighbours, and (b) metals conduct electricity, which shows that electrons in the solid may migrate across the crystal bulk on the application of an electric field.

Atoms of most of the metallic elements crystallize in one (or, in different temperature ranges, more than one) of the following lattice structures:

(i) Face centred cubic, or cubic closest packed (Fig. 4a). Atoms in the crystal are located at the eight corners of the cube which may be taken as the repetitive unit of the lattice. A further six atoms are situated at the centre of each face of the cube. Each atom has twelve nearest neighbours, which may be seen by reference to the diagram. For example, the atom at the centre of the top face shown has four nearest neighbours at the corners of that face of the cube, a further four, at the same distance, at the centres of the four adjoining vertical faces and four in the centres of vertical faces of the adjoining cube of the lattice directly above the cube shown. Examples of metals which crystallize in a lattice of this type are Cu, Ag, Ni, and Pt.

(ii) Body centred cubic (Fig. 4b). Atoms are located at all eight corners of the cube which forms the repetitive unit of the lattice and a fur-

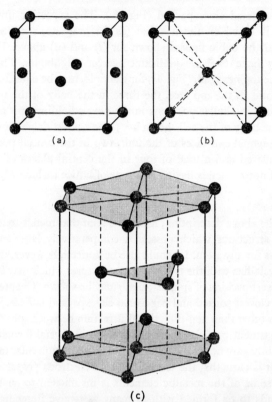

(a)   (b)

(c)

FIG. 4. Most metals crystallize in one, or more, of the above crystal structures.

(a) Face centred cubic. Atoms are located at eight corners of a cube and the centres of all six faces.

(b) Body centred cubic. Atoms are located at eight corners of a cube and the centre point of it.

(c) Hexagonal close packed. Atoms are located at the corners and centre of two hexagons positioned parallel, and a further three atoms are located on a parallel plane halfway between them. These three atoms occupy positions directly above and below spaces between the atoms in the hexagons.

ther atom is found at the centre of each cube. The central atom can be seen to have eight nearest neighbours, and in addition, there are a further six which are at the centres of adjoining cubes which are only ~15% more distant. Metals which possess this lattice include Li, Na, V and Ta.

c

(iii) Hexagonal close packed (Fig. 4c). The repeating unit in this structure is based on the hexagon (as for graphite, see Fig. 2a), in contrast to the cubic figures shown for (i) and (ii) above. Here each atom may have twelve equidistant nearest neighbours. The central atom in the top hexagon, (Fig. 4c) for example, may be equidistant from the six atoms in the top face, the three in the body of the unit and a further three in similar positions in the next adjoining unit above. An atom in the body of the cell shown has three nearest neighbours in each of the hexagonal end-faces of the unit, two in the central plane of the unit considered and a total of four in the central planes of adjoining hexagonal units. Metals having this type of lattice include Mg, Zn, Cd and Os.

From the above description, it may be seen that metals tend to crystallize in structures which possess a comparatively large number of neighbours for any atom. It should also be noticed, however, that not all metals crystallize with the two possible structures which may be formed by the closest packing of spheres; these may be shown (Chapter 2) to be the cubic closest packed and hexagonal close packed lattices. It follows that forces other than non-directional attraction between spherical equal sized constituent particles must be involved in crystal formation. The bonding forces are not of the same type as those in molecular or covalent crystals. It is clear that the total number of electrons possessed by the atoms of some of the metallic elements is insufficient to enable directional bonds to be formed with as many as twelve immediate neighbours. Furthermore, the mobility of electrons in metals contrasts with the non-conducting properties exhibited by many covalent crystals. If we consider lithium metal as an example it may be seen that it is not possible to describe the crystal as covalent since each atom possesses only three electrons in all, and two of these are contained in an inner shell (helium structure) which is unlikely to be disturbed on solidification of gaseous molecules to the crystalline metal. The concept of the single $2s$ electron of the lithium atom forming covalent bonds to the eight nearest neighbours, and, in addition, remaining sufficiently mobile to migrate in an electric field is clearly at variance with the usual representation of a covalent bond. It must be concluded, therefore, that the covalent crystal model discussed in the previous paragraph does not provide an adequate description of the bonding forces in metals.

In the discussion of the properties of certain covalent crystals, for example graphite and bismuth, it was implied that on reduction of the interatomic distances between covalently bonded groups, van der Waals bonds began to show some of the properties characteristic of metal crystals. Thus, while the metallic interatomic forces represent a different bond type to the three classes considered hitherto, it may possess certain features in common with each of these types.

A qualitative model of the metallic crystal, considered early in the development of metal theory, regarded the atoms of a metal lattice as being ionized and the electrons so removed had considerable freedom of motion within the volume defined by the boundary surfaces of the solid. The cohesive energy of the solid must thus result from electrostatic attraction between the positive ions located at fixed lattice positions and the 'electron gas' which permeated the whole metallic particle. This somewhat qualitative representation has been developed to describe the metallic bond in greater detail so that now it is possible theoretically to account for a number of the more important metallic properties. The metallic bond differs from the other bonds so far described; but it should be remembered that in several solids it may be modified to form bonds intermediate between 'pure metallic' and some other type. For example, in the sequence As, Sb, Bi, attractive forces intermediate in character between van der Waals bonds and metallic bonds are observed and these increase the metallic character of the solid with decrease in distance between the successive layers in the lattice.

Two main approaches to the theoretical descriptions of the metallic bond have been made through molecular orbital and valence bond methods. These are not to be regarded as being in conflict but should be considered as largely complementary, each approach being designed to consider somewhat different aspects of the forces involved.

Molecular orbital theory
This approach considers the formation of covalent bonds between neighbouring atoms in the solid and has been largely developed by Bloch. The formation of a metallic crystal may be regarded as bringing together two metal atoms, then adding a third and continuing this process until a solid crystallite, containing a large number of individual atoms, has been formed. The original separated, neutral metal atoms, in the gaseous phase, which subsequently aggregate to form the crystal, initially possess discrete energy levels into which an electron may be accommodated. But electrons cannot be maintained at intermediate positions on the energy scale. When a diatomic molecule is formed by the combination of two such single atoms, three effects on the disposition

of electron accommodating levels may be recognized: (i) the energy levels of the innermost electrons, including completed inner shells, are not significantly different in the diatomic molecule from those in the atoms which have combined to form the molecule; (ii) the valence electrons form the bond which links the pair of atoms. Where one electron level is present in the reactant atom, molecule formation is accompanied by the modification of the two single levels, one initially present in each atom to a pair of levels which are common to the two atoms and the formation of these results in the generation of the chemical linkage. The two levels in the molecule are separated by a small energy difference (Fig. 5).

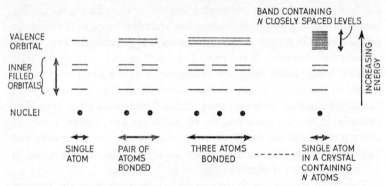

FIG. 5. Schematic representation of the formation of an energy band, of permitted electron accommodating levels, from the orbitals of constituent atoms of the solid as the crystal is built up by addition of single atoms.

(iii) Outer, unfilled electron levels of the original atoms may be modified to yield levels common to both atoms (as in (ii) above).

On continuing to build the crystal, by addition of a third atom to the dimer molecule, modification of the available electron levels by a type (ii) process again occurs to yield a group of three levels common to the molecule as a whole and all of the three levels are separated by small energy differences. Through the continued addition of single atoms to the assemblage, the orbitals of the group may be similarly modified as the number of atoms in the 'molecule' increases. The changes in electron accommodating energy levels with aggregation, as described above, may be diagrammatically represented in Fig. 5. This shows schematic extrapolation from the trimer to consider the available electron levels in a crystal where one level contributed by each atom in the lattice is common to the crystal as a whole. The resultant energy levels in the bonding orbitals are very closely spaced on the energy scale for a crystal of any appreciable size. This is usually termed an *energy band* since the large number of levels between the extreme values may be regarded as approaching a continuum, or band of permitted levels. The solid may therefore be regarded as a giant molecule in which the bonding is not located between individual atoms but is common to the crystal as a whole. The bonding may also be regarded as a covalent structure in which not all the available orbitals are occupied. A more detailed consideration of the band structure of solids will be given in Chapter 3.

Valence bond theory

The alternative approach has been largely developed by Pauling, who made calculations to determine the bonding energy which may be derived from resonance between the various possible covalently bonded structures of the lattice units. The interatomic distances in the metal lattice are such that covalent bonds may be formed between neighbouring atom pairs. We have seen that each metal atom has usually about twelve nearest neighbours and each atom possesses insufficient valence electrons to form covalent bonds with all of them. The valence bond theory attributes the stability of the lattice to energy derived from resonance between the numerous possible covalent structures. In addition to these purely covalent bond arrangements, there are also numerous structures involving ionized atoms and these increase the number of available structures which contribute to stability, and the multiplicity of such structures may result in a relatively large resonance energy. This model differs from that described for covalent crystals in that much of the cohesive force of the metal is derived from resonance between partially filled orbitals, the possibilities of resonance being increased by the presence of a larger number of nearest neighbours than is predicted by the 8-N rule.

The two different theories of metals outlined above have found particular fields of application in dealing with different metallic properties. The molecular orbital approach has been found more useful in considering phenomena involving the migration of electrons while the valence bond theory has found greater importance in theoretically accounting for the arrangement of atoms in the solid lattice. Both theories indicate that resonance energy between overlapping orbitals of neighbouring atoms provides an appreciable fraction of the crystal bonding energy but that electrons may readily resonate between the multiple structures provided by the partially filled orbitals available. This contrasts with the situation in covalent solids where all electrons are localized in filled orbitals and are thus unable to migrate to a neighbouring unfilled orbital on application of an electric field. These properties of solids will be considered in Chapter 3 where a more detailed account will be given of the band theory and its applications to the theoretical description of a number of different types of characteristic behaviour of solids.

The hydrogen bond

Normally the hydrogen atom can form a single covalent bond, but in situations where it is placed in a suitable environment it may form a second relatively weak ($\sim$5 kcal mole^{-1}) link with certain electronegative species. Such bonding is often observed when hydrogen is attracted

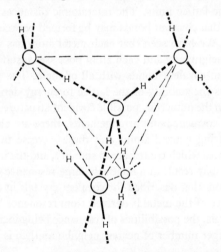

FIG. 6. Schematic representation of bonding of the water molecule in ice. Hydrogen bonds shown dotted, covalent bonds shown by full lines. The four bonds about any oxygen atom are *approximately* tetrahedrally directed.

towards oxygen and many instances of modified reactivity of organic molecules attributable to hydrogen bonding are known. The hydrogen bond can also influence the molecular orientation in the solid state; an important example of this effect occurs in ice. The relatively high melting point of ice, compared with those for other substances having comparable molecular weight, results from hydrogen bonding in the solid. Crystallographic studies show that in ice each H_2O molecule is tetrahedrally co-ordinated and this results from the tetrahedral co-ordination of each oxygen atom through covalent bonds to two hydrogen atoms and through two hydrogen bonds with hydrogen on neighbouring molecules, as shown schematically in Fig. 6. This structure of the lattice unit leads to a relatively open molecular structure possessing a small number of nearest neighbours and has a low density. Ice floats on the denser phase, water, since a part of the hydrogen bonding of the solid is lost on melting through increase in thermal vibrations of the molecules in the homogeneous phase. In contrast, hydrogen sulphide gives a solid in which hydrogen bonding does not play a significant part. In the hydrogen sulphide crystal, each molecule is surrounded by twelve nearest neighbours and it melts at a lower temperature ($-85°C$) than water though the molecular weight of the substance is greater.

CHAPTER TWO

The Crystal Lattice

1. PROPERTIES OF CRYSTALS

The lustre, transparency and colours of naturally occurring crystals have attracted considerable attention through the ages, and particularly good specimens have been prized as gems from the time of our earliest records. Such naturally occurring single crystals are often very regular in shape and may be symmetrical; for example, in some substances one half of the crystal is a mirror image of the other. Examination of the constituent crystals of a freshly broken coarsely crystalline rock often shows that all crystals of a particular type (those having the same colour, lustre, texture, etc.) have similar shape. The same conclusion may be reached from examination of the residue after evaporation of a solution of an inorganic salt, in natural circumstances or in the laboratory, where all crystals of a single substance are of strikingly similar shape. Distinctive features, which may be deduced from a more general examination of the shape of crystals which occur in rocks, which are left by evaporation from solution or which have been prepared by chemical methods, may be summarized:

(i) The external crystal faces are almost invariably planar.

(ii) Crystals of a particular substance, even when prepared by somewhat different methods, usually have the same shape.

(iii) The angles at which planar crystal surfaces meet are often constant for different crystals of the same substance.

Each of these points will now be considered in greater detail.

(*i*) *Planar crystal surfaces.* Crystals of very many ionic salts are bounded by planar surfaces. It is possible to grow crystals which have curved bounding faces through control of flow or diffusion of saturated solution to the crystal during growth. This is, however, an artefact imposed by external control of conditions, and it is true to say, that under the most favourable growth conditions, crystals have planar surfaces. The number of such faces present, however, varies from one salt to another. Sodium chloride crystallized from water yields cubic crystals having six planar faces, and well formed crystals of potash alum often have 26 planar surfaces. The number of faces depends also on growth conditions. Ammonium perchlorate crystallized from water gives crystals which are flattened plates but the number of planar bounding surfaces which are present depends on the conditions which obtained during the growth of the particular crystal.

When a crystal is subjected to an externally imposed stress it is observed that rupture occurs most readily in a limited number of directions which bear some simple geometrical relationship to the original faces of the crystal and the new surfaces so exposed are also planar. This phenomenon is known as *cleavage*. The cleavage planes, i.e. the new faces exposed on rupture, of a cubic single crystal of sodium chloride are usually parallel to the original faces of the cube.

(*ii*) *Crystals of the same substance are usually the same shape.* For this heading it was necessary to specify that crystals are *usually* of the same shape, since several factors are known to cause variation in the external form of crystal. Different shapes may be observed for two forms of a particular inorganic salt which contain different amounts of water of hydration; here the chemical compositions of the crystalline phases are different. Substances with identical chemical composition may crystallize in two different forms which are known as *allotropes*. For example, crystal shapes for carbon as graphite or as diamond are different. Similar characteristics are observed for rhombic, monoclinic and plastic sulphur; the last mentioned does not form a true lattice and the solid does not crystallize as a preferred shape, but may be moulded by mechanical pressure.

In a wide variety of systems it is found that crystals having the same chemical composition and identical arrangement of atoms (molecules or ions) in the lattice have a similar external shape. Sometimes, however, the conditions obtaining during crystal growth may modify the external geometric shape of the product solid without changing the lattice structure. Two crystals of a single substance, with the same lattice but different shapes, are said to be of different *habit*. On habit modification the relative areas of different faces change but the angles between such faces remain constant. A two-dimensional representation of crystals having different relative development of faces, but with constant interfacial angles, is shown in Fig. 7.

The crystal habits of inorganic salts prepared from solution may be influenced by the presence of other substances in the mixture from which the crystals are grown. Sodium chloride crystallized from water yields

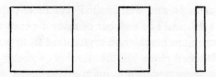

FIG. 7. Diagrammatic representation, in two dimensions, of changes in crystal habit with retention of constant angles between boundary lines.

crystals of cubic habit, as stated before, but, if the water solution contains an appreciable amount of urea, the resultant crystals have octahedral habit (an eight-sided regular figure, see Fig. 8). The addition of small concentrations of particular organic molecules, often dyestuffs, (~0·1% weight of inorganic salt) to water solutions of inorganic compounds, may significantly influence the habit of the crystals of the

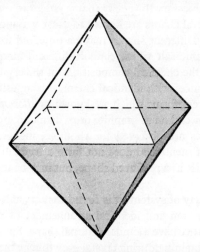

FIG. 8. Octahedral shape of sodium chloride crystal obtained from water solution containing urea. The crystal represented is the ideal habit; real crystals show deviations from such perfect regularity unless conditions of growth are extremely closely controlled.

residue after solvent evaporation. For example, potassium perchlorate crystallizes from water as plates, or as solid prisms for which the crystal dimensions in three mutually perpendicular directions are approximately equal; the habit is controlled by the exact growth conditions. However, if a small amount of the organic dye, Alizarin Red S, is added to the solution, potassium perchlorate crystallizes as large numbers of long thin needle-like crystals known as *dendrites*. These are large numbers of fine crystallites, randomly oriented, with no preferred direction of alignment in the crystallite mass. The habit of individual crystals (grown in the presence of dye) apparently shows preferred growth in *one* dimension in contrast with the approximately equal growth rates in *two* or *three* dimensions during crystallization from pure water. Numerous examples of such habit modification are known.

An organic dye present in the solution may or may not be retained in the growing crystal. An interesting example of dye retention is termed the *hour-glass* effect in which retention of the dye is confined to certain regions of the crystal. A somewhat stylized representation of this phenomenon is shown in Fig. 9 where dye has been retained in the solid during growth of one face of the crystal so that the solid contains a record

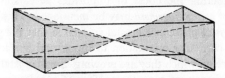

FIG. 9. Diagrammatic representation of the 'hour-glass' effect. Dye, present in the solution from which the crystal was grown, has been retained in two regular cone-shaped volumes, for which a cross-section parallel to an end surface is rectangular in shape.

of the development of this face during growth. The shaded region in the product is approximately the shape of an hour-glass. An example of such behaviour is the retention of the dye fuchsin in potassium sulphate crystals, though the shape of the crystal is more complex than that represented in Fig. 9.

It is probable that habit modification of the type discussed in the present section results from the adsorption (attraction of a substance to the *surface* of another phase; this term will be discussed more fully in Chapter 4 in relation to surfaces) of the additive in the crystallizing solution to the crystal surfaces, so that the relative rates of growth of different faces is altered. To account for the habit modification of sodium chloride, observed after addition of urea to the solution, it has been suggested that a complex is formed between salt and urea and the presence of this substance on the octahedral faces of a small crystal *reduces* the rate at which this face can grow. The faces which present the largest area in the final crystal are those which develop most *slowly* during growth. The manner in which this comes about is represented diagrammatically in Figs. 10(a) and (b); these are perspective drawings and sections through part of a growing crystal. Fig. 10(a) represents the particular situation in which the surface area of the inclined faces increases progressively while the area of the face at the top of the figure remains constant. From the sections A–A' shown it may be seen that the rate of normal advance of the top face is greater than that of the inclined faces. As a more general example, Fig. 10(b) shows the situation where the rate of development of the inclined faces is even slower and the top face decreases in area and will finally disappear. The presence of urea, or the organic dyes mentioned, in the crystallizing solutions modify the relative rates of development of different faces in the small crystals originally formed in the solutions, compared with the relative rates of normal advance of the same solid surfaces from water solutions.

While considering the effect of impurities at crystal surfaces the phenomenon of *epitaxial growth* may be mentioned. This is the growth of a second crystal phase at a crystal surface so that the growing crystallites bear a particular orientation to the crystal surface of the different substance on which they are growing. Small crystallites of potassium permanganate grown on the surface of a potassium perchlorate crystal are all aligned so that corresponding surfaces of the crystals of the former salt point in the same direction although each individual crystal is formed at some distance from a neighbour on the supporting surface and these (i.e. $KMnO_4$) do not touch. This demonstrates that the properties of the lattice at one planar crystal surface can influence the growth of a second crystal at its surface.

There is a considerable literature on the preparation of single crystals of inorganic substances and this involves numerous experimental approaches. All possible methods will not be discussed in detail here but the interested reader is referred to the excellent account given by Buckley in *Crystal Growth* (Wiley). It is necessary to exert very careful control over conditions of growth in order to obtain well-formed crystals of appreciable size. To prepare single large inorganic crystals, two main conditions must be met: (a) the solution must have equal ease of access to all external crystal surfaces, and (b) the degree of supersaturation of the solution must be controlled at a suitable value. It is usual to suspend a small crystal of the substance to be grown, known as a *seed crystal*, in the crystallizing solution so that ions may approach it from all sides with equal probability. When a crystal is placed on the flat bottom of a vessel the relative rate of growth of the lower faces is

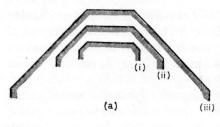

(a) A particular situation where the area of the top surface remains constant. The surface area of the inclined faces increase (i–iii) but, as can be seen from the cross-sections, the rate of normal advance of these faces is slower than that of the end face, the area of which remains constant during growth.

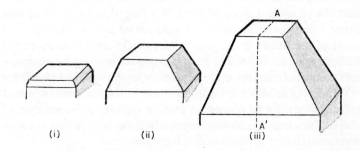

(i) (ii) (iii)

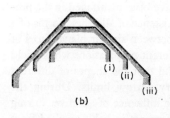

(b) For this crystal the rate of normal advance of the inclined surfaces is relatively slower than that of the top face, compared with the example shown in Fig. 10(a), as may be seen from comparison of the cross-section diagrams. The area of the top boundary surface progressively decreases and will eventually disappear following further crystal growth beyond (iii).

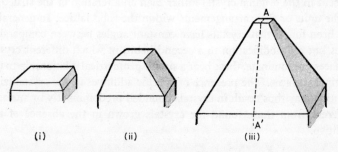

(i) (ii) (iii)

FIG. 10. Those surfaces of a crystal which advance at the lowest rate during growth comprise the greatest surface area of the resultant crystal.

reduced since the supersaturated solution from which the crystal is being grown is unable to diffuse readily to the lower surfaces of the crystal. If the crystallizing solution, the mother liquor, is too highly saturated with salt, a cluster of numerous small crystals may be produced instead of a single large one.

Single crystals of a metal can be prepared by taking a small crystallite of the substance and suspending it with the lower surface just touching the surface of a bath of molten metal. On slowly raising the solid crystal, growth occurs at the lower end. Other methods include moving a heated region slowly along a piece of metal in a long thin container so that melting occurs from the multicrystalline region and, on cooling after passage of the heated zone, growth of a single crystal occurs as the solidified region advances. The growth of crystals of many metals necessitates control of pressure and temperature conditions, and possibly a catalyst, during solidification from the melt. It may be mentioned that small diamonds can be formed on chilling carbon, in the presence of nickel catalyst, from a reaction mixture which has been heated to a high temperature during application of a high pressure.

(iii) *Constant angles between planar faces for different crystals of the same substance.* Some exceptions to this rule have been mentioned in the preceding section, one example being the existence of allotropic forms of a single element. However, when angles between similar planar faces of crystals from a single batch, or from different preparations which yield the same habit, are measured, it is found that the shapes of different crystals are usually constant within very narrow limits. During the account (in the preceding section) of the influence of additives during crystallization, it was suggested that differences in habit resulted from changes in the relative development of particular surfaces which were present in the original crystal rather than an alteration of the structure of the units or their arrangements within the solid lattice. In general it has been found that crystals have constant angles between comparable faces but on modification to a second habit, in which different crystal surfaces predominate, these bear a simple geometrical relationship to the original surfaces. The presence of specific additives in the crystallizing solution may thus result in crystals bounded predominantly by surfaces different from those found for crystals grown in the absence of the additive.

2. QUANTITATIVE EXAMINATION OF CRYSTALS
To make quantitative studies of crystals and to present the results

obtained from such measurements, it is necessary (i) to measure the angles between crystal faces, and (ii) provide a descriptive 'label' for different faces, to facilitate exchange of data and discussions between workers in the field.

Goniometers. A goniometer measures the angles between faces of a crystal. The simplest form is a protractor with an arm pivoted at the centre of the scale. To measure the angle between two faces of a crystal, one such surface is aligned at the protractor 0° edge, the pivoted arm is brought in contact with the second surface and the position of the other end of this arm is noted on a circular scale ($\pm 0.5°$).

For accurate work this simple device has been superseded by instruments in which the planar crystal surfaces are used to reflect an incident light beam. In one form, the crystal is positioned at the centre of a circular table the edge of which is inscribed with an angular scale. A telescope, incorporating cross-wires illuminated by a light source, is focused on one face of the crystal, so that both the cross-wires and their image reflected from the crystal are coincident, and the position of the telescope on the scale noted. A second reading is then made for the second face and the angle between the faces may thus be found. An alternative experimental arrangement incorporating separate light-source and telescope has been used. In this instrument the crystal is mounted with an edge at the centre of a circular table, which has a scale inscribed on the edge, and it is rotated to bring the image of the light-source coincident with the telescope cross-wires and the position of the crystal on the angular scale is noted. The angle through which the crystal must be rotated to bring the image of the reflected ray from a second crystal face coincident with the telescope cross-wires is measured and, from the geometry of the system, the angle between the faces can easily be found.

Symmetry in crystals

The regularity of shapes of crystals has been mentioned several times in the above paragraphs and it is now necessary to define terms used in descriptions of the symmetry of crystals.

Plane of symmetry. Any plane drawn through a crystal so that it divides the crystal into two halves, each of which is a mirror image of the other, is a plane of symmetry of that crystal. A crystal may have several planes of symmetry. A cube has nine as may be seen by consideration of Fig. 11(*a*). A plane of symmetry bisects four of the edges of the cube; three such planes can be found for the cube. Six further planes

of symmetry pass through opposite edges of the cube and diagonally
bisect pairs of opposite faces.

Axis of symmetry. An axis of symmetry is a line drawn through the
crystal such that during rotation of the crystal, using the line as the axis
of rotation, the crystal presents exactly the same appearance more than
once during rotation through 360°. Again, considering the cubic crystal
as an example, axes of symmetry exist (*a*) through mid-points of opposite faces (the crystal presents exactly the same appearance four times

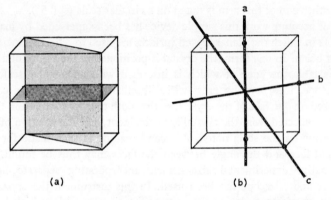

(a)   (b)

FIG. 11. (*a*) Planes of symmetry in a crystal of cubic habit.
(*b*) Axes of symmetry in a crystal of cubic habit.

during rotation through 360° about this axis; this is a fourfold axis of
symmetry), (*b*) through mid-points of diagonally opposite edges, two-
fold axes of symmetry, and (*c*) through diagonally opposite corners,
threefold axes of symmetry (Fig. 11*b*).

Centre of symmetry. This is a point in the crystal such that *any*
straight line through it cuts the crystal surfaces at equal distances on
either side of it. Again considering a cubic crystal as an example, the
centre of gravity is a centre of symmetry; the axes of symmetry, amongst
an infinite number of lines through this point, are bisected by it.

Inversion symmetry. This type of symmetry is found in those crystals
which present the same appearance after rotation through a specified
angle (often 90°) followed by inversion through a point.

Enantiomorphism. Normally a crystal of a substance grown from a
solution possesses identical symmetry elements to those of all the other
crystals of that substance formed in the same batch. However, with a

number of salts a crop of crystals may be divided into two groups which are related to each other as object and mirror image. Crystals from each group have closely similar habits, but are non-superimposable; such a pair are termed *enantiomorphs*. Symmetry of this type is observed for sodium chlorate.

The above descriptions of the symmetry elements have considered the geometrical properties of the shapes of crystals of good habit. The boundary surfaces of the solid are not the only physical properties which are controlled by the symmetry of the lattice arrangement of units in the solid. For example, where a temperature change occurs in a crystal which has the property that it does not possess a centre of symmetry, a positive electric charge is developed at one end of an axis of symmetry while a negative charge is developed at the other. This is known as *pyroelectricity*. Also *piezoelectrical* properties, the appearance of electrical charges on compression, are shown by most of those crystals which do not possess a centre of symmetry. From the detection of such properties it is possible to obtain information about the symmetry elements for a particular solid. Further information can be derived from examination of the shape of depressions formed in the surface of the solid on dissolving small amounts with a suitable solvent. The depressions so formed are termed *etch-pits*.

Reference axes for crystals
To study quantitatively the solid geometry of crystals it is necessary to select a set of reference axes, co-ordinate axes, to which all measurements made may be referred. While, in theory, it is possible to use any set of axes for any crystal, it simplifies discussion, and also mathematical description of crystal properties, if the axes are selected in such a way that they are related to the symmetry properties of the particular crystal being considered. The descriptions and examples quoted hitherto in the present chapter have been largely restricted to consideration of the highly symmetrical cubic habit, but it must be remembered numerous other crystal forms are of wide occurrence. It has been found useful, therefore, to classify crystalline substances into seven *crystal systems*; all those substances which are grouped in any one system are considered with reference to crystal axes selected by a single set of rules. The selection of axes for the four simplest and most regular of the seven systems is diagrammatically represented in Fig. 12. It should be noted that the habits of these crystals may be alternatively represented

by prisms having a different shape from those shown in Fig. 12. On this model those in Figs. 12(*a*), (*b*) and (*c*) would possess a rectangular cross-section in the plane of two of the axes and the planar faces would taper to meet at a point located in the direction of the third axis. This

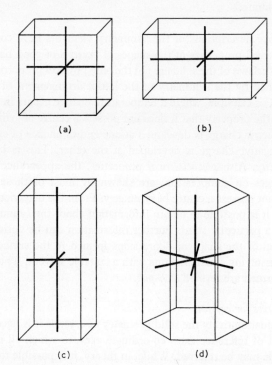

(a)   (b)

(c)   (d)

FIG. 12. The selection of axes in four of the seven crystal systems.

(*a*) Cubic. Three mutually perpendicular axes of equal length.

(*b*) Tetragonal. Three mutually perpendicular axes, two of equal length and the third different; it may be longer or shorter.

(*c*) Rhombic. Three mutually perpendicular axes of unequal length.

(*d*) Hexagonal. Four axes, three of the same length equally inclined at 60° and the fourth, having a different length, perpendicular to the plane containing the other two.

yields a regular octahedron for the cubic system (from Fig. 12(*a*), also see Fig. 8). Fig 12(*d*) may be similarly represented with a hexagonal section in the plane of the three axes and the planar faces taper in the direction of the fourth axis. A brief statement of the rules governing the selection of axes for the seven systems is as follows:

(1) *Regular or cubic system* (Fig. 12a). All three axes of equal length and mutually perpendicular. Substances which give crystals of this type include diamond, silver, sodium chloride.

(2) *Tetragonal system* (Fig. 12b). Two axes of equal length and the third being longer or shorter, all mutually perpendicular, e.g. rutile, lead tungstate.

(3) *Rhombic or orthorhombic system* (Fig. 12c). Three axes of unequal length meeting mutually perpendicularly, e.g. ammonium sulphate, iodine, the low temperature form of sulphur.

(4) *Hexagonal System* (Fig. 12d). Three equal axes in a single plane meeting at mutual angles 60° and a fourth axis – this is the only system to include a fourth axis – at right angles to the plane of the other three and not necessarily the same length as them, e.g. graphite, zinc, cadmium iodide.

(5) *Monoclinic system*. Two unequal axes intersecting at an angle ($\neq 90°$) and a third axis (unequal) at right angles to the plane containing the other two, e.g. potassium chlorate, barium chloride, the high temperature form of sulphur.

(6) *Trigonal system*. Three equal axes, equally inclined but not at right angles to one another, e.g. arsenic, antimony, bismuth, calcite.

(7) *Triclinic system*. Three unequal axes; none of the angles between the axes are right angles. This is the only crystal system which shows no elements of symmetry, e.g. boric acid, potassium dichromate.

Law of rational indices

It has been mentioned above that the selection of crystal coordinate axes is somewhat arbitrary. However, the division of all crystals into the seven systems which have been defined above enables the symmetry properties of the crystal habit to be used as far as is possible in the simplification of crystallographic calculations. Extensive usage has shown that these seven systems are the most convenient of the infinite variety of reference frameworks which may be considered for use in the study of crystalline solids. After a system of axes for a particular crystal has been selected, it is then necessary to define a reference crystal face, *the unit face*, which cuts all three reference axes. Again the choice is somewhat arbitrary but experience assists in the recognition of the most suitable crystal surface. Assume the unit face cuts the three reference axes (OX, OY and OZ) at distances a, b and c units from the origin. It is an experimental observation that all other faces of that crystal intercept the axes at multiples of these values; i.e. at da, eb, fc, where d, e and f are small integers. This observation was first made by Haüy and is known as the *law of rational indices*. It is also possible that a crystal face may be parallel to one (or two) axis and therefore cut it (them) at infinity. The experimental law is diagrammatically illustrated on Fig. 13, where, for clarity, attention is confined to the plane con-

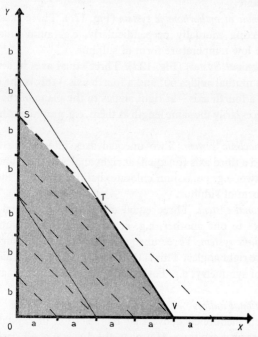

FIG. 13. Diagrammatic representation of Haüy's law of rational indices.
The light dotted lines represent the projection of the unit plane on the OX and OY axes, for which the intercepts are a and b, the face ST of the given crystal is parallel having intercepts $5a$ and $5b$ (that on the OX axis being found by extrapolation). Similarly the intercepts for the face TV are $4a$ and $6b$. The ratio of the slopes of these faces $1:3/2$ are in the proportions of small integers $(2:3)$ in accordance with Haüy's law.

taining the OX and OY axes. Two planar faces of the crystal meet at the point T, one face, represented by the heavy dotted line (ST), may be projected as a parallel set of lines at different perpendicular distances from the origin as the family of (lighter) dotted lines of constant slope $(-b/a)$. Similarly the other face (unbroken heavy line TV) may be projected as the full lines for which the slope is $(-3b/2a)$. The law of rational indices states that the ratio of the intercepts is always $da:eb$ and here the values of d and e are both unity for ST and 2 and 3 respectively for TV. Alternatively, it may be stated that the slope of the projection of any face on this diagram is a small number or a simple fraction of the b/a ratio where a, b (and c) are characteristic parameters of the particular crystal. Fig. 14 shows a three-dimensional representation of intersections of two crystal faces DEF and $D'E'F'$ where both may be

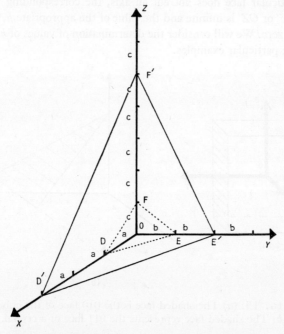

FIG. 14. Illustration of the law of rational indices.

The plane shown dotted, DEF, is the unit plane which cuts the axes at distances a, b and c from the origin. The plane $D'E'F'$ cuts the axes at whole number multiples of these values.

assumed to have been projected on to the three crystal axes by the procedure outlined above for Fig. 13. The intercepts OD', OE' and OF' are simple multiples of OD, OE, and OF. From the diagram it may be seen that $OD'/OD = 3$; $OE'/OE = 2$ and $OF'/OF = 5$. DEF is the unit plane since $d = e = f = 1$.

Miller indices. The previous paragraph discussed experimental observations about the geometrical interrelationships of different faces, and it is convenient to use these observations as a basis for labelling different bounding surfaces for crystals. This approach is due to Miller (1839) who described each crystal face by a set of three numbers h, k and l, which are defined by the formula (symbols are defined with reference to Fig. 14):

$$OD' : OE' : OF' : : \frac{a}{h} : \frac{b}{k} : \frac{c}{l} \qquad (3)$$

If a particular face does not cut an axis, the corresponding value of OX', OY' or OZ' is infinite and the value of the appropriate h, k, or l is equal to zero. We will consider the determination of values of h, k and l for some particular examples.

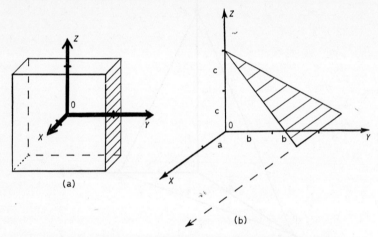

FIG. 15. (a) The shaded face is the 010 face of the cube.
(b) The shaded face represents the 011 face of a crystal.

(i) Faces of a cubic crystal. Three mutually perpendicular axes meeting at the centre of symmetry are selected (cubic system). Consider the (shaded) face of the cube which cuts the OY axis but none of the others (in Fig. 15a). We may write down Eq. (3) above incorporating appropriate values for OD', OE' and OF' as

$$\infty : nb : \infty : : \frac{a}{h} : \frac{b}{k} : \frac{c}{l}$$

From which we find that $h = l = 0$; $k = n$. This, by convention is written $0n0$; no punctuations signs are needed. It is usual to divide through all three numbers by the highest common factor, hence this is the 010 face. Similarly the faces cutting the OX and the OZ axes only are the 100 and 001 faces respectively. Crystal faces parallel to these, but cutting the negative extrapolations of the axes, are the $0\bar{1}0$, $\bar{1}00$ and $00\bar{1}$ faces respectively.

(ii) A face of a crystal which is parallel to the OX axis and which cuts the OY and OZ axes at distances $2b$ and $2c$ from the origin respectively (Fig. 15b) can be labelled, or *indexed*, since the three integers of the Miller system are known as the *Miller indices*, by application of Eq. (3)

$$\infty : 2b : 2c :: \frac{a}{h} : \frac{b}{k} : \frac{c}{l}$$

thus $k = l$ and $h = 0$, hence this is the 011 face.

(iii) Considering the DEF face on Fig. 14 we find that $h = k = l = 1$, therefore this is the 111 or *unit face*.

(iv) $D'E'F'$ on the same diagram may be indexed from

$$3a : 2b : 5c :: \frac{a}{h} : \frac{b}{k} : \frac{c}{l}.$$

Whence $\qquad\qquad \dfrac{3a}{a/h} = \dfrac{2b}{b/k}$ or $3h = 2k$

and $\qquad\qquad \dfrac{2b}{b/k} = \dfrac{5c}{c/l}$ or $2k = 5l$

$$3h = 2k = 5l \qquad h = \tfrac{2}{3}k, \; h = \tfrac{5}{3}l.$$

Put $h = 1$, therefore $\qquad k = \tfrac{3}{2}$ and $l = \tfrac{3}{5}$.

This is the $1\,\tfrac{3}{2}\,\tfrac{3}{5}$ face.

It is usual to convert these to integers. Here multiply through by ten; thus this is the 10.15.6 face. Such high index surfaces are not often found for crystals grown from solution; the values used here were selected as an example to provide a more difficult calculation of Miller indices. When numbers greater than nine are used it becomes necessary to place full-stops in the index expression to separate the three terms.

It should be noticed, from the above examples, that there is an inverse relationship between the intercept distance on the axis and the Miller index. This reaches a limit with those faces which are parallel to an axis where the appropriate index is zero. Also, the indices in example (iv) above, 10.15.6, were found from a face which intercepted the axes at distances $3a$, $2b$, $5c$ from the origin respectively.

Unit cells and lattice planes

The previous chapter was concerned with the nature of the bonding forces between atoms, considered on a molecular scale, and an account of the factors which influence the positioning of ions within small volumes of the solid. The present chapter has discussed some aspects of the growth of crystals and the geometry of large particles of crystalline solids which contain very large numbers of the repetitive units of molecular dimensions which were previously discussed. It is now necessary to bring together the results from the micro (Chapter 1) and the macro (present chapter) approaches by consideration of the structure of the crystal lattice in greater detail, and also the relationship between the whole crystal and the shape of the smallest repetitive unit from which it was formed.

It has been mentioned that different preparations and different samples of the crystals of a given substance yield solid particles having constant habit in which close agreement of angles between corresponding surfaces of different crystals was found. Also, for any particular crystal, there is a simple relationship between the relative intercepts of different faces on the crystal axes. These observations lead Haüy to suggest, in 1784, that the crystal is composed of a regular three-dimensional array of very small crystal units each of which is the same shape as the whole crystal. Subsequent research has given a very large measure of support to this picture of the crystalline solid. While some slight modifications have been suggested, and also the nature of the lattice units have been more fully worked out, the main idea suggested by Haüy is still acceptable. The basic concept is illustrated in two dimensions in Fig. 16 where the repetitive unit is the four-atom square, one such square being shown connected by full lines (left-hand bottom corner). The array shown is derived from continued repetition of this unit over the region of pattern illustrated to give a figure in which the angles between the bounding rows are the same (90°) as those between the bounding edges of the repetitive unit.

The repetitive unit of a lattice is termed the unit cell. Fig. 17 shows the sodium chloride unit cell, an example of the cubic system. It may be seen that the positions of the Na^+ and Cl^- ions may be interchanged without changing the lattice. If we assume the ions at the corners of the large cube (Fig. 17) are Na^+ (filled circles, smaller radius) it can be seen that each of these eight ions are situated at the corners of eight different such cubes which meet at these points. A further six Na^+ ions in the centre of each of the outer faces of the cube are each common to two adjacent cubes. The cell may thus be seen to contain $8 \times \frac{1}{8} + 6 \times \frac{1}{2} = 4$ Na^+ ions. Similarly the 12 chloride ions at the mid-point of each edge are common to the edges of four different cubes so that the unit cell

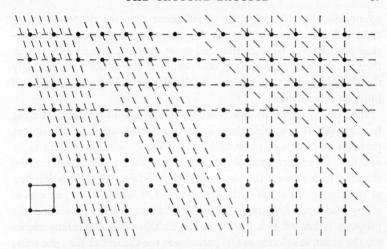

FIG. 16. Two dimensional lattice array formed by regular repetition of the unit enclosed by the full lines. Parallel families of lines (dotted) may be drawn through dots at regular intervals.

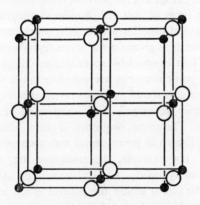

FIG. 17. Unit cell of the sodium chloride lattice. Dark spheres represent sodium ions.

contains $12 \times \frac{1}{4} + 1 = 4$ Cl$^-$. The unit cell contains $(Na^+Cl^-)_4$; more complex unit cells may contain a larger number of ionic 'molecules'.

An infinite number of possibilities exist for the distribution of the positions of the centres of atoms or ions within the repetitive unit of the lattice, but these may be grouped into a limited number of divisions defined by geometrical criteria. The shapes of such cells are classified according to the same set of definitions as those described above in connexion with the selection of reference axes for examinations of crystal shapes. This emphasizes the close connexion between geometrical properties of large crystals and those of the unit cells from which they are derived. However, in description of the lattice unit, not only the shapes of such cells but also the disposition of ions within each cell must be considered.

It has been shown by Bravis (1848) that a total of fourteen different lattice types is possible. Considering the arrangement of constituent particles or groups of particles in unit cells of the cubic system as an example, three arrangements of particles within a cubic cell may be found, which possess the property that whichever particle is selected as the corner of the cube, the arrangement of surrounding particles is always the same. An arrangement of lattice constituents possessing this property is known as a *space lattice*. The three possible arrangements for the example selected are (i) particles at the corners of the cube only, (ii) particles at the corners of the cube and also in the centre of each face (Fig. 4a), and (iii) particles at the corners of the cube and also at the centre of symmetry (Fig. 4b). All possible cubic lattices may be derived from these three types of unit cell. Similar consideration of the geometric arrangement of particles within cells, which have shapes defined by the axes relationships given for the seven crystal systems, shows that there is a total of fourteen possible space lattices. Slight modifications of the selection of particular cells are possible but a total of fourteen Bravis lattices accounts for all possible crystallographic arrangements.

The space lattice represents the arrangement of repetitive units within the crystal. The atoms, or groups of atoms which constitute the individual units, known as *point groups*, may themselves possess symmetry elements. For example, the carbonate ion, $CO_3^{=}$, possesses planes and axes of symmetry. Clearly there is an infinite number of ways in which the atoms within the general group may be arranged. However, in crystals it is found that only point groups having two-, three-, four- or sixfold symmetry axes may be incorporated into repetitive lattice structures. With this restriction on atomic arrangements it is found that a total of 32 different point groups can occur in crystal lattices.

In this discussion of the unit cell, or the prism from which the lattice is derived, emphasis has hitherto been placed on the three-dimensional nature of the repetitive unit. However, it is also possible to regard the crystal as a set of parallel planes, in each of which the centres of atoms are disposed in a repetitive array, and which are stacked together in a regular manner. Fig. 16, for example, may be regarded as part of a section through a sodium chloride crystal in which alternate positions are occupied by Na^+ and Cl^- ions. In this particular example (and not as a general result) the three-dimensional lattice consists of these identical planes stacked so that positive ions occupy positions vertically above negative ions at the same spacing as that between nearest neighbours within each plane. The repetitive unit in the plane in Fig. 16 has been represented as a square, but this array may be alternatively regarded as the various possible sets of parallel equidistant dotted lines shown, with the property that the atoms on each line are spaced at regular intervals. Five sets of such parallel lines are shown, from which it may be seen that the more widely spaced the atoms on each line the smaller the perpendicular distance between successive lines. Identical considerations may be applied to any three-dimensional lattice through representing the lattice as repetition of the prism which is the unit cell or as sets of parallel planes in which the atoms or ions are located as a regular array. Since the dimensions of all the unit cells of a lattice are equal and, in general, the lengths of the three axes are in the ratio $a : b : c$, it follows that planes through the atoms in the solid bear identical geometrical relationships to each other as those which were generalized for external crystal surfaces through the law of rational indices. Moreover, Miller indices may be used to label such planes of atoms in exactly the same way as these have been used to define crystal faces. The 100 crystal face of the sodium chloride cube is a co-planar surface array of the 100 faces of the constituent unit cubes at the surface of the solid. The 110 face may be seen to be formed by the plane of atoms parallel to the OZ axis and through the 45° set of dotted lines in Fig. 16. The octahedral surfaces of sodium chloride crystallized in the presence of urea are crystal faces composed of arrays of the 111 faces of the constituent cubes of the lattice.

The importance of this method of representation of the crystal lattice results from the experimental observation that every planar array of atoms may act as a weak reflecting surface for radiation of suitable wavelength. To observe this property it is necessary to use radiation having a wavelength of the same order as the distance between atoms in the lattice, i.e. X-rays. Crystals are found to behave as a three-dimensional X-ray diffraction grating. In order that maximum reflection from the lattice shall be given, it is necessary for the reflected beams from successive planes of atoms to be in phase. In Fig. 18(b) an incident X-ray beam of wavelength λ, impinges at an angle θ on a crystal having lattice spacing (d). The path difference for reflection from successive planes is $AOA' = 2d \sin \theta$. In order that reflection shall be a maximum this must equal an integral number of wavelengths, $n\lambda$, so that:

$$2d \sin \theta = n\lambda$$

which is known as the Bragg equation. Measurements of the values of θ for which reflection maxima are observed enable information about the spacing between successive crystal planes of the lattice (d) to be obtained. The reflected beam may be detected using a Geiger-Müller counter, an ionization chamber or a photographic film which possesses particular sensitivity in the region of X-ray wavelengths. Some experimental methods are described in the following section.

3. X-RAY EXAMINATION OF CRYSTALS

A useful experimental technique for the determination of X-ray diffraction patterns is shown in Fig. 18(a). The crystal is held at the centre of a table which is calibrated with an angular scale. The crystal mounting is provided with an arm to measure changes in the angle of incidence, and the detector is similarly fitted with a vernier scale so that its displacements also may be determined. In some forms of apparatus the crystal table and the detector mounting are mechanically coupled so that the latter is made to rotate at twice the angular velocity of the former, ensuring constant equality of the angles marked θ in Fig. 18(a). This apparatus enables a number of values of θ, for which the Bragg relation is obeyed, to be measured experimentally. For a cubic lattice in which all the planes of atoms have equal scattering power, aligned so that the 100 planes are vertical (Fig. 16a) it would be expected that, for monocromatic X-radiation, diffraction maxima would be given for obedience to the equation with $n = 1, 2, 3 \ldots$ and, from the Bragg relation it is seen that $\sin \theta_1 : \sin \theta_2 : \sin \theta_3 \ldots : : 1 : 2 : 3 : \ldots$ since d is a crystal parameter and does not vary during rotation. Such a relationship has been experimentally observed for potassium chloride (both ions of this salt have approximately equal scattering power). The actual values of θ_1, θ_2, θ_3, etc., for which the equation is obeyed are, of course, determined by the wavelength of the incident X-radiation used.

An alternative experimental arrangement employs a rigidly held film curved to form a cylinder for which the axis is held vertically to the plane of the table in Fig. 18(a); the film takes the place of the detector shown. Monochromatic X-radiation is obtained by filtering radiation, resulting from electron bombardment of a metal, through a thin film of

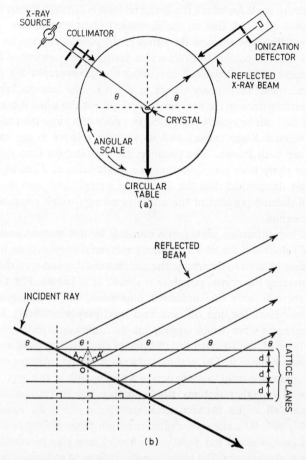

FIG. 18. (a) Experimental method used to measure X-ray diffraction phenomena.

(b) Reflection from successive lattice planes; the distance AOA' is the path difference corresponding to reflection from successive lattice planes.

a second metal. Copper radiation, filtered through nickel, yields the single CuK_α line almost exclusively. When using this technique the specimen usually consists of a small volume of finely crushed powder having a randomly oriented assemblage of small crystallites. This is positioned at the centre of the table and continually rotated during exposure to the X-ray beam to ensure that the radiation meets the crystal planes at every possible value of θ for which diffraction may occur. Every angle for which the Bragg relation is satisfied results in the appearance of a dark line on the developed photographic film. Since diffraction from any plane in the lattice of the powder is given for both $+\theta$ and $-\theta$, the positions of diffraction maxima are symmetrical about the incident beam. Powder X-ray diffraction photographs for nickel oxide and nickel carbide are shown in Fig. 19. The distance between corresponding lines on the film (after development and when it has been laid out flat) can be readily converted to values of θ since the radius of the cylindrical X-ray camera and its position relative to the sample crystal are both known. The distance, on the film, between the two relatively sharp lines corresponding to a single value of d can be more accurately determined than the distance of a single line from the relatively ill-defined position of the undiffracted ray, which consists of a broad maxima.

An X-ray diffraction photograph obtained by this method enables a series of values of θ, for which the Bragg relation is obeyed, to be found. These may be used to determine the dimensions, a, b and c, of the unit cell, providing the crystal structure is simple or is known. For a cubic lattice there is only one unknown dimension, a, in the equations ($a = b = c$ since the unit cell and axes meet perpendicularly). Hence the number of lines which appear on the diffraction photograph is relatively small, the 100, 010 and 001 planes all diffract to yield maxima at the same value of θ. The presence of a cubic crystal structure may be readily confirmed from examination of a photograph of this type. Unit cells based on other systems where there are only two unknowns, tetragonal (all angles between axes are 90°, $a = b \neq c$), hexagonal (60°, 60°, 60°, 90°, one axis different length from the other three), trigonal (angles equal but $\neq$90°, $a = b = c$) may also be established from such photographs. But more complex cells yield numerous diffraction maxima on the film from which the determination of all the lattice parameters may be very difficult. The determination of size and shape of complex unit cells is possible in principle; but in practice results are doubtful since it may not be possible to make measurements with sufficient accuracy to distinguish between alternative possibilities. The determination of any but the simplest unit cell from diffraction data requires considerable skill and experience, since one method of approach to the problem is to attempt to guess the arrangement of atoms which gives the X-ray photograph and work out the values of θ at which the assumed structure would yield maxima. These are then compared with the experimental data and adjustments made to the dimensions of the

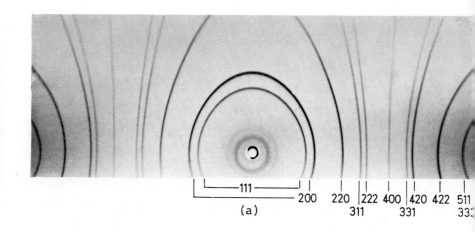

L———111———┘ ┴ ┴   ┴   ┴ ┴   ┴   ┴ ┴   ┴   ┴   ┴
L—————————— 200   220 │222 400 │420 422 511
(a)   311   331   33?

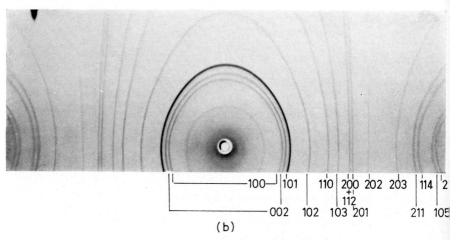

L——————————100—┘ │101   ┴ 110 │ 200 202 203 │114 │'2
                                    +│
                                    112
L——————————— 002   102 103 201   211 105
(b)

FIG. 19. Powder X-ray diffraction photographs for
(a) nickel oxide   ⎱ Including Miller indices for planes giving
(b) nickel carbide ⎰   some of the stronger diffraction lines.

unit cell originally assumed in order to reduce or remove the observed discrepancies. Successive approximations are made until optimum agreement is reached.

Some of the steps in the calculation of expected positions of diffraction lines on a photographic film are illustrated in the following simple example.

Nickel oxide is known to have a face-centred cubic lattice with unit cell edge, $a_0 = 4\cdot168$ Å; it is desired to calculate the position of the ten lowest angle diffraction lines. A diffraction powder photograph for nickel oxide is shown in Fig. 19.

Notes: (i) The planes of atoms which can reflect radiation are oriented at angles to the crystal axes which may be defined by the Miller indices and it can be shown by the methods of solid geometry that the spacings of the various crystal planes, d, are given by

$$d^2(h^2 + k^2 + l^2) = a_0{}^2.$$

(ii) Not every possible combination of values of h, k and l necessarily yields a diffraction line. Where the phase difference for reflection from successive planes differs by half a wavelength no resultant beam is observed. It is therefore necessary to operate the selection rules which are listed in specialist crystallographic texts for various crystalline substances. The selection rule to be applied to the crystal being discussed states that in order that a diffraction maximum shall be observed the values of h, k and l must all be odd or all be even.

(iii) When considering the application of Miller indices to crystal faces it was stated that conventionally the three numbers were divided by the highest common factor. In X-ray work however, it is usual to retain multiple values to indicate the reflections for which the Bragg relation is obeyed with $n > 1$. Thus a 300 plane represents a value of $n = 3$ in the Bragg equation corresponding to reflection from a plane having spacing at $1/3$ that of the 100 plane.

(iv) The scattering power of X-rays varies with the atomic number of the element concerned and the intensity of the beam reflected from a plane containing oxygen ions will be less than that from a plane of nickel ions. This can result in interference effects so that lines on the photograph are not necessarily detected for every possible calculated position, since some may be too weak to detect.

(v) The calculations may be carried through as shown at head of next page, assuming $\lambda/2 = 0\cdot77$Å for CuK$_\alpha$ radiation (nickel filtered).

It is possible to reverse this procedure by starting from a series of

Miller indices	$h^2+k^2+l^2$	$\sqrt{(h^2+k^2+l^2)}$	$\sin\theta = \lambda\sqrt{(h^2+k^2+l^2)}/2a_0$	$\theta°$
111	3	1·732	0·3199	18·7
200	4	2·000	0·3694	21·7
220	8	2·828	0·5224	31·5
311	11	3·317	0·6126	37·8
222	12	3·464	0·6398	39·8
400	16	4·000	0·7388	47·6
331	19	4·358	0·8051	53·6
420	20	4·472	0·8260	55·7
422	24	4·899	0·9048	64·8
511, 333	27	5·196	0·9597	73·7

experimentally determined values of θ, for which it is known that the Bragg relation must be satisfied, and calculating a series of values of $\sqrt{(h^2 + k^2 + l^2)}/a_0$ for the lattice. If the lattice is cubic, a_0 is the only unknown and, since the theory states that the square root term must be a whole number, a series of a_0 values can usually be found, one for each line on the film, from which a mean value of a_0 can be determined. As may be seen from the example, h, k and l do not take every possible value, but the combinations of values of indices for which diffraction maxima are given may be deduced, since these form a related sequence through the operation of a selection rule.

A similar procedure is possible for those lattices which contain two unknown parameters in place of the single a_0 considered in the above example. Graphical aids to the evaluation of such data have been given in specialist texts. Less symmetrical lattices greatly increase the difficulty of determining unit cell parameters.

The range of uses and the sort of information which is obtainable from X-ray studies (using the methods and the apparatus described above) may be summarized:

(i) *Determination of lattice type and unit cell parameters*. This has been described above.

(ii) *Qualitative analyses*. Crystal phases may be recognized. In principle, every crystalline substance in a very small volume of specimen (~ 1 mm^3 or less) gives a characteristic diffraction pattern which may be recognized. If, for example, a small amount of the product from a chemical reaction is known to contain nickel and carbon, X-ray studies may be used to determine whether this is a mixture of the elements or if the nickel carbide phase is present. Examinations of this type are most reliable when comparisons of the diffraction of the unknown substances are made with photographs obtained from authentic specimens of the expected components, since the relative intensities of the lines may be compared in addition to their positions on the film. If the strongest lines in a photograph, obtained for an authentic solid, are absent from the photograph for an unknown substance then it may be concluded that this phase is not a major component though it could be present in small traces. There may be uncertainty in comparisons made between experimental patterns and those calculated theoretically since, if the full selection rules of the latter are not known, the theory may predict lines at positions where diffraction maxima are not, in fact, observed.

(iii) *Alloys and intermetallic compounds.* Changes of lattice constant in metals may occur on alloy formation; these may be measured by X-ray methods. Such examination also enables a mixture to be recognized as an alloy, a mixture of the elements, an intermetallic compound or a mixture of all three such phases.

(iv) *The lattice parameters of some naturally occurring minerals,* e.g. *garnet, are controlled by the chemical composition.* X-ray measurements coupled with measurements of other physical properties such as density and refractive index may be used to determine the composition of a fragment of a natural mineral. X-ray studies have played an important part in the recognition and classification of clays and minerals occurring in nature.

(v) *Crystal size and orientation.* In the experimental method described above, it was assumed that the crystallites in the powder specimen were sufficiently small to present diffracting planes at every possible orientation to the X-ray beam. Several factors may modify this random state: (a) If the crystals of the specimen were grown under conditions tending to align crystal axes in a common direction, this may be detected on the X-ray photograph as a more intense darkening in certain regions of the diffraction line since more diffracting planes are aligned in one direction as compared with another direction. (b) The presence of a small number of relatively large crystallites gives an effect similar to (a) except that more intense spots in the pattern are more localized in area and are sharper. Where the sample consists of a number of small crystals, lines composed of clusters of very variable numbers of spots may be recognized in place of lines of almost constant intensity found when using a very fine powder. (c) Where the size of crystals is very small indeed the numbers of atoms or ions in each particle may be too small to yield a

E

sharp diffraction pattern. This results in broadening of the diffraction lines so that the value of d varies between limits, and each line appears more diffuse. Formulae have been developed to enable semi-quantitative information about crystal size distribution to be obtained from samples showing the above effects.

(vi) *Coefficient of expansion.* Measurements of the interlattice spacing of a crystal, thermostatically controlled at several known temperatures, may be used to determine the coefficients of expansion in the directions of each of the major axes.

A variation of the above experimental approaches to the determination of interlattice spacing, is to align a small single crystal of the compound being investigated so that it rotates about a crystal axis during exposure to a beam of X-rays (having homogeneous wavelength) while the diffraction maxima are detected on a cylindrical film. On development, the photograph shows series of darkened points of diffraction maxima located in parallel lines, the distance between such lines may be used to determine spacings between successive planes of the lattice. The crystal may then be realigned and spacings on the other axes found.

The final experimental approach to be described here is that due to Laüe. In this method the crystal is not rotated during exposure to a narrow incident beam of X-rays. Now, in the description of the experimental technique using a powder sample, given above, it was stated that it is necessary to use a cluster of a very large number of small crystallites so that diffracting planes are oriented at every possible angle to the incident beam, ensuring that the sample would yield diffraction maxima at every angle for which the Bragg relation was obeyed. The chance of a particular crystal being oriented at an angle for which a diffraction maximum will be given, is small. Hence, in the Laüe method it is necessary to use a white X-ray beam, which consists of radiation having a range of wavelengths, in order that an appreciable number of diffraction maxima shall be observed through variation of λ in the Bragg equation. Such a photograph consists of a series of single dark spots arranged in a pattern about a central maximum, located by the undiffracted beam. This type of pattern may yield information about the shape of the unit cell, and, of more practical importance, the planes and axes symmetry. This technique has been largely used in preliminary studies to give information which can be subsequently used in conjunction with studies by the other methods for the elucidation of more complex lattice structures.

The scattering power of the planes of atoms in the crystal is controlled by (i) the density of component particles, and (ii) the density of electrons around the constituent atoms or ions. In a crystal, such as potassium chloride, both ions are isoelectronic so that the efficiency of planes of chloride ions in yielding X-ray diffraction maxima is similar to that of potassium ions. The cubic diffraction pattern is therefore given in which all lines on the photograph obtained are approximately equal intensity. The same is not true of sodium chloride, however, since Na^+ and Cl^- contain 10 and 18 electrons respectively. This significant difference results in this salt yielding a diffraction pattern of the face-centred cubic type. This can be seen from consideration of Fig. 17 where the chloride ions (18 electrons) are arranged in a face-centred cubic lattice. The sodium ions occupy a similar arrangement but their scattering power (10 electrons) is less. This again emphasizes the necessity to consider both positions and scattering power of ions in the lattice when making predictions of diffraction patterns. This point was mentioned above in connexion with the calculation of the position of lines on the nickel oxide pattern.

In recent years considerable advances have been made in the application of X-ray techniques to the elucidation of the structure of complex naturally occurring molecules including proteins. Several factors have contributed to this advance, one is the technique of introducing a heavy atom into the molecule. This particularly large scattering centre is bonded in the molecule at a position which may be characterized by chemical tests, and also its position in the unit cell of the solid may be located by X-ray techniques. The structures of some of the first complex molecules to be elucidated by this approach were those which contained a heavy metal atom, for example, vitamin B_{12} studied by Hodgkin.

The X-ray pattern of the solid results from radiation scattering by the electron clouds of the constituent atoms. If a structure of the molecule is assumed, and chemical evidence may be useful in suggesting possible trial structures, the X-ray pattern from the trial structure may be calculated. From comparisons between the observed pattern for the crystal under consideration and those calculated from the trial model, it may be possible to modify the structure originally assumed in such a way as to improve agreement between the theoretical and the observed patterns. If the molecule is complex, the calculations involved may be prolonged. A considerable advance in the solution of such problems has resulted from the application of electronic computers which reduce the amount of labour necessary to carry them through.

4. STRUCTURE OF SOLID SUBSTANCES

Hitherto the present chapter has been concerned with the external form of crystals of good habit, experimental methods by which information about crystal lattices can be obtained and conventions used in the communication of such data between workers. Chapter 1 was largely concerned with the description and characteristics of forces between the constituent lattice units (atoms, molecules or ions). The positioning of such units relative to each other within the unit cell was not discussed in detail but only mentioned with particular reference to the bonding forces and physical properties of the crystal. It is now necessary to consider examples of solid substances having a wider range of crystallographic structures than those discussed before, and particular consideration will be paid to the relationship between bond structure and the arrangement of atoms in the solid. Relatively simple structures including diamond, metals and inert gases have been mentioned above; the remainder of this chapter will therefore be concerned with a wider range of ionic substances, silicates (including natural minerals), organic polymers, and also glasses.

Ionic solids

From measurements of the unit cell edge(s) of many ionic crystals it has been concluded that, when packed in a crystal lattice, many spherically symmetrical ions behave as if they were spheres of well defined radius. At first sight this model apparently contradicts modern electronic theory which describes the outer shell of an ion as being a charge cloud in which the probability of finding an electron at positions beyond the maximum electron density decreases with increasing distance from the central nucleus. The two concepts are qualitatively reconciled by considering that, at a certain distance from the nucleus, the electron density very rapidly decreases to a small value beyond which the probability of finding an electron is extremely small. This is consistent with the form of the repulsive term given in the section on energy of ionic crystals in Chapter 1. Ions, derived from a single atom, may then be regarded as a spherical charge cloud with a fairly well defined outer bounding edge. The following ionic radii have been deduced from X-ray measurements of the unit cell edges of many compounds in which they occur. The values vary within narrow limits, depending on the other ions in the particular salts, and slightly different values are quoted by different workers.

Li^+ : 0·60	Be^{++} : 0·31	$O^=$: 1·40	F^- : 1·36
Na^+ : 0·95	Mg^{++} : 0·65	$S^=$: 1·84	Cl^- : 1·81
K^+ : 1·33	Ca^{++} : 0·99	$Se^=$: 1·98	Br^- : 1·95
Rb^+ : 1·48	Sr^{++} : 1·13	$Te^=$: 2·21	I^- : 2·16
Cs^+ : 1·69	Ba^{++} : 1·35		OH^- : 1·53
Fe^{3+} : 0·65	Fe^{++} : 0·77		
La^{3+} : 1·15	Ce^{4+} : 1·01	Lu^{3+} : 0·93	
NH_4^+ : 1·46			

All values are in Ångström units.

The following generalizations about ionic radii may be made:

(i) For isoelectronic ions (ions having the same number of electrons in the charge cloud) the ionic radius decreases with increase in cationic charge and increases with increasing anionic charge. This may be seen from the following sequence of ionic radii:

$$Al^{3+}(0·53) < Mg^{++}(0·65) < Na^+(0·95) < F^-(1·36) < O^=(1·40)$$

The greater the positive charge on the central nucleus the more tightly bound, and the more closely held to the central nucleus, are the (constant number of) electrons in the charge cloud.

(ii) For a given element the ionic radius increases in the series cation < (neutral atom) < anion. For a constant nuclear charge the charge cloud will occupy a greater volume the greater the number of electrons it contains.

(iii) There is a decrease in the ionic radii with increase in atomic number in the series of lanthanons which is known as the *lanthanide contraction*. This results from the relatively small screening effect of electrons accepted into the 4*f* shell so that the outer electrons of the ion are more strongly attracted by the increasing positive nuclear charge. Thus, lutetium, atomic number 71, has a smaller ionic radius (Lu^{3+} – 0·93Å) than lanthanum (La^{3+} – 1·15Å), atomic number 57. A second result of this contraction is that the ionic radius of zirconium (Zr^{4+} – 0·80Å) and hafnium (Hf^{4+} – 0·78Å), 5th and 6th period of the Periodic Table respectively, are extremely close. The chemistry of this pair of elements is probably more closely similar than between any other pair of elements outside the lanthanons.

(iv) Ions such as NH_4^+, OH^- and several others may be regarded as spherical to a good degree of approximation. Values for the ionic radii of these two species have been included in the table above. Many ions are, however, asymmetric and cannot be regarded as approximating to spherical shape, e.g. the azide ion N_3^-, in which all three nitrogen atoms are collinear. Other ions again may be regarded somewhat intermediate in behaviour; for example, alkali metal and ammonium perchlorates crystallize in the rhombic system at low temperatures due to 'interlocking' of the constituent ions. Above a transition temperature, however, the crystal transforms to cubic structure and it seems probable that free rotation of the perchlorate ion becomes possible in the crystal which now may be regarded as consisting of approximately spherical ions.

Both molecular and ionic crystal lattices result from non-directional bonding where each unit, molecule or ion, tends to surround itself with as many nearest neighbours as possible. The distance between successive units (i.e. molecules or ions) in the former crystal type is greater than that of the latter. In both classes of solid the shape of the unit cell of the lattice is dependent on the shape of the species from which the crystal is formed. However, two factors operate in ionic crystals which are not present in molecular solids; these are (i) the relative sizes of the two (or more) ions, and (ii) the relative numbers of ions of opposite charge signs.

Relative sizes of ions

If ions of both signs were of equal radii these would form a lattice having closest packing of spheres, as is observed, for example, with the (molecular) crystal of solid inert gas. We will now consider a sequence of compounds in which the radius of one of the ions progressively decreases relative to the other. It is found experimentally that such a series of crystals adopts lattices in which the smaller ion shows a progressive decrease in the number of nearest neighbours. The relative sizes of the two ions in a crystal is defined by the radius ratio, r_+/r_-, where r_+ and r_- are the radii of the cation and anion respectively. This definition usually gives a ratio less than unity, since, for most ionic substances, the radius of the negative ion is greater than that of the positive ion. The number of nearest neighbours of any ion is known as its *Goldschmidt co-ordination number* or the co-ordination number. In the particular example for which $r_+/r_- = 1$ the co-ordination number would be 12 for both ions. For solids in which $r_+/r_- < 1$ the co-ordination numbers for the ions of a particular salt may be predicted from geometrical calculation of the limiting radius ratios for possible structures. The type of calculation used is illustrated in Fig. 20 where (a) represents a limiting case of square coplanar co-ordination, in which each of the four anions just touch the surface of the central cation (assumed to be a sphere) and each one also touches two other anions within the square planar arrangement shown. If the size of the cation is

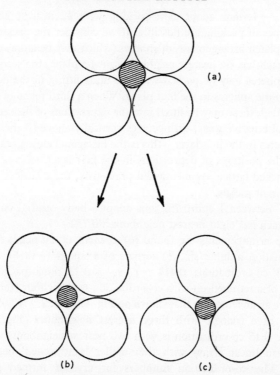

FIG. 20. (*a*) Limiting case of stable planar fourfold co-ordination in the lattice of an ionic solid.

(*b*) Unstable four-fold co-ordination ⎱ The central ion is relatively
(*c*) Three-fold co-ordination   ⎰ smaller than in Fig. 20(*a*) above.

now reduced slightly relative to the anion two situations are possible and these are illustrated as (*b*) and (*c*) in Fig. 10. In alternative (*b*) the central ion is no longer touching the four anions. Clearly, large ions of similar charge tend to repel one another and since this tendency is not offset by the maximum attractive force due to 'contact' with the cation outer charge field, this structure is unstable. In a crystal with this r_+/r_- ratio the more stable arrangement, (*c*) is adopted where the three surrounding ions touch the charge cloud of the central ion, to which they are attracted, and the forces of repulsion between touching anions are not introduced. Fig. 20(*a*), therefore, represents the limiting radius ratio for fourfold co-ordination and its value may be calculated. By considering other possible packing arrangements the following theoretical limiting r_+/r_- values have been found:

$r_+/r_- = 1$, ions adopt close-packing with 12 nearest neighbours. Two types of packing are possible. If we consider the packing of successive planar arrangements of spheres (which may be atoms or ions) in which each has six nearest neighbours in the plane, the second planar set of spheres may be packed with the units fitting in the depressions between the spheres in the first plane. When a third plane of spheres is then added, these may be fitted into the depressions of the second layer in two alternative ways, with centres vertically above (i) the centres of the spheres in the first layer – this is the hexagonal close packed lattice, or (ii) the positions of depressions in the first layer – this is the cubic close packed lattice. As mentioned previously, these lattices are found for different metals.

r_+/r_- between 1 and 0·732 ions adopt a body-centred cubic lattice where each has eight nearest neighbours: $0·732 > r_+/r_- > 0·414$, two possible arrangements are found (a) corners of an octahedron with co-ordination number six, (b) corners of a square (a in Fig. 20) with fourfold co-ordination; $0·414 > r_+/r_- > 0·22$, ions packed at the corners of a tetrahedron with co-ordination number four (this is an alternative arrangement to that shown on Fig. 17c); $0·22 > r_+/r_- > 0·15$, corners of a triangle with three nearest neighbours (Fig. 17c) and $r_+/r_- < 0·15$ co-ordination is with two nearest neighbours and hence ions form linear arrays with the smaller 'sandwiched' between the larger. The co-ordination numbers for crystals formed from two spherical ions may thus be readily predicted if the radius ratio can be found and very many salts are known in which the lattice structures found by crystallographic measurements are in agreement with those predicted by the above calculations.

From the ionic radii values tabulated in the preceding section, it may be found that the radius ratio value for sodium chloride is 0·525 and, as may be seen from Fig. 17, each ion is surrounded by six ions of opposite sign at the corners of an octahedron in accordance with prediction (a) for the 0·732 – 0·414 radius ratio range above. Caesium chloride (Fig. 21a) where the radius ratio is 0·93, crystallizes with co-ordination number eight, the body centred cube lattice allowing a larger number of nearest neighbours than the sodium chloride lattice. This is known as 8 : 8 co-ordination since each ion is surrounded by eight nearest neighbours ions of opposite sign. A chloride ion at a corner of the cube has eight Cs^+ nearest neighbours at the centres of the eight cubes which meet at that corner and the Cs^+ ion at the centre of the cube has eight nearest neighbours, Cl^- ions, at the eight corners of the cube.

Relative numbers of ions

The arrangement of ions in the lattice is also dependent on the relative number of ions of each sign. Two examples of the lattice found for compounds having the formula AB_2 are described below:

The Rutile lattice. Titanium dioxide crystallizes as rutile in the structure shown in Fig. 21(*b*). The radius ratio is 0·49, and, following prediction (*a*) above, for this range, each titanium atom has sixfold co-ordination. The central atom of the prism is co-ordinated with four oxygen atoms: two located on each of the surface (parallel) diagonals on the top and bottom surfaces of the rectangular unit cell. Each such titanium ion is also co-ordinated with two further oxygen atoms which are situated 'half-way-up' the plane joining the two opposite edges of the cubes which the surface diagonals did not meet. Each oxygen ion is co-ordinated with only three titanium ions: an atom situated within the body of the cell is co-ordinated with the central titanium ion and two of the corner ions on a single edge. The oxygen atoms on surface diagonals are co-ordinated to the two titanium ions at the centres of the two cells which share this common interface (at which the ion is located) and one titanium ion at the corner of the cell. This is known as 6 : 3 co-ordination. Several other dioxides, e.g. SnO_2 and MnO_2, crystallize with this structure.

This lattice is an example of the tetragonal crystal; all three axes of the unit cell are mutually perpendicular with one having a different length from the other two (Fig. 20*b*).

The Fluorite lattice. Calcium fluoride has radius ratio 0·73, which is very close to one of the limiting values listed above (0·732), and in the crystal lattice the ions adopt the alternative having the higher co-ordination number so that each Ca^{++} ion has eight F^- nearest neighbours. The unit cell is shown in Fig. 21(*c*), where the filled circles represent F^- and the open circles Ca^{++} ions. The fluoride ions are located at the corners of a small cube having a common centre with the larger cube in which the calcium ions are located at all corners and the centres of faces. The calcium ion at the centre of the top face of the cube is co-ordinated with the four fluoride ions at the top of the cube inside the cell shown and a further four in the lower half of the group of eight in the adjacent cube above. A corner Ca^{++} ion is co-ordinated with one (i.e. the nearest) fluoride ion in each of the eight cubes which meet at that point. Each fluoride ion is co-ordinated with the four nearest calcium ions, three of these are at the centres of three faces of the larger cube and the fourth at the point at which the three faces meet. The

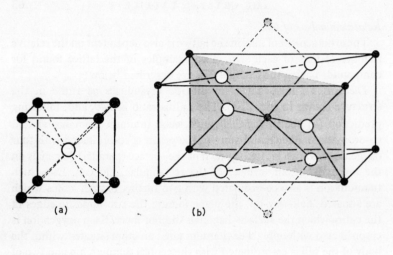

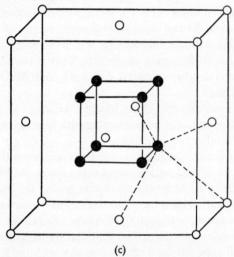

FIG. 21. Unit cells of three ionic solids.

(a) Caesium chloride. 8 : 8 co-ordination.
(b) Rutile (titanium dioxide). 6 : 3 co-ordination.
(c) Fluorite (calcium fluoride). 8 : 4 co-ordination.

In these, and similar diagrams, the spheres representing ions have, for clarity, been drawn with reduced radius values. In a real crystal the outer surfaces of the ionic spheres would be expected to touch as shown in Fig. 20.

dotted lines show this for one particular ion in Fig. 21(*c*). BaF_2, ThO_2 and CaF_2 all form crystals having this type of lattice.

This unit cell is classified in the cubic system since it has three mutually perpendicular axes of equal length.

Other inorganic salts. The four crystal lattices described above, NaCl, CsCl, TiO_2 and CaF_2 and numerous other inorganic crystalline substances are formed by the electrostatic attractions between discrete ions. However, if some of the ions, particularly negative ions, are polarizable, the character of the crystal changes so that some of the strong bonding forces become directional and the salt may take on some of the character of covalent and molecular crystals. For example, in mercuric iodide HgI_2, each iodide ion forms one bond and one donor bond, with two different mercury ions, and each mercury ion is tetrahedrally coordinated to four iodide ions so that both ions are located in planar sheets. Such parallel sheets are bonded together in the crystal by relatively weak forces.

The lattice of a crystal of palladium chloride consists of palladium ions located in straight lines and parallel to the axis of these ions are two lines of chloride ions. Each chloride ion may be regarded as bonded to one palladium ion and donor linked to the adjacent metal ion in the chain. The distance between adjacent chains of ions is larger and the attractive forces correspondingly weaker than the bond lengths between atoms within each chain.

With ionic salts possessing asymmetric ions (azide has been mentioned, carbonate and nitrate are other examples,) the bonds within the ion are largely covalent and the crystal structure is influenced by the shape of the complete charged unit. The shape of the unit cell is governed by similar general principles to those discussed above together with the additional factor due to shape; more detailed accounts for particular examples may be found in specialist crystallographic texts.

Many ionic solids contain water of crystallization. This may be firmly bonded to the metal atoms, $[Al(H_2O)_6]^{3+}$ in alums, $[Ni(H_2O)_6]^{++}$ in hydrated nickel salts, and these ions comprise one of the charged units from which the lattice is formed. Ammonia, and many other ligands, may be similarly held to a central atom by donor bonds; for example, in the salt $[Ni(NH_3)_6]^{++} (ClO_4)_2{}^{-}$.

In other crystalline substances water may act as a 'packing material' and is then incorporated into interstices in the solid left vacant by the arrangement of the other ions. Hydrogen bonding between such water and other species in the lattice increases the stability of the crystal structure.

Isomorphism. Isomorphic substances are those in which the atoms of one element have replaced those of a different element without appreciable alteration of crystal structure. Much of the early interest in the subject was directed towards the use of isomorphism to indicate the valence states of elements by comparative methods. For example, it was concluded from the isomorphism of the two salts $Na_2HPO_4.12H_2O$ and $Na_2HAsO_4.12H_2O$ that in each salt the phosphorous and the arsenic atom was bonded in a like manner. This technique was used to determine valence, for use in atomic weight measurement, by Mitcherlich, who observed that potassium sulphate and potassium selenate were isomorphous and hence concluded that the formulae were identical except that the atom of sulphur in the sulphate ion was replaced by an atom of selenium in the selenate. It was then possible to compare the atomic weights of the two elements. Other groups of isomorphic substances include aluminium, chromium and ferric oxides (M_2O_3); the spinels, Fe_3O_4 $(FeO.Fe_2O_3)$, $FeCr_2O_4$ $(FeO.Cr_2O_3)$, $NiFe_2O_4$ $(NiO.Fe_2O_3)$ and the alums $K_2M_2^{3+}(SO_4)_4.24H_2O$ where M^{3+} may be aluminium, chromium or iron.

Accurate measurements show that the angles between crystal faces may be slightly different for different members of an isomorphous series. When a solution, containing substances which may form isomorphic crystals, is evaporated the resultant solid phase may be a *solid solution* in which the constituents are randomly mixed throughout the lattice in a similar manner to the mixing of ions in a liquid. However, not all solid solutions are formed from isomorphous constituents; one solid may be dissolved in a second of somewhat different lattice structure, hence the formation of solid solutions cannot be used as a criterion of isomorphism. Other factors which limit the importance of isomorphism as a tool for investigation of crystals are that (i) substances containing ions having similar bonding do not always yield isomorphic crystals, and (ii) crystals which are isomorphic do not always contain ions which have similar bonding.

Silicates

To describe and discuss the structures of a large number of inorganic substances is not within the scope of this book. The selected, relatively simple, examples given above referred to packing of spherical ions and brief mention has been made of crystals in which the ions contain a small number of covalent bonds. Silicates contain larger groups of covalently bonded atoms and such groups are linked in the crystal lattice through ionic forces. The diversity of structures and compositions which are known to exist in the innumerable minerals which occur in nature originally made the classification of silicates appear very complex. This subject has, however, been greatly simplified by the recognition of certain underlying principles which may be briefly summarized as follows:

(i) In classifying naturally occurring silicate minerals it is more useful to consider the lattice structure as the reference factor, rather than chemical composition. The latter may be dependent on the temperature at which the given crystal was formed, the availability of elements in the matrix from which the crystal grew and other factors which are, as yet, imperfectly understood. The nature and arrangement of bonding within the lattice is usually used to define a group of minerals and chemical composition is less significant, though there are often close connexions between the two. End members of solid solutions may be represented by idealized formulae, for example, Mg_2SiO_4 and Fe_2SiO_4, whereas the generalized series solid solutions between these limits may be $(Mg, Fe)_2SiO_4$.

(ii) Each silicon atom is normally attached to four oxygen atoms by tetrahedrally directed bonds. Such bonds have considerable covalent character but also have some ionic character so that we may regard the basic repetitive unit as $[SiO_4]^{4-}$ with some $Si^{4+}(O^=)_4$ character.

(iii) $[SiO_4]^{4-}$ tetrahedra may link through oxygen bridges to form $[O_3Si—O—SiO_3]^{6-}$. This process may be repeated to form polymeric chains . . . $SiO_2^{2-}—O—SiO_2^{2-}—O—SiO_2^{2-}—O$ . . . Such chains may cross-link to form sheets. Linkages between sheets may yield a three dimensional lattice.

(iv) Isomorphic replacement of elements may occur. This can be of two types: (a) Replacement of silicon by another element, the most common substitution being aluminium which also may co-ordinate with four oxygen atoms. This replacement (Si^{4+} by Al^{3+}) must be accompanied by accommodation of a further positive ion in the crystal in order to preserve electrical neutrality. (b) Isomorphic replacement of positive ions in the lattice. When considering structures and compositions of particular minerals it must be remembered that aluminium may provide replacement of both (a) and (b) types. Therefore, a certain fraction of the aluminium in the solid may be contained in the anion and the remainder may provide positive ions in the ionic part of the lattice.

(v) Water in the solid may be present as free molecules hydrogen-bonded to surfaces, water of hydration or as hydroxyl groups. If hydroxyl groups are present they may be considered to be negative ions in the lattice and such oxygen must be distinguished from that incorporated in a $[SiO_4]^{n-}$ tetrahedron.

Some representative examples from the main divisions into which silicates have been classified will now be described.

(1) Isolated $[SiO_4]^{4-}$ groups

(i) *Olivines*. These contain separate $[SiO_4]^{4-}$ ions, and have been mentioned above as $(Mg,Fe)_2 SiO_4$. In addition, solid solutions of this series are known which contain the Mn^{2+} ion.

(ii) *Garnet*. The generalized formula of garnet may be represented $M_3M_2'{}_2Si_3O_{12}$ where M is a divalent element Ca^{2+}, Mg^{2+}, Fe^{2+} or Mn^{2+} and M' is a trivalent element Al^{3+}, Fe^{3+} or Cr^{3+}. It is possible to measure the amount of iron in two different positions in the lattice by analytical determination of the proportions in the two oxidation states. Samples having the composition of end members of the series are very rarely found in nature; most crystals contain a mixture of two or more of the limiting compositions in a solid solution. Diagrams relating variation of composition with physical properties such as unit cell edge, refractive indices and density have been published and these may be used to estimate the composition of a particular crystal.

(2) Small groups of $[SiO_4]$ tetrahedra

(i) Minerals containing the $[Si_2O_7]^{6-}$ ion are comparatively rare; one example is melilite which may be represented $Ca_2MgSi_2O_7$. However, silicon in the anion can be replaced by aluminium and to achieve electrical neutrality one of the cations may be replaced by a trivalent ion; aluminium may again be the replacement. Since Al^{3+} ionic radius (0·55 Å) is small it tends to replace the magnesium ion (0·71 Å) rather than the larger calcium ion (0·99 Å).

(ii) Cyclic linking of six $[SiO_4]$ units occurs in beryl to form the anion unit which has the formula $[Si_6O_{18}]^{12-}$. In the solid the constituent atoms within each ionic ring are bonded largely by covalent linkages, and the charged anions are electrostatically attracted to beryllium and aluminium cations. Each beryllium ion is tetrahedrally bonded to oxygen atoms on four different anionic rings and each aluminium ion is co-ordinated to oxygen in six different rings; the overall chemical composition may be represented $Be_3Al_2Si_6O_{18}$. The arrangements of ions in the solid is such that channels through the centres of successive anion rings penetrate the crystal and enable small gas molecules to diffuse through the mineral. A second example of a solid with similar structure is the mineral cordierite $Al_3Mg_2Si_5AlO_{18}$, in which each covalently bonded anion ring contains a single aluminium atom.

(3) Continued linking of $[SiO_4]$ tetrahedra (Metasilicates)

Repetitive linking of tetrahedra can lead to a chain structure of the form shown diagrammatically in Fig. 22(a), for which it must be understood that the silicon to oxygen bonds are tetrahedrally directed. The bonding within the anion unit has considerable covalent character. The ionic bonding between the octahedrally or tetrahedrally co-ordinated cations of the mineral and the oxygen of the anion is relatively weaker so that minerals containing this structure show a fibrous character with the greatest strength along the direction of the anion (c axis). An example of a mineral of this type is diopside $MgCa(SiO_3)_2$.

Cross-linking between two such chains can occur to yield a macro-anion consisting of joined hexagonal units, Fig. 22(b), found in amphiboles, a class of naturally occurring minerals. Again, tetrahedral disposition of linkages is found; the charged ions (represented as —O^- in the diagram) are above and below the other atoms which are close to a planar surface. Asbestos, a well known fibrous type material having strong bonds in one dimension but not in the other two, is an example of an amphibole. Both types of chain silicates described here show extensive isomorphous replacement of cations by other metal ions of comparable ionic radii.

(4) Sheet silicates

Repetitive linkages between parallel chains of tetrahedra yield approximately planar macro-anions (Fig. 22c). Those oxygen atoms, covalently bonded to two silicon atoms, and also the silicon atoms are close to a single plane while the charged (—O^-) species are, by virtue of the tetrahedral bonding, all raised to a plane somewhat above the mean level of the other atoms. The crystal of the solid is formed by parallel arrangement of such covalently bonded anionic sheets with cations interspersed between then.

This macro anion is present in talc where pairs of such sheets are linked by ionic forces to an array of magnesium ions located between them, both sheets being oriented so that the side bearing the charged oxygen species faces the cations. Three of the oxygen atoms are bonded

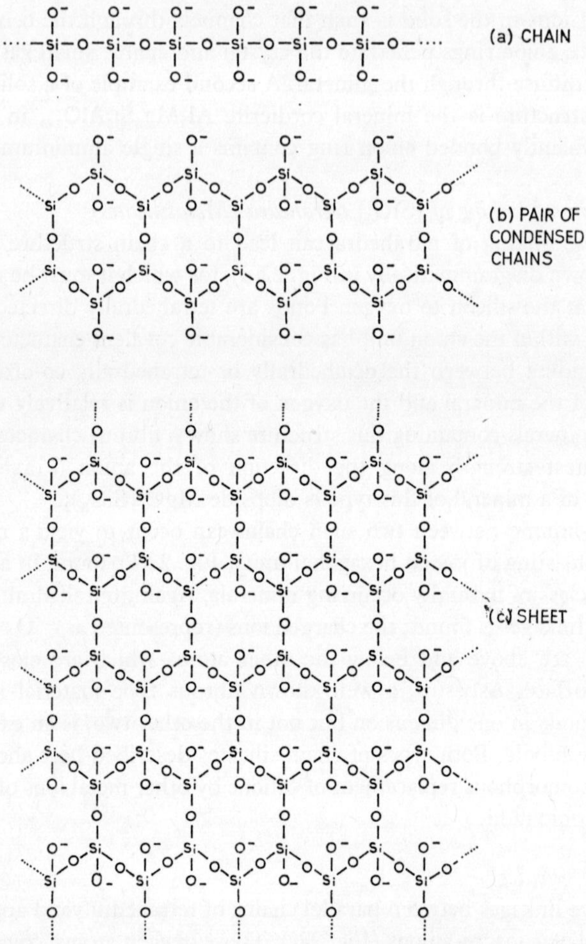

FIG. 22. Anion structures in silicates.

In each ion the Si–O bonds are tetrahedrally directed. In (c) the oxygen ions (—O⁻) lie above the plane which passes close to the centres of all other atoms.

to hydrogen ions so that a single unit from the polymer may be schematically represented, see facing page.

Repetition of this unit yields sheets from which talc is formed, neighbouring sheets being weakly linked by van der Waals forces which results in a very soft solid, and, like graphite which has a somewhat similar structure, may be used as a lubricant.

Si_6O_9 covalently bonded rings $\quad\quad$ } covalently bonded
$O_6(OH)_3$ oxygen ions 'above' plane of rings } together (Fig. 22c).
Mg_9 cation plane
$O_6(OH)_3$ } as above. $\quad\quad\quad\quad\quad\quad\quad$ } covalently bonded
Si_6O_9 $\quad\quad$ } together (Fig. 22c).

Such sheet structures are also present in the micas, which may be regarded as being structurally derived from talc through the replacement of a fraction of the silicon atoms by aluminium together with intercalation of potassium ions between successive sheets. The idealized structure for the mineral muscovite may be represented similarly to that given for talc above:

$\vdots$

Si_3AlO_6 $\quad$ covalent ring system $\quad$ } covalently bonded $\quad$ } electrostatic
$O_4(OH_2)$ $\quad$ charged surface of ring } $\quad\quad\quad\quad\quad\quad\quad\quad\quad\quad$ } bond
Al_4 $\quad\quad$ cation array $\quad\quad\quad\quad\quad\quad\quad\quad\quad\quad\quad\quad\quad$ } "
$O_4(OH)_2$ } as above $\quad\quad\quad\quad\quad\quad$ } covalently bonded
Si_3AlO_6 }
K_2 $\quad\quad$ cations between successive sheets. $\quad\quad\quad\quad\quad$ } "

$\vdots$

This structure represents an idealized composition, since isomorphous replacements can occur to different extents. Most naturally occurring micas resemble garnet in so far as they consist of mixtures or solid solutions of end members of isomorphic replacement series. The idealized formula of muscovite is $KAl_2(OH)_2(Si_3Al)O_{10}$. A similar substance is the mineral phylogophite ($KMg_3(OH)_3(Si_3Al)O_{10}$) in which aluminium cations have been replaced by magnesium. Further replacement of silicon in the anion by aluminium may be accompanied by incorporation of divalent calcium ions between successive sheets in place of potassium.

The softness of talc has been emphasized and attributed to very weak bonding between successive planes. Electrostatic bonding between successive sheets by the monovalent potassium ions in muscovite is weaker than the covalent bonds within each sheet, so that these solids exhibit a pronounced plane of cleavage at which the solid is fairly readily mechanically ruptured in the plane parallel to the macroanion. When divalent calcium ions are present between successive pairs of anionic sheets the mineral becomes harder, more brittle and the cleavage planes are less well developed.

Clay minerals. Those minerals which have been found in clays,

F

kaolinite ($Al_2(OH)_4Si_2O_5$), halloysite, montmorillonite and others, are difficult to investigate experimentally since they form rather small crystals and isomorphous replacement reactions yield products of highly variable composition. Many such minerals resemble mica in that they exhibit well defined cleavage planes. Kaolinite has a layer type lattice in which the repetitive units are all aligned in the same direction so that there is a resultant dipole normal to each plane:

$$
\text{Covalent bonds}
\left\{
\begin{array}{l}
\vdots \\
(OH)_9 \\
Si_6O_9 \\
O_6(OH)_3 \\
Al_6 \\
\vdots
\end{array}
\right\}
\left.
\begin{array}{l}
\text{repetitive unit in kaolinite} \\
\text{electrostatic bond.}
\end{array}
\right.
$$

Clays are formed by weathering of the minerals in rocks and this may involve hydrolysis of the aluminosilicate reactant so that many clay minerals contain appreciable numbers of hydroxyl groups. Clays also usually interact readily with water; the hydroxyl groups confer hydrophilic character, so that the interlayer distance (the c distance of the unit cell) of montmorillonite (and similar substances) varies with the amount of water contained in the mineral. The interlayer distance increases as the clay is hydrated, through penetration of water between the lattice units, and contracts on removal of this water. Many clays exhibit colloidal properties and disperse in water through complete rupture of the bonding between successive planes on hydration.

(5) Three-dimensional silicates

(i) *Silica.* Linkage between [SiO_4] tetrahedra to form planar anions has been considered above, and the formation of solid silica, SiO_2, may be regarded as continuation of the condensation process to the limit, to yield a covalent neutral macromolecule. Slightly different possible spatial dispositions of the tetrahedral [SiO_4] units are present in the α and β forms of each of the three SiO_2 crystal structures; quartz, cristobalite and trydimite.

(ii) *Felspars.* Isomorphous replacement of part of the silicon in a three-dimensional lattice necessitates inclusion of positive ions to preserve electrical neutrality. In the felspars, which are minerals of widespread occurrence and important constituents of many rocks, the [$(Si,Al)O_4$] tetrahedra are linked in a three-dimensional array with inclusion of alkali or alkaline earth metal ions in the lattice to preserve electrical neutrality. The pair of minerals albite $(Na(AlSi_3)O_8)$ and anorthite $(Ca(Al_2Si_2)O_8)$ form a continuous series of solid solutions since the positive ions have comparable ionic radii. Solids of this type, containing other alkali metal ions, are also known.

(iii) *Zeolites.* The three-dimensional framework of some zeolites are very much more open than that of the polymeric structures considered under (i) and (ii) above, and small molecules, e.g. water, can diffuse through the channels within the open framework of the lattice. The lattice of the solid is rigid so that the lattice parameters, unlike those of the clays, are not varied by hydration and dehydration.

If a part of the lattice silicon in such a structure is replaced by aluminium the positive ions, necessary to balance charges, may be incorporated within the pores of the solid, at the surfaces of every channel in the open structure of the polymer. Since diffusion of solutions through the open lattice network is possible, such electrostatically attracted cations may be exchanged for those in solution, a process which may be compared with an ionic double decomposition reaction with the important proviso that one of the ions involved must be retained at the surfaces of the channels within the zeolite macroanion. For example, in a sodium zeolite the sodium may be replaced by potassium by washing thoroughly with a solution containing potassium ions. This process has been used for water treatment through the replacement of calcium ions in 'hard' water by sodium ions from a sodium zeolite and the calcium ions are retained in synthetic zeolites which have been developed for this purpose. The zeolite may be regenerated after use by washing with a brine solution so that the calcium ions are replaced by sodium, and the silicate may be used once again for purification of a further volume of hard water.

Zeolites may be penetrated by particular molecules but not by different, more bulky, molecules. Barrer has shown that straight-chain hydrocarbons may travel through the bulk of certain solid zeolites while branched chain isomers cannot enter or be accommodated in the narrow pores.

Ultramarine is a felspathoid which has an open rigid anion framework, $[(Al,Si)O_4]$ units, which incorporate negative ions within the lattice. Sodalite, $Na_4Al_3Si_3O_{12}Cl$, is one example of a substance of this type, but many compounds having a number of different anions, giving solids of different colours, are known.

Organic polymers

Many high molecular weight substances are known, in which the properties of the solid materials result from the bond disposition in the series of repetitive units which comprise the constituent polymeric macromolecules. The polymers considered in the present section are derived from organic compounds and, thus, carbon-carbon linkages provide the main bonding in the structural units of each molecule, though other elements may occupy regular positions in the repeating pattern. Such polymeric substances are of wide occurrence in nature and a series of synthetic polymers form the basis of an important plastics, fibres and elastomers industry. The reason for the technological interest in polymers is that the properties of these manufactured substances can be controlled to a considerable degree of accuracy to yield materials possessing properties desirable for specific uses and which can be prepared on a large scale. Similarly, living organisms produce highly specific polymeric structures adapted to the needs of each particular species. The present account will, however, be concerned with the relationships between structure and physical properties of synthetic polymers, since these are more fully understood than the complex structures which occur in nature. For a more general account of polymers the reader is referred to an appropriate text, since the present section is concerned with solids only.

Most polymeric structures are comprised of atoms linked through covalent bonds; those directed valence forces which do not form part of the main polymer chain may be satisfied through linkage to hydrogen, methyl, phenyl or other groups. The arrangement of bonds within the repetitive unit of the polymer molecule may be in the form of (i) extended chains, to yield linear molecules, which may possess regularly spaced, short side-chains (i.e. $-CH_3$), (ii) branched chains, derived from a predominantly linear structure or (iii) extensively cross-linked bonding between constituent units, to yield a polymeric structure extending in three dimensions. It is usually found that those polymers formed from compounds which possess only two functional groups in each molecule yield linear chain-type polymers which may soften on warming. Polymers derived from compounds which contain more than two functional groups in each monomer unit may contain a three-dimensionally linked structure and, since these substances may increase the extent of cross-linking on heating, such materials may harden, rather than soften, at elevated temperatures.

Species (i) and (iii) bear an apparent formal resemblance to fibrous and three-dimensional silicates, though it must be remembered that in polymers: (a) the forces between neighbouring molecules may be largely van der Waals in character, (b) these substances may have a low degree of crystallinity (in contrast with numerous ionic salts), (c) the spatial distribution of individual molecules may be more accurately represented as a tangled skein than as a straight chain and (d) a linear polymer may possess regularly arranged short side-chains. As in other aspects of the study of solids, a classification of polymeric solids into rigidly defined groups cannot be made, hence we will adopt the headings as follows: (i) linear polymers, (ii) three-dimensional synthetic polymers and (iii) natural polymers.

(i) *Linear polymers*. On heating ethylene at high pressure (in the presence of oxygen) polymerization may occur to yield molecules of formula $(-CH_2-CH_2-)_n$, where n may be >200, and there is some chain branching. The structure of polyethylene may be represented as a tangled mass of molecules, containing regions of crystallinity, and regions in which the alignments of adjoining chains are so irregular that the atoms cannot be regarded as forming a crystal lattice. The solid is strong; this results from the interlocking of adjoining zig-zag units of the chains in the lattice, the branching of individual molecules in the solid and the considerable length of each chain. X-ray measurements for crystalline regions have shown that the unit cell dimension along the chain axis is close to the value found for the same parameter in crystals of n-triacontane. Furthermore, both long-chain paraffins ($\sim C_{30}$) and polyethylene exhibit the property that changes in methods of crystal preparation can cause minor variations in lattice structure. Neighbouring chains in the polyethylene lattice interact through van der Waals forces; this is reflected in the relatively large coefficient of expansion found for one dimension of the lattice unit cell.

The absence of regular, closely-spaced side-chains in the polyethylene structure enables the close approach of neighbouring chains. The adoption of such a structure may be inhibited through the introduction of substituents into the monomer. In natural rubber the 'backbone' of the polymer molecule again consists of a chain of carbon atoms, but it differs from polyethylene in that (i) it is unsaturated and (ii) it possesses substituents; the repetitive unit may be represented as shown at the top of page 76. This is an isoprene, $CH_2=C(CH_3)-CH=CH_2$, polymer; two such units are shown in the formula but it may be mentioned that isoprene is not the intermediate involved in biosynthesis. Since all the olefinic bonds are *cis*, the nearest pairs of methyl groups are oriented in

$$\left[-CH_2-\underset{\underset{CH_3}{|}}{\overset{\overset{CH_3}{|}}{C}}=CH-CH_2-CH_2-\underset{\underset{CH_3}{|}}{C}=CH-CH_2- \right]_n$$

different directions. This polymer is most remarkable for its ability to stretch under tension to many times its original length. X-ray evidence shows that there is no significant ordering in unstretched rubber. When a force is applied, however, the molecules slide past one another, re-arranging to give an ordered structure, shown by the development of ability to show an X-ray diffraction pattern; the degree of order increases with the extent of stretching, Relaxation of the tension results in a return of the molecules to the random configuration of the unstretched material.

The composition and structure of gutta-percha are closely similar to those of rubber except that, since all the olefinic bonds are *trans*, the methyl groups do not exhibit the alternation of disposition mentioned for rubber and the repetitive unit may be represented (all methyl groups on the same side of the chain):

$$\left[-CH_2-\underset{\underset{CH_3}{|}}{\overset{\overset{CH_3}{|}}{C}}=CH-CH_2- \right]_n$$

In contrast to rubber, this substance at room temperature is a hard, non-elastic solid, though it may be moulded to desired shapes at elevated temperatures. Thus it is seen that the detailed structure of the units in the polymer molecules may exert profound influence on the properties of the resultant solid.

Examples of solids in which the polymer molecule has a structure similar to that of polyethylene, but in which the properties of the solid have been varied by the introduction of regular substituent groups are provided by the extensive group of vinyl-type polymers,

$$(-CH_2-CHX-)_n,$$

which include polypropylene, $(-CH(CH_3)-CH_2-)_n$, polystyrene, $(-CH(C_6H_5)-CH_2-)_n$, and polyvinylchloride, $(-CHCl-CH_2-)_n$. Many of these polymers are relatively tough, do not readily corrode and have found extensive applications in plastic kitchen-ware, insulators, etc. A variety of properties is shown by polymers within this family,

e.g. $(-CH(CN)-CH_2-)_n$, synthetic fibre;
$(-C(CH_3)(CO_2CH_3)-CH_2-)_n$, glass-like; $(-C(CH_3)_2-CH_2-)_n$ is

rubbery, an elastomer. Polymers of other types may be elastomers, e.g. the sulphur-containing 'thiokols' in which the structural unit is probably $(-CH_2-CH_2-S(:S)-S(:S)-)_n$.

A second family of linear polymers, used extensively as fibres, include polyamides such as:

$$Nylon\ 66\ (-CO.(CH_2)_4.CO-NH.(CH_2)_6.NH-)_n$$

formed by the condensation of hexamethylenediamine and adipic acid (each of which contain six carbon atoms, hence '66') into long chains. Another type of fibre is a polyester, formed by condensation of terephthalic acid and ethylene glycol

$$(-O.CO.C_6H_4.CO.O.(CH_2)_2-)_n$$

In the formation of such molecules, significant chain-branching does not occur. These molecules contain dipoles, which may enable some electrostatic attraction to occur between neighbours, so increasing the strength of the solid. When warm, the polymer may be drawn to a fine thread; this may be further elongated by cold drawing and the resultant fibres are used for textiles, filaments, cords, etc.

(ii) *Three-dimensional synthetic polymers.* When a constituent monomer, of the polymer, bonds with more than two adjacent groups, an inelastic, hard solid containing a three-dimensional system of covalent linkages may be formed. One example of such a solid is a phenol-formaldehyde resin. These two compounds condense in the presence of a basic, or acidic, catalyst, by reactions of the type

$$2C_6H_5OH + HCHO \rightarrow HO-C_6H_4-CH_2-C_6H_4-OH$$

where the methylene group may be *ortho* or *para* to the hydroxyl group. This process may continue to give further linking of the aromatic nuclei through methylene groups attached at both the *ortho* and *para* positions of each ring; since there are three such positions on each nucleus, bonding may extend in three dimensions. In the preparation of such a solid by a manufacturing process, the mixture may be partially polymerized and dried. Polymerization is subsequently completed, for example, by heating in a mould in admixture with hexamethylenetetramine (a source of formaldehyde). From such a process castings, with dimensions accurate to fine limits, can be obtained. This property of hardening with heating contrasts with the behaviour shown by linear polymers, described in the previous section.

Heat-moulded plastics have found wide application in numerous fields, including children's toys, tableware, electrical fittings, etc.

The mechanical properties of the solid are commonly modified by the incorporation of a filler in the reactant mixture.

Another example of a resin with a three-dimensional cross-linked structure is that formed by the condensation of urea and formaldehyde. The urea molecule condenses with formaldehyde to give units of this type:

$$-CH_2-N-CH_2-$$
$$|$$
$$C = O$$
$$|$$
$$-CH_2-N-CH_2-$$

where each methylene unit shown is also directly linked to the nitrogen atom of another urea type unit and the structure extends in three dimensions. A similar resin is formed through condensation of melamine with formaldehyde.

(iii) *Natural polymers.* Polymers in nature include proteins and polysaccharides such as starch and cellulose. Natural rubber has already been mentioned, but a review of these substances is outside the scope of the present monograph. Certain types of bonding which can occur in such systems may be briefly mentioned:

(*a*) Cellulose is a linear polymer of glucose, and the strength of bundles of such fibres is probably increased by cross-linkages and also hydrogen bonding between hydroxyl groups in neighbouring, largely linear, molecules.

(*b*) Proteins are condensation products of α-amino-acids, in which the structure may be represented:

$$\ldots -NH-CHR-CO-NH-CHR'-CO- \ldots$$

The groups R and R' on successive units of the chain vary considerably. Some twenty such groups are common. These groups may possess substituents which form hydrogen bonds between neighbouring chains. Also these groups may contain acidic or basic functional groups which result in electrostatic attractions ($-COO^-H_3N^+-$) between neighbouring molecules.

5. 'SEMI-SOLID' STATES OF MATTER

It was emphasized in Chapter 1 that the division of matter into solids, liquids and gases is not an absolute classification and several substances of intermediate properties are known. Two examples of such behaviour are briefly described here, liquid crystals and glasses, both of which show some properties characteristic of solids.

Liquid crystals. Certain solids do not give a homogeneous isotropic liquid phase on melting but retain some of the properties of the solid phase; for example, liquid crystals retain some properties of the crystal lattice. Liquid crystals are formed by some of those substances in which one molecular dimension is very much greater than the other two. It is believed that in a liquid crystal every molecule does not exhibit motion completely independent of all others but these are retained in groups of aligned molecules which are loosely bonded together. Limited X-ray diffraction patterns can be obtained for liquid crystals, showing that there is some ordering, of the type which occurs in solids but which is absent from liquids. These X-ray observations contrast with the diffuse haloes which are the characteristic diffraction patterns for true liquids.

On heating liquid crystals the lateral bonding between molecules is overcome to yield the random independent molecular motion characteristic of liquids. The transitions from solid to liquid crystal and liquid crystal to true liquid both occur at sharp characteristic temperatures, for example:

Substance	Solid ⇌ liquid crystal ⇌ liquid	
Ethyl-*p*-azoxybenzoate	114°	121°C
p-Azoxyanisole	116°	135°C
Dibenzalbenzidine	234°	260°C

Glass. Glasses exhibit some of the properties of solids but in other ways resemble liquids and are classified as a separate state, the vitreous or glassy state which is most conveniently regarded as being intermediate in character between solids and liquids. Unlike true solids, glasses do not have a sharp melting point but soften over an appreciable temperature range to yield a liquid. On cooling, the liquid may reverse the process, hardening over an appreciable temperature range. On heating aged glass, crystals may separate, a process known as devitrification. X-ray diffraction patterns of glasses consist of a small number of diffuse haloes in place of the sharp diffraction lines or points observed for truly crystalline solids. This property has one particular use in that a glass fibre may be used as a support for crystalline materials in experimental determinations of X-ray diffraction patterns. In contrast to these properties of the liquid state, glass can withstand a shear and, if sufficiently strained, rupture like a solid, but cleavage planes are not found.

Glasses are formed on cooling mixtures of silicon dioxide and/or boron trioxide with the oxides of group IA or IIA metals. Such mixtures yield the familiar material used for windows and for containers. These substances are not the only glasses and other substances which yield glassy or vitreous states include glucose, phosphoric oxide, arsenic oxide, germanium dioxide and beryllium fluoride.

The absence of a crystalline structure in a glass has suggested that it may be regarded as an extremely viscous supercooled liquid. A pictorial representation, in two dimensions, of bonding in a glass is shown in Fig. 23(a), where the oxide units are joined in random array of cyclic

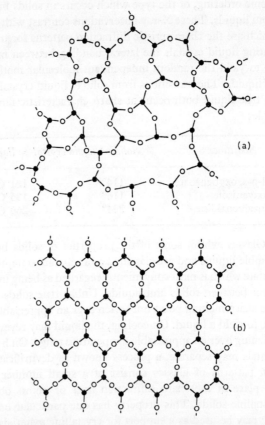

(a)

(b)

FIG. 23. (a) Stylized and somewhat exaggerated representation of the distortion from regular bonding in a glass formed by condensation of units of an R_2O_3 oxide.

(b) Crystalline structure resulting from regular repetitive pattern derived from the same constituent units as in (a).

units of different size in which no regular order occurs, in contrast
to the regular bonding of the same unit in the crystalline solid, Fig.
23(*b*). In a silica glass, such bonding of the tetrahedra extends in three
dimensions. This random bonding between different lattice units in
glasses results in varying degrees of strain in different bonds so that, on
warming, mobility of some of the lattice units becomes possible at a temperature below that at which other, less strained, linkages attain mobility.
Thus, on heating, a gradual 'loosening' process occurs giving softening
over an appreciable temperature range rather than a sharp melting
point which is characteristic of true crystalline solids where all similar
bonds have closely similar strength.

CHAPTER THREE

Band Theory of Solids: Dislocations, Defects and Impurities in Solids

1. BAND THEORY OF SOLIDS

The first chapter of this book was concerned with the relation between certain physical properties of pure solids, including hardness, melting point and crystal lattice, and the strength, directional and polar characteristics of the bonding within and between the crystal lattice constituents. This account of the bonding forces was largely concerned with the short-range linkages, the attractions (and repulsions) between nearest and next-nearest neighbours which are closely spaced in the lattice. An alternative method by which a theoretical description of solids may be developed is to consider the properties of the crystal as a whole. The results of this approach, as discussed in the present chapter, are usually referred to as the *band theory of solids*. A short account of the application of this approach to metals has been given in Chapter 1. In the present chapter we will be concerned with the application of band theory to a wider range of both metallic and non-metallic solids.

Many of the more important problems, to which the band theory of solids has been applied, are in describing and accounting theoretically for the properties of those solids which show deviations from ideal behaviour and also the characteristic behaviour of those crystals which contain impurities. Consideration of particular systems which have been studied and of results explained through the band theory will be discussed in the latter part of this chapter. Before an account of such investigations can be presented, a description of the types of local variations which can occur within the lattice structure of a solid is appropriate. In Chapters 1 and 2 it was assumed implicitly that, in those crystals which were considered as examples, each solid consisted of a perfectly regular repeating array of atoms (ions or molecules) as described by the definition of a lattice. One exception to this perfect pattern, which has been mentioned, is that each atom within the lattice is not held rigidly at the lattice point. Thermal vibration leads to oscillation about the idealized location, the latter point being defined with reference to the average position of other lattice units. In a real solid, however, several types of deviation from the perfect behaviour can, and do, occur. At the edges of crystals, the forces between constituent lattice units are unsymmetrical and thus the strength of bonds in this region differs from the corresponding forces between similar units in the bulk solid. The properties of solid surfaces will be discussed in Chapter 4.

Deviations from perfect behaviour which are known to occur within the bulk (and sometimes also at the surfaces) of solids may be classified in the following main divisions:

(1) Distortion of the lattice through departures from perfect alignment of repetitive units. This type of imperfection is termed a *dislocation* and the effect is embodied in the relative positioning of many lattice units with respect to each other and to adjoining regions of perfect lattice.

(2) A lattice position may be unoccupied and/or a component unit of the lattice may be located within the solid at a position in the repetitive array other than that at which the greater proportion of such units are accommodated. Each absent or misplaced atom (or ion) is known as a *defect*.

(3) The solid may contain impurity atoms (ions or molecules). Two types of impurity systems are possible: (i) excess of one of the constituent units of a binary (or ternary, etc.) substance, resulting in deviation from the exact stoichiometric composition of the compound, or (ii) atoms (or ions) which are not a constituent of the pure substance.

Examples of all three types of behaviour will be given below.

The occurrence of such imperfections, though present in low concentration, may profoundly influence the electrical properties of the bulk crystal since electrons associated with such regions may be capable of removal from the distorted region and may subsequently migrate through the complete volume of the crystal. Such behaviour is most readily considered theoretically through the band theory, which is concerned with the energy distribution of the electrons within the crystal as a whole. The band theory seeks to explain those properties determined by the overall electron assemblage in the complete crystal and these include electrical conduction (and other electrical properties) and spectra. This approach contrasts with the 'nearest neighbour' bonding which was the main topic considered in Chapter 1. It is not intended to imply that there is a contradiction between the two approaches, but that these should be regarded as complementary, each accounting for certain observed characteristic types of behaviour of particular crystals more satisfactorily than the other. Although historically, and in the introduction to the metallic bond given in Chapter 1, particular attention was paid to the application of the band theory to metals, it must be emphasized that this model has been applied to many non-metallic crystals and here we are concerned with the *band theory of solids*.

The detailed mathematical development of band theory is outside the scope of the present monograph. The qualitative account below is intended to outline some of the more important assumptions made together with the steps used in the quantitative development of the model.

The concept of electrons forming an 'electron gas', which executes random motions within metallic crystals, has been mentioned in Chapter 1 in connexion with the metal bond. The energy of such 'gaseous' electrons would be expected to be temperature-dependent and therefore this model predicts that the specific heats of conducing solids would be higher than those of insulators. This simple representation is shown to be untenable since it has been observed that both types of solid obey the Dulong and Petit rule with approximately the same degree of accuracy. From this experimental result it must be concluded that either the energy of the 'free' electrons within a conductor does not change significantly with temperature or only a small fraction of those electrons responsible for the conducting properties of the solid are capable of 'free' motion within the crystal. To determine which alternative operates in real crystals, it is necessary to consider the 'electron gas' concept in greater detail.

The 'electron gas' model considers the metallic crystal as a potential well, within which electrons are accommodated. The crystal surface represents the edge of this well and a large rise in potential occurs at these boundaries so that an electron can only surmount this barrier after attaining considerable energy. At high temperatures it is experimentally observed that electrons do leave the surface of metals, and Richardson has shown that the energy distribution of such electrons obey the predictions of Maxwell-Boltzmann distribution law, a result which is in accordance with the requirements of the 'electron gas' model. It must therefore be concluded that only a small fraction of the electrons can execute random motions within the solid.

The qualitative electron gas model may be refined by considering the interactions between the electrons and the periodic potential field within the crystal due to the positively charged atom nuclei. It is known from observations on the properties of electrons that these possess the characteristics of a wave motion; for example, they may exhibit diffraction phenomena. A crystal can, therefore, be considered to be a periodic potential field in which a wave-motion is accommodated. In the section on X-ray diffraction (the previous chapter) it was seen that the direction of progression of wave-motion (X-rays) within a crystal may be modified by the constituent electrons of the lattice components. A somewhat similar phenomenon may occur between the outermost electrons of the lattice units and the potential variation within the solid. The wavelength of the electrons and the internuclear spacing of covalent, ionic and metallic crystals, are such that interaction can occur. It is possible to make calculations to predict the behaviour of electrons in the periodic potential of the solid from which the form of the energy levels at which electrons may be accommodated within a lattice may be deduced. Each energy level in which an electron may be present can be regarded as a permitted solution of the Schrödinger wave equation for electrons within the solid. The results of calculations using this equation show that electrons in the solid may be accommodated only in bands between limiting permitted energy levels and that the positions and widths on the energy scale, of such permitted bands of levels are a property of both lattice and constituent components of a particular solid. These permitted energy bands are derived from the electron levels of the constituent atoms (or ions). A solid may possess several such permitted energy bands separated by forbidden regions within which no electron may be accommodated.

Consider a fragment of a metallic solid which contains a large number (N) of atoms, each of which contributes a single electron to an energy band of the solid crystallite. This energy band may contain the maximum number $2N$ electrons since each atom in the crystal contributes one level to the solid as a whole and the Pauli exclusion principle states that each level may contain two electrons having oppositely paired spins. In the solid at $0°K$ the electrons occupy the lowest levels available and for the particular band system described above the $N/2$ lowest levels will be doubly occupied and the upper $N/2$ states within the band will be empty. On heating the solid, a small number of those electrons in the uppermost filled levels, in the median region of the band, may acquire some thermal energy and so be promoted to the unoccupied levels immediately above the filled levels and singly occupy a number of these. The energy separation between successive levels, within each permitted band of a crystallite of appreciable size, is very small so that the assemblage of closely spaced levels can be regarded as a *band* of permitted levels. Since only a small fraction of the electrons are promoted on heating, this total contribution to the specific heat is small. Once promoted to a singly occupied level the electron may readily migrate through the solid so that on application of an electric field, the solid shows conducting properties. These promoted electrons constitute the 'electron gas' of the solid but represent only a small fraction of the electrons contained within the band.

The distribution of electrons in such a conducting solid is schematically represented in Fig. 24(a). The inner electrons are associated with particular nuclei and would require appreciable energy to surmount the barrier to transference to a neighbour. Such a process cannot occur where these levels are already doubly occupied. The outermost electrons are accommodated within the band where any electron present in a singly occupied level may migrate throughout the solid without the necessity for surmounting energy barriers between successive atoms. The dotted line (Fig. 24a) represents the half-filled band, the levels below the dotted line being doubly occupied at $0°K$. The position of the electron potential energy on the energy scale is known as the *Fermi level*.

Fig. 24(a) represents the band structure of a conducting solid. Other dispositions of electrons and levels may be envisaged. Two possibilities, for simplicity only showing the outer levels, are given on Figs. 24 (c) and (d). To facilitate comparison, the outer level of Fig. 24 (a) has been included as Fig. 24 (b).

Fig. 24 (c) represents an insulating solid. All the levels in the filled band are doubly occupied so that the motion of a particular electron in one direction must always be exactly counterbalanced by components of motions of other electrons in the opposite direction. When an electric field is applied across the solid no net charge transfer can occur; this is a characteristic property of a solid insulator. The filled band is termed the *valence band*, since these electrons contribute towards the bonding of the solid; the empty band is the *conduction band*. For the particular solid shown in the diagram (Fig. 24c), the separation of the two bands is relatively large, and, at low temperatures, thermal energy is insufficient to promote electrons across the gap from the valence to the conduction band. If the distance between the bands is progressively reduced, considering a series of different solids, a point will be reached where the bands are separated by a sufficiently small gap to enable

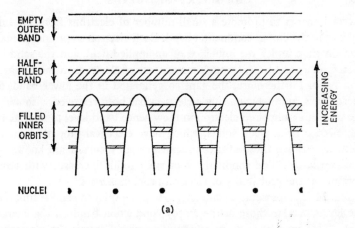

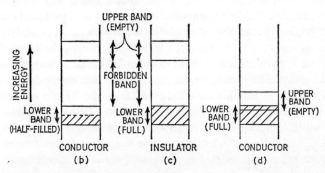

Fɪɢ. 24. Diagrammatic representation of band structure in different types of solids.

(a) Conducting solid showing inner orbits, the lower band of the solid is half-filled and the upper band empty; the upper two levels, only, are shown at (b).

(c) Upper bands only shown for an insulating solid, the lower band is full, and is separated from the upper band by an appreciable energy gap.

(d) A conducting solid in which the filled lower band overlaps the higher empty band.

The inner, filled orbits have been omitted from (b)—(d). >0°K promotion of electrons from the lowest energy levels can occur.

thermal energy to promote a small number of electrons from the full valence to the empty conduction band. Each electron so promoted may then migrate under the influence of an applied field, and the solid is, therefore, a conductor, through movements of electrons in the conduction band. Furthermore, the gaps so generated in the lower band, at those levels from which a single electron has been removed, also allow the remaining unpaired electron in the valence band level to migrate in the electric field. Such solids, which have electrical properties intermediate between those of a conductor and an insulator are known as *semi-conductors*. The conductivity of such solids increases with temperature as the probability of electron promotion rises.

Fig. 24 (*d*) represents a conductor. Here the valence band is full, but the levels overlap those of the empty conduction band on the energy scale. This may be seen by reference to nickel metal; the electronic structure of the outer orbits of the nickel atom may be written $3s^2 \, 3p^6 \, 3d^8 \, 4s^2$. This representation implies that the outermost orbit is filled ($4s^2$) but that an inner shell ($3d^8$) is incomplete. It was stated above, however, that at $0°K$ the electrons will doubly occupy the lowest level on the energy scale. From detailed examination of conducting properties of this (and similar metals) workers in this field have concluded that the energy bands in metallic nickel, derived from the $3d$ and $4s$ levels of the atoms, overlap and electrons are distributed between them so that the former contains, on average, 9·46 and the latter 0·54 electrons per atom. Thus it is concluded that where successive bands overlap the electrons are accommodated at the lowest available energy states and do not exclusively enter one particular band to fill it before starting to enter another. Group II metals show similar behaviour; it has been concluded that the band derived from the outer (*s*) electron level must overlap other levels since solid elements in this group, for example, zinc, show conducting properties.

The resistance of a good conductor is small, of the order of 10^{-4} ohms cm^{-1} while the value for an insulator may be as high as 10^{22} ohms cm^{-1}. It is difficult to account for such considerable differences (a factor $\sim 10^{26}$) by a model based on variations in retention strength of electrons within the bonds between the lattice components. However, the demonstration of a forbidden region on the energy scale, supported by band theory calculations, provides a more reasonable theoretical explanation for the scale of the observed differences.

It is possible to increase the conductivity of insulators by application of a high strength electric field across the solid. Through such a force, the energy of electrons moving in the field direction within the solid is increased and it may be possible for these to acquire sufficient energy to be promoted to the conduction band. Where there is an appreciable energy gap between valence and conduction bands, very high field strengths, $>10^5$ volts cm^{-1}, may be necessary before conductivity is observed.

The resistance of a metallic conductor rises with temperature, since increase in the vibrational energy of atomic nuclei reduces the regularity of the periodic potential field within the solid, with consequent reduction in the ease of electron mobility. When deciding whether a given solid exhibits metallic conduction or if it is a semi-conductor, two factors must be considered: (i) the resistance of a semi-conductor is usually higher than that of a metal since the electrons giving conducting properties must be promoted across the energy gaps before they are able to migrate in an electric field, and (ii) since thermal energy increases the number of electrons in the conduction band of a semi-conductor, such solids contrast with metals by showing a rise in electrical conductivity with temperature increase.

The band theory of solids considers the electronic structure of a complete crystal, whereas the valence bond approach directs attention to the electronic properties of specific small regions of the lattice units. Since both models have been applied to the theory of solids, we must consider points of similarity between them. In a conductor (e.g. a metal) each atom possesses a number of orbitals oriented towards its neighbours but the number of available electrons is insufficient to doubly occupy all these electron-accepting levels. Conduction results from the transference of an electron from an orbital of one atom to that of its neighbour, a process which in a conducting solid may be repeated progressively across the crystal during the application of an electric field. It may also be noted that the energies of electrons in corresponding orbitals on different atoms are not equal, due to thermal energy within the lattice. Furthermore, as electrons are supplied to the same orbitals of different atoms in the solid (envisaging the solid being progressively built up in a similar manner to that described for band theory) a repulsion term arises resulting in a decrease in the energy of accommodation of successive electrons within the lattice. This resembles the progressive variation of energy for electron accommodation in successive closely spaced levels within each band as described by band theory. Thus it may be seen that there is a close resemblance between both descriptions.

Considering an insulator, on the valence bond treatment, it is found that the highest energy orbitals of the atoms (or ions) which comprise the solid, are all doubly occupied. The transference of an electron from atom A_1 orbital to the corresponding orbital on neighbouring atom A_2 is accompanied by a similar change in the reverse direction so that no net charge migration in the solid occurs. If, however, an electron on atom A_1 is promoted through the appreciable energy gap to a higher orbital on atom A_2 (or on atom A_1) then the electron may migrate in the empty higher energy orbitals of the atoms (or ions) across the solid, and conducting properties are found. This is closely comparable to the promotion of an electron across the gap between valence and conduction bands as represented in Fig. 24(c). Suitable disposition of atomic orbitals in the crystal, on the energy scale, may yield a situation formally similar to that shown on Fig. 24(d). The band theory and valence bond approaches thus yield closely comparable alternative descriptions of bonding within solids.

Consider the band theory of solids applied to the four classes of solid defined in Chapter 1.

(i) *Molecular crystals.* The distance between atoms on neighbouring molecules is usually larger than those found in primary bonding and the resulting lattice parameters are too large to emphasize the wave nature of the electron. Such solids are insulators since the energy required to ionize such a molecule and transfer an electron from that molecule to a neighbour is relatively large. Although these solids may be formally considered through the band theory, the usefulness of this approach is limited.

(ii) *Covalent crystals.* The valence electrons are localized at the interatomic bonds within the lattice and are not easily removed from these positions. Such solids possess the band structure of an insulator in which there is an appreciable energy gap between the valence band, corresponding to the localized electrons in the doubly filled orbitals which provide the primary valence forces, and the empty conduction band which corresponds to the outer unfilled atomic orbitals.

(iii) *Ionic crystals.* The electrical properties and spectra of ionic crystals will be discussed below in greater detail. Many ionic solids do not conduct electricity by the migration of electrons except under particular conditions. For example, radiant energy of a suitable wavelength may promote an electron from the full valence band to the conduction band where it may thereafter migrate in an electric field; conducting properties observed during illumination are termed *photoconduction.*

(*iv*) *Metals*. The application of both band theory and the valence bond approach to metals has been discussed above.

Direct measurement of band energy levels in a solid should, in principle, be possible from spectral investigations. The experimental difficulties, however, are very much greater than might be expected at first sight. Absorption bands of interest often occur at wavelengths in the short-wavelength vacuum ultra-violet region. Furthermore, solids have high extinction coefficients and readily reflect radiation from all surfaces so that it is often necessary to use thin films and single crystals. For these reasons, those spectral investigations which have been undertaken have largely studied volatile solids. The greater part of reported work in the literature has been concerned with Group I halides, for which thin films of evaporated material can be obtained. Such spectra consist of a small number (2–4) of rather broad absorption bands in which the fine structure cannot be resolved since vibrational energy changes contribute to the energy of electronic transitions.

A difficulty which arises in the interpretation of those spectra which have been experimentally determined is that energy levels may exist in the solid at which electrons may be accommodated in positions between the valence and the conduction bands. Such trapping levels are regarded as resulting from transference of an electron from the negative to the positive ion to produce a pair of *atoms* in the ionic solid. This species, which may have a significant lifetime, is known as an *exciton*, and is a pair of energetic species which remain bound together during migration through the lattice (the lattice constituents remain immobile). Since the charged species of an exciton do not dissociate, its motion does not result in conduction. In the assignment of spectral absorptions to specific electronic processes within the solid, conductivity measurements must be made during illumination to determine whether a particular absorption maximum may be attributed to exciton formation or whether an electron has been promoted to the conduction band.

2. DEPARTURE OF SOLIDS FROM IDEAL BEHAVIOUR

Dislocations
Dislocations are regions within the solid at which the regularly repeating lattice array shows a discontinuity or a distortion from the ideal alignment of units within the crystal.

It has been stated above that the planar external surfaces of real crystals are composed of repetitions of a particular face of the unit cells, often low index faces; for example, a cube may be composed of 100, 010 and 001 surfaces. This must be regarded, however, as an idealized representation since it is known that real crystals are formed from a conglomerate of small regions ($\sim 10^{-5}$ cm cubes) of almost perfect lattice domain; but each such domain is aligned at a slight angle with respect to its neighbours. The lattice within each small region must be regarded as *almost* perfect, since it may contain defects, the nature of which will be discussed below. Any real crystal consists of a mosaic of such blocks joined together by regions of imperfect lattice known as *grain boundaries*. Clearly, the degree of disorder within individual grain boundaries depends on the relative disposition of adjoining attached blocks, the elastic properties of the solid and such externally imposed factors as conditions obtaining during preparation and subsequent treatment and storage of the particular crystal. There may be an almost infinite number of variations in detailed arrangement of lattice units within such regions. It has been found, however, that it is possible to represent the disorder in such regions through appropriate repetition and combinations of two fundamental types of dislocation, the edge dislocation and the screw dislocation.

Edge dislocation. This may be represented as the insertion of part of an extra plane of atoms (or ions) into a perfect lattice so that it lies parallel to the other crystallographic planes. The situation may be represented as being similar to that found if a page of a book is bisected in a direction parallel to the spine and the detached half-page removed. That part of the cut page which remains is comparable to the inserted plane of atoms and the remaining complete pages represent complete crystal planes. At the edge of the cut page, the adjoining complete pages tend to close towards each other to occupy the thickness formerly occupied by the removed paper and these pages are no longer strictly planar. Similarly, in a crystal there is a region of imperfect lattice beyond the end of the 'extra inserted plane of atoms' in which distortion of the adjoining crystallographic planes results in occupation of the space within the crystallite, Fig. 25(a). The edge of the 'extra inserted plane' is not necessarily a straight line but may have an irregular form comparable to that of the edge of a page roughly torn from a book.

The parameter used to measure dislocations quantitatively is known as the *Burgers vector* which may be found as follows. A path is drawn in a real crystal by moving from lattice point to lattice point around the dislocation edge, and avoiding the region of greatest disorder (along the edge of the 'extra inserted plane') to return to the lattice point from which the circular route started. An exactly comparable path, between successive comparable lattice points is then drawn for a region of perfect crystal and the two paths compared. If the path in the real crystal encircles a dislocation edge the points of starting and completing the comparable path in the real crystal will not coincide. The separation distance, the Burgers vector, is at right angles to the dislocation edge and the

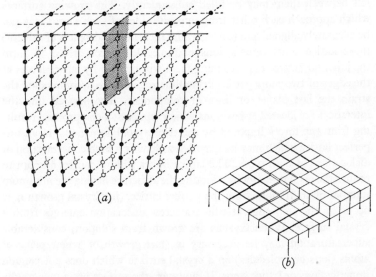

FIG. 25. (a) An edge dislocation.
(b) A screw dislocation. (Reproduced, with permission, from *Discussion of the Faraday Society*, 1949 **5**).

magnitude represents the vector sum of the dislocations within the enclosed path.

Screw dislocations. If a circular path is traced on a plane of atoms around a screw dislocation, again somewhat removed from the region of greatest disorder, it will be found that this path describes a helix progressing in the direction of the dislocation. A diagram showing one cycle of such a helix as a crystal surface is shown in Fig. 25(b). It may be seen that the Burgers vector of a screw dislocation, obtained following the procedure outlined in the previous paragraph, is parallel to the line of the dislocation.

Properties of dislocations. The degree of disorder close to a crystal dislocation line is considerable and therefore an appreciable amount of energy must be required to modify the normal lattice structure to enable it to be formed. The factors which control dislocation generation are incompletely understood but such regions of disorder are known to be formed and retained during crystal growth by at least two types of process: (i) crystal growth does not always proceed by equal rate of addition to every point on the boundary surface but may be *dendritic*. This means that small regions of crystal grow outwards and the voids left between them may be filled subsequently. The growing surfaces which approach each other from opposite sides of such a void may not be accurately aligned and (disregarding inclusion of droplets of solvent) those lattice units (atoms, ions or molecules) incorporated to form the junction between approaching faces will be held by lattice forces at the edges of two more perfect crystalline regions. To accommodate the strain the last planes or lines of components incorporated into the interstices are located at positions which represent a compromise resulting from the forces imposed by the two crystalline regions, in an imperfect lattice which may be regarded as having a high concentration of dislocations of both types. The lattice forces will, of course, attempt to reduce the crystal energy by adopting the structure having the minimum number of aberrations from the perfect lattice. (ii) Crystal growth may occur on the step edge at which a screw dislocation emerges from a crystal surface. When crystals are grown from solution, considerable supersaturation may be necessary to start growth of a new plane of atoms (ions or molecules) on a crystal surface which does not contain imperfections or lattice steps. If, however, the surface has a topography like that shown in Fig. 25(*b*), growth, by the addition of atoms to the emergent 'step', can readily occur and the crystal continues to increase in size in a solution of low supersaturation. Spiral growth, attributed to growth around a screw dislocation, has been observed for crystals of many compounds, particularly with large organic molecules, the development of which can be readily observed. The spiral form may originate in the unstable seed crystal before significant amounts of more perfect crystal have been formed.

Dislocations are also produced when crystals are subjected to mechanical deformation or to the thermal stresses which may occur when being grown from a melt. Two mechanisms by which dislocations can move through the solid are *glide* or *climb*.

In movements through glide, the dislocation progresses in a direction parallel to its Burgers vector and examination of models has shown that during this process individual atoms are moved distances which are small compared with the lattice parameter. This is a low energy process which can occur at low temperature. In climb, the movement of a dislocation is at right angles to the Burgers vector. For example, in climb of an edge dislocation, atoms (or ions) must be added to or removed from the edge of the 'extra' plane which terminates within the solid. Climb, therefore, is a higher energy process and only occurs at higher temperatures. Both processes allow dislocation movements within the solid, and, since these represent lines of high energy in the lattice, interactions between them can occur. Theoretical treatments have suggested that two dislocations having equal and opposite Burgers vectors may disappear by coalescence, so reducing the lattice strain, but those of similar sign tend to repel one another. The ease with which such combination processes can occur depends on whether glide or climb is necessary to enable the dislocations to meet. At elevated temperatures both processes may occur readily and the number of dislocations in a particular crystal may be reduced by holding it for a time at a temperature slightly less than the melting point. This process is known as *annealing*. By altering the number of dislocations in a solid it is possible to vary the mechanical properties, since movements of the lattice under strain occur preferentially in the high energy regions, the dislocations. This has considerable technological importance. Cold working of a solid, usually a metal (i.e. subjecting it to stresses and strains well below the melting point) increases the concentration of dislocations to produce a hard springy material, in which the movements of dislocations are prevented by their proximity to each other. Annealing results in a softer, more malleable product in which the movements of dislocations are less restrained.

Impurities in a solid may be accommodated close to dislocation lines with less strain energy than within the 'perfect' lattice. Impurities within the distorted regions may stabilize the dislocations by reducing the total strain energy which is imposed on the solid through filling the void spaces. Impurities also tend to 'anchor' dislocations at a particular place since both cannot readily move together through the solid.

Defects
The term defect is used to describe both missing and misplaced atoms (or ions) from positions in the ideal crystal lattice (also combinations of these) and to systems involving incorporation of foreign ions within the solid. It is now generally accepted that a pure crystal may possess two different types of imperfections which are called *Schottky defects* and

Frenkel defects named after the research workers who first suggested their existence. Both types do not necessarily occur in the same crystal and they are not associated with the presence of impurities. Defects may occur close to, or at, dislocation lines, and also in more perfect regions of crystal.

Schottky defects. An ionic crystal containing Schottky defects has an equal number of cation and anion vacancies. Such defects can be regarded as displacement of cations and anions from a number of random

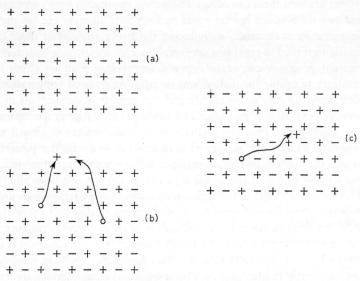

FIG. 26. Schottky and Frenkel defects.

(*a*) Region of perfect lattice, every point occupied.

(*b*) Schottky defect formation; one ion of each sign removed from the lattice point and transported to the crystal surface.

(*c*) Frenkel defect formation: an ion, usually a cation, removed from the lattice point and transported to an interstitial lattice position.

lattice positions, to the crystal surface, as shown in Fig. 26(*b*). This is illustrated for an ionic solid. Atoms from a metal crystal, or molecules from within a molecular crystal, may be similarly transferred to the surface leaving lattice vacancies.

Frenkel defects. A Frenkel defect is formed (Fig. 26*c*) by the transference of an ion from a normal lattice position to an interstitial (i.e. 'between lattice points') position in a different region of the crystal. It is usually the cation which is transferred in this way since this is often the smaller ion and thus more easily accommodated at the inter-lattice point.

It is possible to suggest other types of defect, for example interchange of an anion and cation. But experimental support for the occurrence of this species has not been forthcoming. Certain other types of defect have been suggested in the literature.

Dislocation generation is a high energy process and may occur as a result of kinetic factors operating during crystal growth or from the application of stress to the solid. In contrast, the formation of defects, Schottky and Frenkel types, requires very much less energy since the distorted region is limited to a small number of lattice units and does not extend any appreciable distance through the lattice. The presence of defects results in an increase in crystal entropy, due to the large number of possible combinations of defect location which are possible for the relatively small proportion of such vacancies in the solid. From this it follows that any crystal, at temperatures $>0°K$, contains an equilibrium concentration of defects, the number of which may be calculated by thermodynamic methods. For example, Frenkel defect formation may be treated as a reversible chemical reaction of the type:

lattice ion (L^+) + interstitial vacancy (I)

$$\leftrightharpoons \text{interstitial ion } (I^+) + \text{lattice vacancy } (L)$$

where the symbols in brackets denote the equilibrium concentration of these species. The equilibrium constant for this reaction (K) is equal to $\exp(-E_v/kT)$ where E_v is the energy required for defect formation, and we may write:

$$K = I^+L/IL^+ = \exp(-E_v/kT).$$

If the equilibrium vacancy concentration is small $I^+ = L$ and

$$I^+ = \sqrt{(IL^+)} \exp(-E_v/2kT).$$

A comparable calculation may be made to determine the equilibrium concentration of Schottky defects. Refinements to such calculations have been made to allow for changes in density accompanying defect formation and for local strains in the vicinity of the perturbed lattice region.

Although experimental evidence has shown that defects of the Schottky and Frenkel types may occur in different ionic crystals, it is believed that some crystals contain appreciable numbers of one type and insignificant amounts of the other, while a different substance contains a preponderant amount of the alternative defect. Frenkel defect formation is favoured in those solids where there is a disparity between the ionic sizes of the constituents so that the smaller cation can leave its lattice position, and migrate between the larger anions to a point which does not form part of the regular lattice array. Ions in strained interstitial lattice positions will be relatively more stable in those solids which have a high van der Waals energy and high dielectric constant. All these relevant factors are favourable for Frenkel defect formation in silver bromide and it is believed that this type of defect predominates and the same is probably true of silver chloride. In the alkali halides, however, it is considered that Schottky defects predominate; in sodium chloride the dielectric constant and the van der Waals energy are very much lower than in the silver halides.

3. ELECTRICAL CONDUCTIVITY OF IONIC SOLIDS

Electrical conduction of solids, through migration of electrons within the conduction band, has been discussed above. In insulators an alternative current-carrying mechanism may be possible. The presence of defects in ionic solids enables conduction to occur through ionic migrations. Since there are three possible current-carrying species, three transport numbers are necessary to define the proportions of the current carried by each entity, so that:

$$t_+ + t_- + t_e = 1$$

where t_+ and t_- are the proportions of current carried by cations and anions respectively and t_e the electronic conductivity. The magnitude of each of the three numbers is a measure of the relative ease of migration of each species.

The measurement of transport numbers of ions in solids is experimentally difficult. In principle a method similar to that used for ionic solutions may be applied. Three weighed blocks of the solid to be investigated are clamped together in series in a constant temperature environment and a measured current passed through them for a known time. The three blocks are subsequently separated and analysed, thus the weight of material which has migrated can be found. The low conductivity shown by many solids of interest, together with the possibility of losses by vaporization and/or decomposition at higher temperatures, restrict the usefulness and reduce the accuracy of the method. Furthermore, the current-carrying properties of such solids are profoundly influenced by the presence of very small amounts of impurities in the crystal. Transport numbers, for the same substance, as measured by different workers, often show poor quantitative agreement and results must therefore be treated with reserve. Nevertheless, significant trends have been recognized which are useful in deciding which types of defect predominate in a particular compound. Transport number measurements have shown, for example, that many ionic halides carry currents by the migration of ions (t_+ or $t_- > t_e$). Other compounds, usually those in which the composition may significantly deviate from the stoichiometric value (for example, some oxides and sulphides of transition metals) may carry current through electron migration in the conduction band, or $t_e > t_+$ or t_-.

When an electric field is applied across an ionic solid which contains Frenkel defects, the interstitial (defect) cations may migrate if the thermal vibration energy, or the field strength, is sufficiently great to allow the positive ion to surmount the energy barriers which separate the successive relatively more stable interstitial positions at which the ion may be accommodated. In other words, an ion must force itself between neighbours, located at regular lattice positions, to travel from one interstitial position, at which it may be accommodated with relatively low strain energy, to the next. At elevated temperatures such ionic migration can result in conducting properties of the solid; transport number measurements have shown that for the silver halides t_+ is very close to unity.

The migration of a vacancy from one lattice position to the next in a particular direction is equivalent to the transference of an appropriate ion one step in the opposite direction and thus Schottky defects may also confer conducting properties on the solid. Transport number studies for various ionic solids which contain this type of defect, the alkali halides, e.g. NaCl, NaBr, KCl, etc., have shown that both ions migrate in an electric field at elevated temperatures ($> \sim 500°C$) and that t_- increases with temperature.

The electrical conductivities of several alkali halides have been shown to vary with temperature in the manner shown diagrammatically in Fig. 27. At low temperatures the conductivity varies for different specimens of the same compound (A–D) but the rate of increase with temperature is close to a constant value for the particular salt. At higher temperatures the differences between samples are reduced or eliminated and all values tend towards the single line. These observations, characteristic of ionic crystals, are explained on the model that, at low temperatures, current is carried by ionic migration along crystallite surfaces and dislocation lines and through the disordered grain boundary region.

The structure of such regions is strongly influenced by the history of the particular crystal (grain boundary structure developed during growth, annealing, crushing, impurities, etc.) and it is a characteristic property of each individual sample. At higher temperatures, however, migration of ions through the bulk of the lattice provides the greater part of the current-carrying power. Differences in degrees of local disorder between samples are no longer significant since surfaces, grain boundaries, etc.,

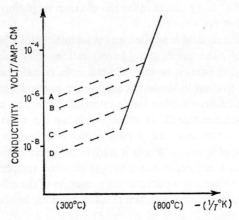

FIG. 27. Variation in electrical conductivity of sodium chloride (or sodium bromide) with temperature. Dotted lines A–D refer to data obtained for different samples of the same salt, at higher temperatures all samples give results close to the single line.

comprise only a small proportion of the total lattice. The more perfect regions of crystal are virtually identical between different specimens of a particular salt, and migration in these regions at high temperature results in closely similar quantitative behaviour between different specimens. Slight modifications of this basic model have been suggested in which attempts have been made to establish the nature of the species which controls the low temperature conduction process.

4. IMPURITY SYSTEMS

In a compound, which exists as a liquid or as a gas, every similar molecule must contain the same number of atoms of the same elements bonded in the same proportions through identical linkages. The removal of an atom or replacement of an atom of a different element in a molecule of a gaseous compound results in the formation of a different substance. Solids show somewhat different behaviour in that it is possible for a crystal of a particular compound to exist over a limited composition range. A small proportion of foreign species incorporated within the lattice may result in small changes in the crystal energy and distortion of the unit cells in the small volume of lattice in the vicinity of the impurity but the identity of the phase is unchanged.

Two general types of impurity systems may be recognized: (i) *Non-stoichiometry:* This is the slight variation of the proportions of the constituent elements of a compound, usually between fairly narrow limits, without the introduction of species other than those present in the ideal solid. The electrical and spectral properties may be significantly altered by such composition variation. (ii) *Impurity.* Impurities, that is, species other than those present in the ideal compound, may sometimes be incorporated in the solid with little more than local perturbation of the band structure of the crystal, though in different systems the presence of such defects may cause significant changes in the electrical and spectral properties of the crystal. Both types of impurity system will be discussed.

Non-stoichiometry
Much of the research into properties of substances of this type has been concerned with systems most readily investigated experimentally: binary ionic salts, and, in particular, alkali halides and transition metal oxides.

Excess potassium in potassium chloride. When potassium chloride is heated in potassium vapour the crystals take on a blue colour which is due to the formation of a spectral absorption centre having a maximum in the 600–700 mμ wavelength region. Accurate measurements have shown that the number of absorbing centres (measured spectroscopically) is, within experimental error, directly proportional to (i) the stoichiometric excess of alkali metal which has been taken up by the crystal, and (ii) the changes in crystal density, attributed to the formation of anion vacancies, which accompany excess metal incorporation. These results are explained by the model that excess metal *atoms* are incorporated at appropriate lattice positions as *ions* and the electrons resulting from the ionization process are trapped at the anion vacancies, which must be formed at the time that additional metal atoms enter the ionic solid. The vacancies which trap the electrons, or *F-centres* as they are usually called, may thus be represented as a negative electron charge held at a vacant lattice position surrounded by six potassium ion nearest neighbours, and which, in the ideal lattice, would have been occupied by a chloride ion. Spectroscopic studies have shown that, in addition to the absorption band in the visible region mentioned above, there is a second absorption band in the ultra-violet region which is associated with the presence of F-centres. This band is close to the maximum wavelength at which lattice-ion absorption occurs and it results from differences between the energy of lattice ions adjoining an F-centre and those in normal lattice positions.

When irradiated by light having wavelength within the F-centre absorption region, crystals containing F-centres become photoconducting, showing that either such radiation promotes electrons directly from the F-centre to the conduction band, or that the excited state so reached is close to the conduction band. Solids containing F-centres are paramagnetic; this is consistent with the above model in which the lattice vacancies are represented as containing an unpaired electron.

Much of the early research on such defects was concerned with potassium chloride, but similar behaviour has been observed for other alkali halides. The term *colour-centre* has been applied to the range of comparable defect structures which occur in ionic solids. More complex defect structures than that discussed above, involving more than one lattice site and trapped electron(s) have been described in the literature to account for absorption bands observed in solids after various chemical treatments. Recently, resonance techniques have been applied to the investigation of the properties of colour centres.

Transition metal oxides and sulphides. In addition to the F-centre, two other important types of non-stoichiometric behaviour have been studied: (i) incorporation of excess of one lattice constituent in the crystal at interstitial positions, for example, zinc oxide containing excess zinc, and (ii) cationic vacancies accompanied by an appropriate number of metal atoms bearing an excess charge, as occurs for example in nickel oxide. The deviation from stoichiometry in such solids is often $<1\%$.

Zinc oxide. Zinc oxide, as prepared, often contains excess metal incorporated as interstitial zinc ions and the electrons removed through ionization remain close to the excess (defect) metal. Crystals containing such defects show semi-conducting properties since the loosely bonded electrons may be readily promoted to the conduction band of the solid where migration through the lattice is possible. From the viewpoint of the band theory, the impurity atom generates a local electron accommodating level somewhat below the conduction band and an electron may be readily promoted from this level to give conducting properties to the solid. This is called n-type semi-conduction since the $n$egative electron, on promotion to the conduction band, is the normal current-carrying species (see Fig. 28a).

Solids in which negative ions are incorporated in interstitial positions have been less fully investigated.

Nickel oxide. Nickel oxide may depart from stoichiometry through nickel ion vacancies; each such vacancy results in the formation of two

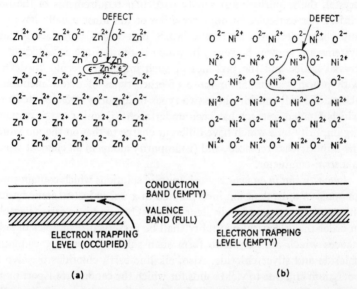

FIG. 28. Representation of two types of semi-conducting oxide in which electrical properties are determined by deviations from stoichiometry.

    (a) ZnO with excess Zn; an n-type semi-conductor.

    (b) NiO with Ni deficiency; a p-type semi-conductor.

Ni^{3+} ions, to preserve electrical neutrality (Fig. 28b). Comparable defects occur in ferrous oxide, ferrous sulphide, cuprous oxide and other similar substances. Such solids exhibit semi-conductivity through a somewhat different mechanism to that described above. Each defect provides an unoccupied impurity level at an energy just greater than the upper limit of the valance band and to which an electron may be promoted, with reduction of the defect ion charge ($Ni^{3+} + e^- \rightarrow Ni^{2+}$) and a vacancy in the valence band is thus generated. Such a 'gap' is known as a *positive hole* and the migration of a positive hole in one direction is equivalent to the migration of an electron in the opposite

H

direction. Thus *positive*-hole migration results in *p*-type semi-conductivity.

Foreign impurity atoms or ions

Atoms or ions, foreign to the lattice, are very often contained in the solid at dislocations or in disordered grain boundary regions. In order that an impurity may be located within the more perfect parts of a crystal, the impurity must satisfy particular requirements of the host lattice. For example, an impurity atom or ion must usually have size and shape close to that of the lattice unit which it replaces. Many systems are known, however, in which impurities are accepted into a crystal lattice and the presence of such impurities results in defects with properties similar to those of other types of defect mentioned above. We will consider here two types of impurity defect systems on which detailed research has been undertaken: (i) ionic crystals containing impurity ions which have different charge to that on the ion which the impurity has replaced, and (ii) impurity atoms in an element which is a semi-conductor.

Impurity ions in an ionic crystal. In solid solutions which contain small amounts of a divalent ion incorporated in a uni-univalent ionic lattice, the excess charge on each divalent ion must be offset by a cation vacancy in order that electrical neutrality shall be preserved. Examples of substances which are known to form such solid solutions are cadmium chloride and silver chloride. Also, alkaline earth chlorides dissolve in potassium chloride to yield solids for which the cationic transport numbers approach unity, showing that the cation vacancies facilitate the migration of positive ions through the solid. This mechanism is closely similar to that of ionic conductivity which results from migration of positive ions through Schottky defects.

Nickel oxide is an insulator and the semi-conducting properties observed for this solid result from defects caused by departure from stoichiometric composition. The defect concentration in a particular sample depends on the exact conditions which obtained during oxidation of the particular sample, so that different preparations very often show different electrical properties. It has been found possible to stabilize the concentration of defects in different preparations by the incorporation of the lithium oxide since each lithium ion in the crystal must be accompanied by the formation of an Ni^{3+} ion to preserve neutrality of the nickel oxide lattice. Thus the defect concentration and, through this, the electrical properties of the solid may be controlled by the proportion of additive present. Such solids, with stabilized electrical properties, which may be reproduced for different preparations fairly readily (unlike the pure solid), have been used for the manufacture of components for electrical apparatus.

Impurities in a semi-conducting element. In pure crystalline germanium, each atom donates one electron to each of four paired-electron bonds which are directed to each of its four neighbours in the lattice. This results in a filled valence band for the solid and there is a small energy gap between this and the next available electron accommodating levels which form the conduction band. Pure germanium is an intrinsic semi-conductor but appreciable energy is required to promote electrons to the conduction band, and the conducting properties of the element are increased by the presence of certain impurities in the lattice, for example arsenic or gallium.

An atom of arsenic, Atomic Number 33 (which occupies the position adjacent to germanium, Atomic Number 32, in a horizontal row of the Periodic Table) introduced into the germanium lattice tends to adopt the bond structure imposed upon it by the lattice neighbours. However, in doing so, there remains in excess a single electron which cannot be directly accommodated into the host lattice band structure. An impurity electron-accepting level is generated, therefore, just below the position of the conduction band on the energy scale and the 'excess' electron is held in this position by electrostatic attraction to the arsenic atom, which has thus become a centre of positive charge (Fig. 29a). The electron in this impurity level may acquire the thermal energy necessary for promotion to the conduction band, so that solids having defects of this type exhibit *n*-type semi-conduction.

A somewhat similar situation arises on the incorporation of gallium, Atomic Number 31 (also adjacent to germanium in the Periodic Table), into the same host lattice. But this system shows the significant difference that the impurity atoms have insufficient electrons to enable each atom to conform to the germanium lattice bond disposition. Again, an impurity level is established in which an electron may be accommodated in the vicinity of the defect atom but at an energy level just *above* that of the valence band (Fig. 29b). When this level contains an electron the gallium atom bonding may conform to that of its neighbours and its occupation results in a positive hole in the valence band. Gallium impurity confers *p*-type semi-conductivity on germanium.

The Hall effect. If a semi-conductor carrying a current is placed in a magnetic field positioned at right-angles to the direction of current flow,

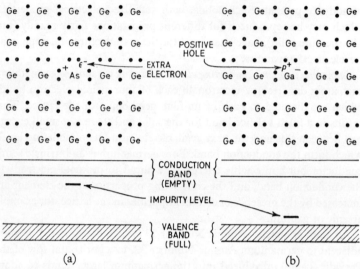

FIG. 29. Representation of impurity semi-conduction in germanium.

(*a*) *n*-type semi-conduction, arsenic impurity.

(*b*) *p*-type semi-conduction, gallium impurity.

a potential is developed in a direction perpendicular to the plane containing directions of both current and field. The development of this potential is known as the Hall effect, and results from movement of migrating current-carrying species within the solid under the influence of the magnetic field. The direction of the induced potential enables a decision to be made as to the charge sign of the migrating entities, i.e. whether the semi-conductor is *n*-type or *p*-type.

5. SOLID SOLUTIONS

A series of solid solutions is a set of solid mixtures having the same two (or more) components crystallized in the same lattice arrangement but in which the composition and lattice parameter progressively change together. Several of the systems described in the previous section are solid solutions, e.g. arsenic in germanium. The present section is concerned with a classification of some of the types which have been recognized.

A number of solid binary systems may form alloys (or mixtures) ranging from pure substance X, through all possible compositional ratios X/Y to pure substance Y, without the appearance of a new phase. An example of such behaviour is the solid solution series formed between silver and gold which can exist over the whole composition range. Other solid solution systems may form a stable phase only within definite composition limits and outside these limits a new crystal lattice is found.

The atoms of two elements in a binary solid solution may be randomly dispersed over the available lattice positions (Fig. 30a), or show a regular arrangement with respect to each other; the latter arrangement is known as a *superlattice* (Fig. 30b). The crystallographic transformation by which a superlattice is formed from a random solution is known as an *order-disorder* transition (Fig. 30a → b).

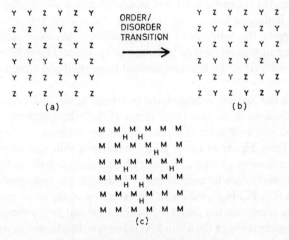

FIG. 30. Types of solid solution.

Two main types of solid solution may be recognized: (i) a substitutional solid solution in which both ions occupy identical positions in the lattice (the silver-gold alloys mentioned above are of this type), and (ii) interstitial solid solutions (Fig. 30c). Where the radii of the constituent components of a solid solution are very different, the smaller atoms occupy positions at the interstices of the lattice of the larger component. Interstitial hydrides, borides, carbides and nitrides of several transition metals are known. Most interstitial compounds are hard and are refractory, though the hydrides are an exception to the latter property since the volatile interstitial hydrogen atoms may be removed on heating in vacuum.

Interstitial hydrides. The most fully investigated system of this type is palladium hydride; heated palladium metal will absorb many times its own volume of gaseous hydrogen. This hydride is also formed following discharge of hydrogen ions at a palladium electrode. Hydrogen atoms on the surface of the solid, formed by dissociation of a gaseous molecule, or discharge of an ion, may diffuse into the bulk crystal, between the atoms of the metallic lattice, to form an interstitial solid solution. This results in an increase of the lattice parameter, compared with that of the pure metal, and some reduction in the electrical conductivity of the palladium, though its metallic character is retained. Hydrogen continues to be absorbed into the lattice of the metal until the composition $PdH_{0.6}$ is reached. Comparisons have shown that the outermost partly filled band of the metal is filled at this composition of the solid solution, if each hydrogen atom makes available a single electron to the band structure of the solid. After this composition has been reached, the tendency to absorb further hydrogen is reduced. The stability of the solid results from the bonding derived from the band structure of the crystal.

When the hydride is heated, the hydrogen atoms diffuse from interstitial positions in the bulk to the metal surface where they may combine in pairs, and molecules of hydrogen gas are evolved. Hydrogen may diffuse from higher to lower pressure across a thin wall of palladium metal, each atom passing as a result of intermediate hydride formation. This property may be used to purify hydrogen gas since probable impurities (O_2, N_2, H_2O, etc., with the exception of D_2 which may form a deutride phase) do not dissolve in the lattice and hence are prevented from passing through the solid. Several metals, in addition to palladium, show similar ability to absorb relatively large volumes of hydrogen, these include, Ta, Ti and Th.

Interstitial borides, carbides and nitrides. Examples of such compounds include TiB, TiC, TiN, HfC, TaC and MoC. These substances may be formed by direct reaction of the metal with the second constituent, the latter entering the lattice at high temperature to form the interstitial compound. An alternative route for preparation is through reaction of the heated metal with an appropriate volatile compound, for example a hydrocarbon to form a carbide, or ammonia to form the nitride.

The formation of such solids requires an expansion of the pure metal lattice but the resultant phase shows metallic electrical conductivity from which it is seen that a metal-type band structure is retained in the interstitial compound. These substances have particularly high melting points, several values are $>3000°K$, and their hardness may approach that of diamond. These properties show that the band structure in such solids results in greater bonding strength within the lattice than is present in the softer, more easily fused, metals.

Interstitial metallic compounds contrast sharply with the ionic, salt-like carbides of the more electropositive metals, for example CaC_2, Na_2C_2 and Al_4C_3. Carbides intermediate in properties between interstitial and ionic classes are known; these possess some metallic character yet do not show the great stability characteristic of the interstitial alloy-type phases. Nickel carbide, one such solid, shows some metallic character but decomposes at $\sim$350°C and is more reactive with acids than the inert interstitial carbides. Cementite, Fe_3C, is also in this group, but it is more stable to heating than the nickel compound.

Intermetallic compounds. Numerous different combinations of two or more metals which form stable crystalline phases may be regarded as compounds which exist in the solid phase only. Results of experimental studies on such mixtures are complicated by solid solution formation, which makes difficult the recognition and characterization of the particular pure phases formed. A comprehensive review of the various substances formed is outside the scope of this monograph, so the remainder of this chapter will be concerned with the principles which underlie the formation and stability of such solid compounds.

The observed ratios of the constituents present in intermetallic compounds are inconsistent with the predictions of the classical valence rules observed for covalent and ionic compounds containing the same metals. Intermetallic compounds do not exist after the crystal has been melted, so that their stability must be related to the bonding forces which may be formed within the crystal lattice. Furthermore, many solid compounds of this type can exist over a range of composition between definite limits, which is a property which may be possessed by solid compounds, but it is not possible for compounds which can exist in the gaseous or liquid states. These characteristic types of behaviour indicate that it is the band structure of the solid which confers stability on any particular crystalline intermetallic phase. Such compounds possess a particular arrangement of the metal valence electrons within an energy band structure which results from an appropriate arrangement of atomic nuclei in the lattice. This is the basis of the *Hume-Rothery* rule, which is applicable to such solids, and which states that for any particular phase the ratio of the total number of atoms to the total number of valence electrons is constant. Thus appropriate mixtures of different metallic elements may form similar lattice arrangements, simultaneously creating a characteristic stable metallic band structure containing the same *average* number of electrons derived from each atom participating in the crystal bonding.

This theoretical model explains the two main relevant experimental observations which have been recorded for intermetallic compounds:

(i) The same lattice structures are found for different mixtures of different pairs of metals, for compositions where the atom/valence electron ratio has the same value. To calculate the number of valence electrons derived from each atom in such a crystal, copper is considered to possess a single electron, appropriate to a Group I element (as in cuprous salts; divalent copper is more characteristic of the hydrated cupric ion) and several Group VIII metals are regarded as zero valent (as in certain organometallic compounds). A series of intermetallic compounds having the same crystal lattice are $CuZn$, Cu_3Al and Cu_5Si, from which it may be seen that all three show a $2 : 3 : :$ atom : valence electron ratio, in accordance with the Hume-Rothery rule. The $CuZn$ compound is β-brass and the type of lattice possessed by all three compounds is the β-brass structure. It would be difficult to account for the existence of the compound Cu_5Si on the rules which apply to the formation of covalent and of ionic compounds of these metals, although its formation is consistent with the Hume-Rothery rule.

(ii) In passing through a compositional sequence of solid solutions from 100% A to 100% B it is found that with different pairs of metals A and B, the same crystalline lattice structures occur in the same order in the series. Since the atom/valence electron ratio must vary continuously in such a series, it follows from the Hume-Rothery predictions that the order in which different lattice structures will be stable is the same for different pairs of metals.

The existence of intermetallic compounds results from the stability of the crystal band structure. More sophisticated derivations of the Hume-Rothery rules than the qualitative observations quoted above have been attempted, using theoretically calculated values of the energy bands within the various solids. Such calculations have shown that for some intermetallic compounds the stable phase corresponds to a completely filled energy band, but the experimental determination of the exact composition at which the most stable compound is formed is often made more difficult by the formation of solid solutions in the mixture, and this complicates attempts to compare experiment and theory.

CHAPTER FOUR

The Chemistry of Solid Surfaces

1. SOLID SURFACES

Before considering the chemistry of boundary regions of solids, it is necessary to discuss just what is meant by the expression 'the surface of a solid'. An atom (ion or molecule) situated within the more perfect crystalline regions of the lattice within the bulk is held in an equilibrium position (discounting random thermal vibrations which represent dynamic equilibria) through lattice forces from those neighbouring lattice units which surround it. However, a similar lattice unit situated in the outermost planar array which forms the boundary layer of the solid is bonded to its neighbours in the crystal only by those lattice forces which are oriented from it in the direction of the crystal bulk. Those crystal bonding forces directed towards the particular lattice unit considered, which would have been derived from atoms (etc.) situated at positions which are not occupied, due to the position of the selected atom at the surface, must either remain unsatisfied or the disposition of crystal bonding forces at the surface regions must be modified. Such crystal force modification must be even more pronounced for those atoms (etc.) located at an edge or a corner of the crystal. Thus, changes in the strength and direction of interlattice forces in the boundary regions may result in differences between the lattice interatomic distances and the arrangement of atoms of units in the boundary layer as compared with those within the crystal bulk. Such lattice distortion of the outermost layer may, in turn, influence adjacent layers so that the effect of the surface may extend several lattice units into the crystal bulk. The surface boundary layer of atoms must, therefore, be regarded as a region at which there may be some departure from idealized behaviour.

When we considered (Chapter 2) the appearance of ionic crystals, which had grown to sufficient size to be observed, it was emphasized that these are almost invariably bounded by planar surfaces. Boundary surfaces of solids which are exactly planar on atomic dimensions is, however, an idealized concept, and real crystals exhibit deviations from

111

the perfect crystal lattice which result from the presence of defects and dislocations. The surfaces of real crystals contain irregularities, dislocations and imperfections so that the total boundary surfaces may be very much larger than the geometric surface area which can be measured on the assumption of perfectly planar surfaces. The outer boundary surfaces of a crystal are damaged by scratches, clefts and holes which run into the bulk of the solid and in many samples these are sufficiently large to be seen by the naked eye, or with a low-power microscope. Also, all surfaces of crystals may possess numerous minor superficial cracks which are of ever decreasing size down to those so fine that they may be regarded either as external surfaces which closely approach at a small angle or alternatively as regions of imperfect lattice containing an array of dislocations and imperfections. Cracks which have dimensions comparable in size with lattice components, occur in crystal grain boundaries. The surface area of a solid may thus be very much larger than that found by measuring external crystal dimensions and assuming planar faces, so that when reporting quantitative studies of the surfaces of solids it becomes necessary to state exactly what is meant, or how a particular value was obtained. Furthermore, the effective area of a particular crystal may differ when that solid is exposed to different reactants, since the surface which may take part in a chemical process may vary somewhat with the nature of the second reactant. For example, the smaller molecules of one fluid reactant may penetrate the finer cracks of a particular crystal to a greater distance than the more bulky molecules of a different reactant. Therefore, the effective area of the same solid sample in the two processes is different.

A solid surface must be regarded as a somewhat distorted lattice which extends along the edges of holes, cracks and cavities of such narrow dimensions that departures from the ideal lattice, in some places, are to be more conveniently regarded as combinations of dislocations and defects. Such surface distortion penetrates in the direction of the more perfect lattice regions but the influence progressively diminishes at increasing distance from the surface.

Many of the most important, and most completely studied, reactions of solids take place at or in the distorted boundary lattice and it has been shown that many reactions are confined to this region. The present chapter is largely concerned with such chemical processes, the final chapter (5) will be concerned with reactions where the interface, at which such chemical changes occur, progressively penetrates the solid. This division, while convenient, must be regarded as somewhat arbitrary since a reaction limited to the surface at one temperature may progress into the bulk of the solid when heated slightly more strongly. Some overlap between these two divisions is inevitable, therefore, since there is no absolute demarcation line. Solid-solid interfaces are difficult to study directly; a description of some of the inherent problems is deferred to the next chapter.

It is convenient to start an account of surface chemistry with a definition of the terms used. Atoms (ions or molecules) bonded to the surface of a solid, but differing from the constituents of the lattice and not penetrating the boundary edges of the crystal, are said to be *adsorbed*. This contrasts with the *ab*sorption of hydrogen by palladium, discussed previously, where the hydrogen atoms enter the bulk lattice to occupy interstitial lattice positions at appreciable depth below the metal surface. Much of the study of chemistry of solid surfaces has been concerned with the investigation of the nature and properties of the bonds established between adsorbed molecules and the constituents of the solid at the lattice boundary layer. Two general types of adsorption are distinguished: (*a*) *physical adsorption*, where the attractive forces between solid and the adsorbed species are weak (often van der Waals bonds are responsible) and (*b*) chemical adsorption, or, more usually, *chemisorption*, where primary valence bonds result in a strong attractive force between adsorbent (solid) and adsorbate (adsorbed species). It should be emphasized that, while these general types of adsorption describe a large number of well defined systems, some of which will be mentioned later, examples of intermediate behaviour are also known. An exclusive division into two classes cannot be made since molecules are capable of being attracted to solid surfaces by bonds within the whole range of strengths of chemical association.

Direct study of the properties of solid surfaces

Surface energy of solid surfaces. The total strain energy of the surface regions of solids, due to distortion of the lattice (as mentioned above), is directly proportional to the surface area and is comparable to the surface energy of liquids. It has been found that, in common with the behaviour of liquids, small particles of solid metals reduce their surface area to a minimum by adopting a spherical shape. In contrast, many ionic crystals form stable prisms having planar boundary surfaces. This is believed to result from the somewhat lower surface energies in crystals of this type, and such substances adopt crystal lattices, having, in general, fewer nearest neighbours. Attempts have been made both to measure directly and to calculate theoretically the surface tensions of a number of different solids, but results are often of doubtful validity and the accuracies achieved are probably low.

Topography of solid surfaces. There is evidence that the chemical reactions of solids may start, or occur preferentially, in those regions of the lattice which possess the greatest strain. Many research workers, using evidence from a variety of experimental approaches, have concluded that the most reactive lattice units of the solid may be situated at just those positions in which the lattice bonding is the most highly distorted, i.e. at the end of a dislocation which emerges from the surface, or at the edge of an incomplete plane of atoms at the surface

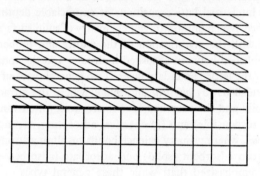

FIG. 31. Representation of a step at the surface of a solid.

(Fig. 31). Some information about the regions of greatest distortion (for example, superficial macro-scratches of individual particles) can be obtained by direct examination using an optical microscope. This approach also allows observations and quantitative measurements of sizes and shapes of individual crystals. The detection of finer structures requires more refined techniques, some of which are described below.

(*i*) *The electron microscope.* This instrument has greater resolving power than the optical microscope, and, like it, gives information about the larger regions of disorder and also the sizes and shapes of crystallites. However, the range of substances which can be directly investigated with it is restricted by the somewhat extreme conditions within the specimen mounting. A thin specimen of the material to be examined is subjected to electron bombardment while being held in a good vacuum.

Crystals of some inorganic salts may be melted by heating from the electron beam, while others, for example some azides, may detonate. Accordingly, it is often a more satisfactory experimental procedure to view in the microscope a replica of the surface of interest. This replica is a thin plastic film, obtained by drying a drop of polymer solution on the surface to be studied. After removal, the replica surface is rendered opaque (i.e. *shaded*) by a thin covering of an evaporated metal film. Such a replica can then be examined in the electron microscope since it is more stable than the original specimen.

Several variations of this technique have been described in the literature. One such method will be described here to show how information about the occurrence of certain features on the surface may be obtained. A small amount of metal is evaporated onto the crystal face of the inorganic salt to be examined. Metallic crystallites are only formed at those points on the crystal surface which are most highly distorted from the perfect lattice. It is in such regions of local high surface energy that the foreign (i.e. metal) atoms aggregate since it is here that they may be accommodated with maximum reduction of free energy both of ionic crystal deformed region and metallic crystallite. A replica polymer film of that solid surface may then be prepared, to which the metal crystallites adhere, and their disposition (on the replica surface) may subsequently be established using an electron microscope. The resulting photograph may be regarded as a map showing the positions of the most highly deformed regions at the original crystal surface.

(*ii*) *Multiple-beam interferometer*. Information about the topography of a very nearly planar surface of a transparent solid can be obtained by interference techniques. The crystal surface to be studied is first coated with a layer of silver, sufficiently thin to follow the detailed topography of the surface and also to transmit visible radiation. The silvered surface of the crystal is then mounted in such a position that it is close to, but making a small angle with, a high quality silvered optical flat. When this reflecting system is exposed to a monochromatic beam of light an interference pattern of lines may be seen along the lines of discontinuity at the edges of lattice planes on the surface of the silvered crystal specimen. Each interference line may be ascribed to a change in the planarity of the surface. Whether a particular line is due to an elevation or a depression of the specimen surface may be established from the direction in which it moves when the angle between the reflecting surfaces is altered. The interference pattern may thus be interpreted as a contour map of the surface.

(iii) The field emission microscope. This instrument is diagrammatically represented in Fig. 32. A very fine annealed point of metal (the emission tip) is held in a high vacuum in front of a phosphorescent screen, supported on a thicker metal loop, and a high potential is applied between tip and screen. The surface of the fine tip nearest the screen, which has been curved during the annealing process, is subjected to very high local field strengths ($\sim 10^8$ volts cm^{-1}) so that electrons are drawn from

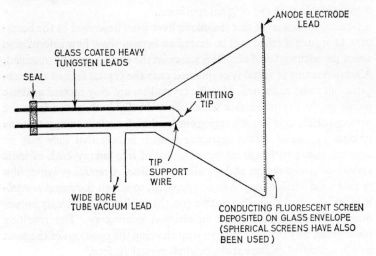

FIG. 32. The field emission microscope.

Several modifications of this basic design have been used.

The apparatus is constructed of glass and built inside an oven to ensure that all surface impurities may be volatilized and removed during evacuation, so that the necessary high vacuum ($\sim 10^{-8}$ mm Hg) may be maintained in the glass envelope during adsorption studies.

the surface of the tip and accelerated to the screen in a straight line. The resultant pattern on the screen is, therefore, most strongly illuminated in those regions which receive electrons from those parts of the metal surfaces, out of which electrons may be most readily withdrawn and the darker areas correspond to regions of the tip having high work function. The pattern on the screen, therefore, gives a very much enlarged representation of the variation in work function over the surface of the small metal tip. Examination of such patterns and comparison with atomic models of the curved annealed metal tip have enabled regions of the illuminated area to be ascribed to emission of electrons from crystallographic planes of known index, which occur on the boundary surfaces of the tip.

In a somewhat similar apparatus, the *field-ion microscope*, the tip is cooled by immersion of the heavy supporting wire in liquid hydrogen and a small pressure of gaseous helium is admitted to the tube. On applying high field strengths, helium atoms are ionized at the metal surface and the ions are accelerated to the screen. The patterns thus obtained on the screen contain sufficient detail to enable the positions of individual atoms in the crystal planes comprising the surface of the tip to be recognized.

(*iv*) *X-ray methods.* The use of line broadening of X-ray diffraction patterns as a method whereby crystallite sizes may be determined has been mentioned in Chapter 2. Low angle X-ray scattering may also be used to measure crystallite sizes. Such X-ray scattering occurs at an angle close to that of the undeflected beam and is inside the lowest angle diffraction line for many solids. A monochromatic X-ray beam is allowed to fall at grazing incidence (angle of incidence $< 1°$) on the powder and, from measurements of the angular intensity distribution of the scattered beam, it is possible to determine crystal sizes.

(*v*) *Pressure porosimeter.* This experimental method is used to investigate the pore structure of solids. The solid, in a constant volume container, is first evacuated to remove gases and the container is then filled with a liquid which does not wet the solid, usually mercury. This liquid exhibits capillary depression and does not enter the finer pores unless forced by an externally applied pressure. Since greater pressures are necessary to make the liquid enter the finer capillaries, the apparent changes in volume which occur when mercury is forced into the pores of the solid at different measured, externally imposed pressures can be used to give information about the pore size distribution.

(*vi*) *Density measurements.* Density measurements may be used to determine total pore volume of a solid. The apparent density of the solid is first measured using a liquid which does not enter the pores. The true volume of the solid phase is then found from the difference in pressures observed when a measured volume of helium is admitted to (i) a calibrated evacuated volume, and (ii) the same volume which now contains a known weight of solid from which the adsorbed gases have been removed by evacuation. From the apparent and the true densities the total pore volume may be found.

2. ADSORPTION OF A SINGLE GAS BY A SOLID

The greater part of the attractive energy which bonds a gaseous molecule to a solid surface may be due either to van der Waals forces (physical adsorption) or to a primary valence force which may result from interactions between the orbitals of the constituent atoms of the gaseous molecule and the unfilled orbitals of atoms at the solid surface (chemisorption). It is usually possible to decide which type of bonding provides the main attractive energy in a particular system by reference to one or more of the following criteria:

(*i*) *Heat of adsorption*. Chemical bond formation is often accompanied by a relatively large energy release and calorimetric measurements for adsorption reactions have shown that heats of chemisorption are very often > 10 kcal mole^{-1}. This is not true for all systems, and examples are known of reactions where primary valence forces are formed between the molecules of a gaseous reactant and a solid surface with a relatively low chemisorption heat. The heat evolved on physical adsorption must always be low, of the order of the heat of gas liquefaction ($\sim$4 kcal mole^{-1}), though it may be somewhat higher when a molecule is adsorbed in a pore.

(*ii*) *Specificity*. Chemisorption is a chemical reaction involving bond formation between the atoms of a gaseous molecule and the atoms or ions at the surface of a solid, and is therefore a specific process. This means that, for appropriate combinations of reactant, the atoms in the gaseous molecule may react by forming bonds with species in the surface of one solid element (or compound) but not with those of a different element. Physical adsorption may occur on any solid surface at low temperatures. Specificity, however, must not be used as the sole diagnostic test, or conclusions may be misleading. For example, the penetration of noble gas atoms into the network of channels of a zeolite type lattice, but not into the lattice of minerals having similar composition but which do not possess a pore structure, was formerly interpreted as showing the formation of occlusion inert gas compounds with certain solids. It is now accepted that only physical bonding is present in such systems but that the zeolite lattice extends the effective surface area.

(*iii*) *Rate of adsorption*. Physical adsorption is normally a fast process so that equilibrium between gaseous and adsorbed molecules is often established within minutes of admission of the adsorbate. The adsorption rate may be reduced if it is necessary for molecules to penetrate long narrow passages within the solid before all internal surfaces reach adsorption equilibrium. Physical adsorption is always reversible so that adsorbed gases may be removed on heating and evacuating the solid adsorbent. Chemisorption may be fast or slow and very often the adsorbed gas cannot be pumped off unchanged. As an example of such a system, oxygen, chemisorbed on charcoal, can only be removed as oxides of carbon on pumping at elevated temperatures.

(*iv*) *Temperature.* Increase in temperature always decreases the quantity of physically adsorbed gas. Any gas may be physically adsorbed on any solid, as the condensation temperature of that gas is approached, in contrast to the specific behaviour shown by chemisorption reactions. The amount of a gas physically adsorbed by a given solid at a particular temperature is dependent on its boiling point. The higher the boiling point the greater the volume of gas adsorbed. Chemisorption may show an increase, both in rate and in volume adsorbed, with increase in temperature. In some systems there is an energy barrier, which must be overcome by an activation process before a chemical bond (between adsorbent and adsorbate) can be formed, as in many homogeneous phase chemical rate processes. Thus in these systems the volume of gas chemisorbed in a given time will increase with temperature as there is an increase in the number of gaseous reactant molecules having sufficient energy to overcome the energy barrier to reaction.

(*v*) *Physical measurements.* Measurements of several physical properties of the reactants may be used to obtain information about bonds formed between a surface and a chemisorbed species. Chemical bond formation on chemisorption may result in changes in the magnetic properties of the solid which result from the formation of linkages between the surface and the adsorbate. Also, differences between the infrared spectra of gaseous molecules and those adsorbed on the solid may be attributed to chemisorption bond formation.

(*vi*) *Volume adsorbed.* Chemisorption cannot extend beyond the formation of a single layer of adsorbed molecules. In contrast, as the gas pressure in equilibrium with physically adsorbed molecules on the surface approaches saturation value, condensation of liquid within the finer pores of the solid occurs. Thus a part of the surface may be regarded as being covered by more than a single layer of molecules. This is *multilayer* adsorption and results in isotherms of the general shapes shown below in Fig. 33.

(*vii*) *Reactivity.* Reaction of a chemisorbed molecule or radical with a gaseous reactant may yield a new gaseous product at temperatures below those at which the same reaction occurs in the homogeneous

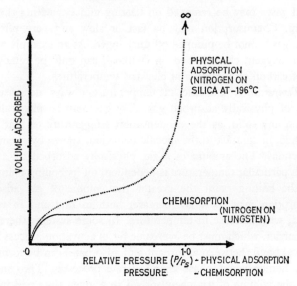

FIG. 33. Typical isotherms for physical adsorption and
for chemisorption.

phase. Such increased reactivity of adsorbed chemical intermediates
shows that modification of the bonding within a molecule has occurred
and such adsorbed radicals play an important part in heterogeneous
catalytic reactions; this topic will be discussed in a subsequent
section.

Adsorption isotherms

The reaction of a single gas with a solid is usually studied in an evacuated
glass reaction vessel of calibrated volume. From this volume a measured
pressure of reactant is admitted to the reaction vessel which contains
the evacuated solid adsorbent. Subsequent changes in pressure with
time are measured, using a McLeod gauge or a Pirani gauge (Fig. 34a).
It is not always necessary to use both gauges, as shown. The McLeod
gauge measures absolute pressure for non-condensable gases, but some
provision for calibration of the non-absolute Pirani gauge must be
included when this gauge is used. The McLeod gauge measures pressure by using mercury to compress the low ambient gas pressure in a
calibrated volume bulb into a capillary of known radius, with sealed
end, and both pressure and volume of gas are measured after compres-

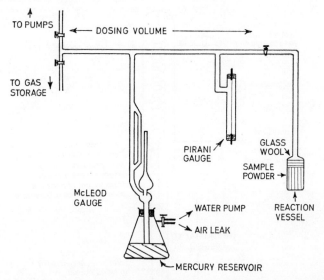

FIG. 34. (a) Apparatus used to measure gas adsorption by a solid.

A known volume of reactant gas is admitted to the calibrated dosing volume and the change in pressure on sharing this reactant with the reaction volume is measured. From such measured pressure changes when the reaction vessel (i) contains the reactant, and (ii) is empty, the volume of gas adsorbed may be determined. Two pressure measuring devices are shown in the sketch.

Notes: (i) A pumping system consisting of a two-stage mercury diffusion pump in series with a mechanical rotary pump can give a vacuum of $<10^{-7}$ mm Hg.

(ii) A refrigerant trap may be included between gauge and sample to remove volatile impurities, for example water vapour.

(iii) The sample is maintained in thermostated surroundings.

(iv) The Pirani gauge measures pressure from the resistance of a heated wire held in the gas. As pressure rises, the loss of heat from the wire increases and so the resistance decreases. This resistance is measured using a Wheatstone net, of which it forms one arm. This gauge is maintained in a thermostated bath. External contact to the fine wire is made through heavy tungsten leads sealed in glass.

(v) The McLeod gauge measures pressure through compression of gas from the bulb into the capillary of known radius by raising mercury in the tube. The pressure and volume of the compressed gas are measured, hence the original pressure may be found by the application of Boyle's law. This gauge may be used in a lower pressure range than that for which a manometer is used.

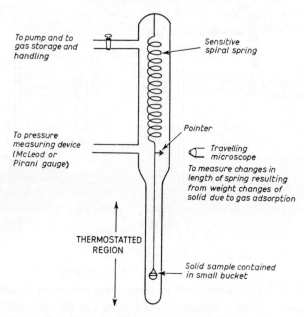

To pump and to
gas storage and
handling

Sensitive
spiral spring

To pressure
measuring device
(McLeod or
Pirani gauge)

Pointer

Travelling
microscope

To measure changes in
length of spring resulting
from weight changes of
solid due to gas adsorption

THERMOSTATTED
REGION

Solid sample contained
in small bucket

FIG. 34. (b) Alternative experimental apparatus which may be used to measure adsorption of gases by solids.

sion. Application of Boyle's law to this compression process enables the original low gas pressure, the only unknown quantity in the equation, to be determined. The Pirani gauge measures gas pressure from the resistance changes of a thin heated metal wire which result from changes in temperature of the wire by losses of heat through gaseous conduction and convection. The rate of heat loss depends on the ambient gas pressure.

An alternative experimental arrangement is shown in Fig. 34(b), where changes in the weight of the solid resulting from gas adsorption are measured using a delicate spring. Both experimental methods enable the determination of adsorption *isotherms*, which indicate the variation with pressure of the equilibrium volume of gas adsorbed at constant temperature, to be carried out. Several other types of experimental apparatus, for example, sensitive calorimeters suitable for heat of adsorption measurements, have been used to gain information about adsorption reactions; these are described in appropriate specialist texts and will not be dealt with here.

Measurements of the equilibrium volume of gas adsorbed at various pressures have been made for numerous gases on a large number of solids. The earliest satisfactory theoretical description of an adsorption isotherm, which gained wide acceptance, was given by Langmuir in 1916. This model, based on dynamic equilibrium, assumes that the surface of the solid consists of an array of equivalent sites on each of which a single molecule may be adsorbed with equal probability and heat of reaction to that for adsorption on any other site. The rate of adsorption is directly proportional to:

(i) the fraction of surface sites which are not already occupied $(1 - \theta)$, where θ is the fraction of sites occupied, the surface coverage;

(ii) the number of molecules striking the surface in unit time, c, and

(iii) the fraction of collisions with the surface which result in a molecular adsorption reaction, α.

Starting from an unoccupied surface, the desorption reaction progressively increases in importance as the surface is covered. The rate of desorption is given by the product of the surface coverage (θ) and a probability constant, v. At equilibrium:

rate of adsorption = rate of desorption.

$$c\alpha(1 - \theta) = v\theta.$$

In this equation c is proportional to gaseous pressure, P, and θ is proportional to the volume of gas adsorbed by unit mass of solid, V. The final formula may be written in a number of different ways, one of which is

$$\frac{P}{V} = \frac{P}{k_1} + \frac{1}{k_1 k_2}.$$

This equation is known as the *Langmuir isotherm*. Plots of P/V against P for data from many different systems have yielded straight lines, for example the adsorption of oxygen, ethylene, or carbon monoxide by silica.

In attempts to extend the theory to include systems for which deviations from this equation have been found, some of the assumptions made in the Langmuir treatment have been modified. For example, the Temkin isotherm is derived using the Langmuir approach, but the Langmuir assumption that heat of adsorption is constant is modified to postulate that the heat of gas adsorption varies linearly with the volume adsorbed. Several other comparable modifications of the original Langmuir equation have been proposed.

The Langmuir isotherm may be alternatively written:

$$\frac{1}{V} = \frac{1}{k_1} + \frac{1}{Pk_1k_2}.$$

In this form it can be readily seen that at high pressures the influence of the second term on the right-hand side diminishes and V tends towards a constant or $V \simeq k'P^0$. At low pressures the $1/k_1$ term is of less importance so that here $V \simeq k''P^1$. From these approximations it can be seen that the index of pressure dependence of volume adsorbed ranges from unity to zero and in the median regions we may approximate the isotherm to

$$V = kP^{1/n} \qquad \text{where } n > 1.$$

This is known as the *Freundlich isotherm*. This equation has found some application in the study of adsorption processes.

Physical adsorption

Physical adsorption investigations have been widely used for the measurement of surface areas and to obtain information about the pore geometry of solids. The isotherms which have been mentioned in the previous section apply to systems in which gaseous molecules are in equilibrium with a monolayer adsorbed phase. This equilibrium may be established for the physical adsorption of gases on solids at low pressures, but as the pressure approaches saturation value, the assumption of monolayer coverage becomes invalid. Brunauer, Emmet and Teller have extended the Langmuir treatment for use in surface area determinations by considering gas adsorption at pressures up to those at which the surface is covered by more than a single layer of adsorbed molecules. The equation so derived, often known as the B.E.T. equation, is usually written in the form:

$$\frac{P}{V(P_S - P)} = \frac{1}{V_m C} + \frac{P(c-1)}{P_S V_m c}.$$

P_S is the saturation vapour pressure, P and V have the same meanings as in the Langmuir equation above and V_m is the volume of gas which forms a surface monolayer. c is a constant which includes a term giving the difference between the heat of gas adsorption in the layer immediately adjacent to the solid surface and that for molecules in positions non-adjacent to the surface, the latter positions are assumed to be similar in character to the liquid phase. There has been considerable discussion in the literature about the validity of some of the assumptions made in the derivation of the B.E.T. equation. Many research workers have now concluded that, while the experimentally measured isotherms fit the equation to a good degree of accuracy, the details of the model from which the equation has been derived are somewhat unsatisfactory. Nevertheless the B.E.T. equation has found extensive use in measuring and comparing the surface areas of solids and no alternative expression has found the same widespread application.

In a surface area determination by the B.E.T. method, the solid sample is first thoroughly evacuated (known as *outgassing*) and then the volumes of gas adsorbed (V) at various gas pressures (P) are measured. It is necessary to be careful that the system has been allowed to reach equilibrium before each measurement is recorded. An apparatus of the type shown in Fig. 34(a), with slight modifications and appropriate choice of volumes, may be used. From the slope and the intercept of a plot of $P/V(P_S - P)$ against P/P_S the value V_m, the volume of gas in the monolayer, may be found, using the B.E.T. equation. The area occupied by each adsorbed molecule at the surface may be estimated if it is assumed that it has a particular shape and occupies the same volume in the adsorbed layer as it does in the liquefied adsorbate. From the number of molecules in the monolayer (V_m) and the area occupied by each on the surface, the surface area of the solid is easily calculated. A convenient experimental measurement of area of solids with surfaces $> 5\text{m}^2\text{g}^{-1}$ is to determine the volumes of nitrogen adsorbed at its boiling point ($-195°\text{C}$) for at least seven values of gas equilibrium pressure in the range $0.05 < P/P_S < 0.3$. The surface area is then calculated from the B.E.T. V_m value assuming the cross-sectional area of adsorbed nitrogen to be 16.2 Å^2. Slightly different values have been used by different workers for this cross-sectional area. Measurement of argon, krypton and xenon adsorption have also been widely used for surface area determination.

The B.E.T. equation does not provide an acceptable fit to the experimental results for the adsorption of gases on solids which contain small pores, since multilayer adsorption may result in condensation and the whole volume of the pores become filled with liquid. The adsorption isotherm on such a solid may show hysteresis. This occurs since certain narrow pores ($\sim$50 Å diameter) may be empty at a particular pressure, P_x, reached after increase from a lower value. But the same pores may remain filled with liquid at the same equilibrium pressure P_x reached after reduction from a higher gas pressure. After reaching P_x from lower pressures, capillary condensation does not occur, but after reaching P_x

from pressures at which condensation does occur, the pore may retain the liquid since the vapour pressure at the surface is reduced as result of the pronounced curvature of the meniscus at the end of the narrow pores. Information about the pore structure of solids has been obtained from detailed examination of such hysteresis loops.

Chemisorption

The above account of physical adsorption has been concerned with the methods by which information can be obtained about the physical properties, area and porosity, of a surface already in existence and which remained chemically unchanged as a result of the adsorption processes. The non-specific nature of physical adsorption was emphasized. It follows, therefore, that provided the solid is stored and treated under conditions which precluded the possibility of chemical changes or thermal sintering (and for the study of reactive solids, very stringent conditions may be required), it is only necessary to remove gaseous and condensable impurities from the reactant and vessel before measuring the physical adsorption isotherm. In contrast, before measurements of the chemical reactivity of a solid surface can be undertaken, it is necessary to establish the chemical nature of the reactant surface and great care must be devoted to the preparation of the solid reactant. The unsatisfied valence forces which exist at the boundary regions of many solids result in the very rapid chemisorption of any gaseous impurities in the vicinity, and the preparation of uncontaminated surfaces of a particular solid may be a matter of considerable experimental difficulty. The surfaces of many metals are very rapidly contaminated in the presence of small gas pressures so that very low ambient pressures must be maintained during the preparation of clean metal surfaces. To illustrate the rapidity with which contamination can occur, it may be mentioned that it has been shown that if a bond is formed between an active surface and every gaseous atom striking it, a surface monolayer of adsorbed atoms may be formed in less than one minute when a gas pressure of 10^{-7} mm Hg is maintained over that surface.

A number of experimental methods which have been used for the preparation of solid surfaces active in chemisorption are described below. Numerous variations of these general methods have been applied to particular systems, or to obtain results appertaining to a particular aspect of the chemisorption process. The study of chemisorption reactions on clean surfaces is at present a particularly active research field.

Metal surfaces

(i) *Compound reduction.* Samples of elementary metals which possess surfaces sufficiently clean to chemisorb gases may be prepared by reduction of a metallic compound, but care must be taken (i) completely to remove the reducing agent – hydrogen may be used to reduce many metals, and is subsequently removed by evacuation at elevated temperature – and (ii) to prevent adsorption of gaseous impurities after preparation and before the reactant gas is introduced. Reduction of a compound, followed by high-temperature evacuation of the product, often gives the metal in a form where the total surface area is low, and, therefore, adsorption of a small volume of impurity contaminates a large fraction of the available surface. The surfaces of such solids, having high bulk/area ratio, can readily be contaminated by diffusion of non-volatile impurities from the bulk or by adsorption of small volumes of contaminants desorbed from the reaction vessel walls. One convenient method of increasing the area/bulk ratio, which is possible for several metals, is to disperse the particles of that metal on the surfaces of an inert high area refractory supporting material. For example, a preparation containing nickel metal, which shows considerable reactivity in the chemisorption of hydrogen, oxygen or hydrocarbons, is formed by heating, in hydrogen, a sample of high area silica which has been impregnated with nickel nitrate solution. The metal nitrate is decomposed on heating to form the oxide which is subsequently reduced by very pure, palladium-diffused, hydrogen for several hours at 430°C. Such reducing gas must not contain significant traces of oxygen or this element will accumulate through preferential adsorption to form surface oxide on the metal particles. Adsorbed hydrogen is finally removed, after reduction has been completed, by evacuation at $\sim 10^{-8}$ mm Hg for some hours at ~ 390°C. The solid is evacuated at a temperature somewhat below reduction temperature to minimize the possibility of part of the water strongly chemisorbed on the silica support migrating onto the metal surface. The surface area of the nickel metal obtainable by this method may be several hundred square metres per gram, and electron microscopy studies have shown that the metal is dispersed as very fine crystallites over the surface of the silica particles. Similar methods have been used to prepare high surface area samples of other metals, for example, platinum supported on alumina, also cobalt on carbon.

(*ii*) *Flashed filaments.* Clean surfaces of high melting-point metals may be prepared by heating a ribbon of metal in vacuum to a temperature sufficiently great to volatilize all impurities. Adsorption studies may be made after cooling the ribbon in high vacuum ($\sim 10^{-9}$ mm Hg). Sensitive gauges have been developed to measure, through ionization of the gaseous molecules, the low pressures of reactant gases involved. This method has been used in the preparation of surfaces for studies of permanent gas chemisorption on metals, including tungsten, molybdenum and nickel.

(*iii*) *Evaporated metal films*. The metal, in the form of a wire, is electrically heated for some hours, with simultaneous evacuation, at temperatures just below evaporation point, to remove gaseous impurities. The temperature is then raised so that a fine deposit of crystallites is evaporated onto the walls, usually glass, of the containing vessel. The total surface area of such multi-crystallite films may be high, particularly if a high melting point metal is evaporated onto a chilled reaction vessel wall; the area may be reduced by sintering on warming. Films of most of the metallic elements, and certain alloys, have been prepared by this method. Since many clean metal surfaces readily chemisorb gases, such a solid reactant must be prepared and maintained under carefully controlled conditions to reduce surface contamination before the chemisorption reaction is studied.

(*iv*) *Field-emission microscope*. Gases adsorbed on a metal change the work function (ease of electron removal) over those regions of surface at which chemisorption has occurred. Chemisorption on the cleaned emitting tip of a field emission microscope results in changes on the appropriate parts of the emission image on the screen and these may be recognized by comparison with the characteristic emission pattern found for a clean tip. The volumes of gas adsorbed are too small to be directly measured, but preferential adsorption of a particular gas on one crystallographic surface rather than another, can be recognized from changes in brightness of the emission pattern.

Experiments have shown that data for the chemisorption of a particular gas on samples of a particular metal, which have been prepared by different methods, show quantitative differences which may be ascribed to (*inter alia*): (i) the presence of impurities contained in the bulk of the solid or chemisorbed on the surface during preparation, (ii) preferential occurrence of different sets of crystallographic planes at the surface of the same metal when prepared by different techniques, (iii) interaction between a metal and a supporting material; in this situation the latter cannot be regarded as inert.

It is probably true to say that the greater part of fundamental chemisorption research has been concerned with the surface reactions of metals or with attempts to prepare metal surfaces free of surface contaminants. Reasons for the concentration of effort on this particular type of reactant solid surface include: (i) interest in the study of some of the most reactive surfaces known, (ii) variations in reactant composition do not occur when an element is studied, and the interpretation of results is facilitated since there is only one possible atomic (or ionic) species comprising the original reactant surface. The surfaces of a compound may contain two or more different species, (iii) the influence of adsorbed surface species on the facility of electronic movements in the metal crystal may give information relevant in extending the band theory of metals to include surface sites; electrical measurements may be readily made at the same time as adsorption measurements, (iv) many metals are active heterogeneous catalysts.

More recently there has been an extension of interest to the study of chemisorption reactions on a number of other compounds, including oxides and sulphides. Comparatively few detailed studies have been undertaken on the surface reactions which occur between gases and ionic crystals (KCl, NaCl, etc.), purely covalent crystals and molecular crystals (many of which show little chemisorption activity), and such systems will not be considered further in the present monograph.

Oxides and sulphides. Solids which show chemisorption activity may be prepared by heating, with evacuation, a sample of the substance to be studied to a temperature slightly below that at which significant decomposition and/or sintering occurs. The presence of a small pressure of gas, oxygen for oxides, etc., during the early stages of heating (it is subsequently evacuated during heating) may enhance the chemisorption activity observed for the final product.

The results of chemisorption experiments involving binary compounds are difficult to interpret fully, since a particular type of adsorbed species may be bonded to the surface through interaction either with surface anions or cations. Furthermore, reactants which yield reducing conditions may produce small crystallites of metal through reaction of the adsorbent. These crystallites are difficult to detect unless they are specifically sought, and such material may be very much more reactive, in a particular chemical process, than the oxide being studied. Also, deviations from stoichiometry within the solid may cause changes in its surface chemistry.

Kinetics of chemisorption

Specificity has been mentioned as one of the factors which enable a decision to be made as to whether a particular adsorption reaction is a physical or chemical process, since a clean solid does not necessarily form primary valence bonds with every gaseous reactant to which it may be exposed. Investigations of the possibility of surface reactions between every possible combination of gas – and – solid system have not been undertaken and so far no general rule has been established which enables predictions to be made as to which gases are chemisorbed by a particular solid, though several trends have been reported. Experimental results obtained for a large number of systems have shown that such reactions can be classified into three main groups:

(*i*) *Rapid low temperature chemisorption.* In such a reaction the activation energy must be low or zero. Rates of these chemisorption processes are usually expressed through the *sticking probability*, which is defined as the fraction of those molecules striking the surface which become chemisorbed. Examples from many systems, which have been shown to exhibit this type of behaviour, include the chemisorption of hydrogen on nickel, platinum or tungsten, of nitrogen on tungsten or titanium and of oxygen on almost all metals except gold.

Sticking probability measurements have been made for many chemisorption reactions on metal surfaces prepared by the flashed filament technique. Results have shown that sticking probabilities of nitrogen, hydrogen or carbon monoxide on tungsten are $\sim$0·5 for chemisorption on clean or on sparsely covered surfaces. At low coverages the value remains fairly constant but as the volume of chemisorbed material increases the sticking probability decreases fairly rapidly. Since the adsorption rate does not vary linearly with coverage, and, indeed, initially remains almost constant, it has been concluded that, on reaching the surface, molecules may be able to enter weakly bonded surface energy states temporarily. Such *precursor states* are believed to be derived from bonding orbitals of the surface atoms and a molecule which is held in such a state may subsequently either become chemisorbed or be desorbed to the gas. In general, sticking probabilities decrease with increase in temperature of the reactant solid.

(*ii*) *Activated adsorption.* Where there is an energy barrier to bond formation between a reactant molecule and the bonding orbitals of the solid, the chemisorption reaction may proceed by a slow rate process. The rates of many such processes have been found to obey the Elovich equation, which is usually expressed in the following form:

$$V = k \log (t + a)$$

where V is the volume of gas adsorbed at time t, and k and a are constants. The adsorption of hydrogen on zinc oxide obeys this equation. The Elovich equation may be derived theoretically on the assumption that the activation energy for adsorption increases linearly with the volume of adsorbed gas, which is consistent with the observed decrease in heat of adsorption with coverage. The same equation may be alternatively derived making the (rather similar) assumption that the surface does not consist of an array of exactly equivalent sites.

Other examples of activated chemisorption reactions include chemisorption of methane on nickel, nitrogen on iron and oxygen on zinc or cuprous oxide. Some combinations of gas with solid show rapid low-temperature chemisorption which is followed by a slower uptake of gas by the solid. The latter slow process may result from (i) reactions of the chemisorbed species with surface impurities, or (ii) slow, possibly activated, diffusion of surface species into fine channels or pores of atomic dimensions within the solid.

When the volume of gas adsorbed at constant pressure is plotted against temperature (an adsorption *isobar*) the graph may show more than a single maximum value. For example, the volume of hydrogen chemisorbed by iron powder decreases somewhat as temperature is increased from $-100°$ to $0°$, it then increases to a maximum value at $\sim100°$ and decreases on further heating $>100°$. These results, and similar observations for other systems, have been interpreted as showing that each adsorption maximum corresponds to the formation of a different chemisorbed species at the surface, i.e. a different gas-solid reaction has occurred.

(*iii*) *No chemisorption.* Chemisorption may not occur to any appreciable extent for one (or more) of the following reasons: (i) There may be a prohibitively high activation energy, so that the reactant molecule is decomposed below the temperature at which chemisorption attains a significant rate. (ii) The desorption reaction may be rapid, for example, hydrogen *atoms* adsorbed on a copper metal film rapidly combine to form molecules which are then desorbed. (iii) The orbitals of gas and solid surface atoms may not yield a stable bonding system, for example the noble gases, neon and argon, are not usually chemisorbed by metals.

Heats of chemisorption

Calorimetric measurements for chemisorption reactions have shown that the heats of surface reaction of successive equal volumes of gas usually decrease progressively with increasing surface coverage. The heats of adsorption of small volumes of hydrogen on iron or on nickel decrease slowly at first from $\sim$35 kcal mole^{-1} at very small coverages ($\theta \sim 0$) to about 28 kcal mole^{-1} at $\theta \sim 0.5$ and then more rapidly as the monolayer is approached. The quantitative relation between heat of reaction and coverage varies for different gases on a given metal and also for the same gas on different metals. Two main types of explanation have been widely considered to account for these observations, and each, or both, may operate in different particular systems. However, the extent to which each contributes in those reactions for which quantitative data is available must be regarded as still open to discussion. (i) There is a repulsive force opposing the approach of two chemisorbed species so that the total repulsive energy between the adsorbed radicals increases with coverage, as the surface becomes progressively more crowded, and (ii) a larger amount of energy may be liberated on adsorption of a molecule at a crystallite edge, corner or other high energy region at which adsorption may preferentially occur, than from adsorption of the same molecule on a more perfect region of the planar crystal surfaces. Furthermore, the heat of adsorption on different exposed crystallographic surface planes may be different. Attempts to apply the band theory of solids to this problem have not as yet yielded any generally accepted conclusions.

The nature of the chemisorption bond and chemisorbed species

Metals. It has been emphasized above that clean metal surfaces are often highly reactive and the heat of chemisorption of a gas on such unsaturated areas of solid surface is often of comparable magnitude to that found for homogeneous phase chemical reactions. It is possible, therefore, that the chemisorbed species bonded to atoms of the metal surface are different chemical entities from the gaseous molecules from which they were derived since the electrons in the reactant have been rearranged to provide primary valence bonding forces with the metal surface. Such bonding rearrangements on chemisorption have been shown to occur when many gaseous molecules react with a clean metal surface. In the present monograph we will consider particular examples taken from studies of hydrogen and hydrocarbon chemisorption on nickel surfaces. These results have been selected because such reactions have been studied by a larger number of different research workers, using widely different techniques, than any other comparable system in this research field. Nickel has been used by many workers as the solid reactant since high-area supported metal samples may be easily prepared, and nickel metal is well known to be a very active hydrogenation and cracking catalyst. Closely similar reactions occur between gases and the surfaces of other metals; some examples will be mentioned below.

It is generally accepted that the hydrogen chemisorption reaction on a clean nickel surface results in dissociation of the *molecule* to yield a pair of hydrogen *atoms* bonded to the metal. Several different lines of experimental evidence point to this conclusion:

(i) When hydrogen, chemisorbed on nickel metal, is exposed to deuterium gas, hydrogen deuteride very soon appears in the gaseous phase showing that interaction between adsorbed hydrogen and the deuterium molecule has resulted in rupture of H–H and D–D bonds. This reaction must occur at the nickel surface since the reaction does not occur at low temperatures in the absence of the metal.

(ii) Comparison between the number of metal atoms in the surface (calculated from the area measured by the B.E.T. method by making reasonable assumptions about the density of atoms in the surface of the most abundant emergent crystallographic planes) and the number of hydrogen molecules which are chemisorbed on saturation of the surface has shown that there is close to 1 : 1 correspondence between the number of adsorbed atoms and the number of surface metal atoms.

(iii) Measurement of the magnetic properties of nickel before and after hydrogen has been chemisorbed has shown that the adsorption of a single molecule (or two atoms) of hydrogen results (on average) in the pairing of 1·4 electrons in the metal. This is interpreted as indicating the formation of two largely covalent bonds between the surface metal atoms and the two adsorbed atoms. Since the formation of two covalent bonds would result in the pairing of two electrons, it is concluded that the chemisorption bonds possess some ionic character. This has been confirmed by dipole moment type measurements.

These lines of evidence show that, on chemisorption, the hydrogen molecule is dissociated at the metal surface and the hydrogen atoms are retained on the metal by a largely covalent link which possesses some ionic character. Hydrocarbons are also dissociatively chemisorbed on a clean nickel surface. Experimental evidence which has led to this latter conclusion includes the following observations:

(i) A part, but not all, of the constituent hydrogen in the hydrocarbon molecules chemisorbed on a nickel surface yield gaseous hydrogen and hydrogen deuteride when these radicals (chemisorbed in the absence of gaseous hydrogen) are exposed to pure deuterium gas. These results show that hydrocarbon chemisorption resulted in dissociation of some of the C–H bonds to yield chemisorbed hydrogen atoms, which are probably bonded to the surface by identical linkages to those formed on dissociative chemisorption of hydrogen molecules. That part of the hydrogen on the surface which cannot be replaced (i.e. undergo exchange) with deuterium probably remains attached to the adsorbed carbon atoms of the hydrocarbon, from which it is not readily transferred to the metal surface where the exchange processes occur. These reactions may be represented:

dissociative chemisorption: $C_xH_y \rightarrow C_xH_{y-z}(a) + zH(a)$

exchange: $\qquad D_2 + H(a) \rightarrow HD + D(a)$

$$D_2 \rightarrow 2D(a)$$

$$D(a) + H(a) \rightarrow HD$$

where (a) signifies an adsorbed species.

(ii) Chemisorption of cyclohexane molecules on nickel results in approximately four times the change in magnetic properties of the metal to that found for the adsorption of a single hydrogen molecule. This is interpreted as showing that four C–H bonds of the hydrocarbon have been dissociated to yield four adsorbed hydrogen atoms and the radical C_6H_8 which possesses four bonds with the metal surface. It is assumed that the effect of the C–Ni bond on the magnetic properties of the metal is the same as that of the H–Ni bond.

(iii) Infrared spectra of hydrocarbons chemisorbed on high area supported nickel metal preparations have shown that the hydrocarbon molecules are not completely dissociated but that a number of C–H bonds are retained in the chemisorbed radicals. It has also been shown the π-bond in ethylene may undergo modification when the molecule is chemisorbed on nickel, but the exact nature of the structure and bonding in the resultant surface species has been under discussion for some years. It has not yet been established whether the surface radical is 'saturated', olefinic or acetylenic (resulting from dissociative adsorption); possibly all three species may be formed on the surface under different reaction conditions (temperature, surface concentration of radicals, presence or absence of added hydrogen).

Experimental investigations have also shown that hydrogen is dissociatively chemisorbed on other metals, including *inter alia* platinum and tungsten; also methane and ethane are dissociatively chemisorbed on tungsten, iron and other metals. From the large quantity of experimental results published it has become generally accepted that an adsorbed radical may have a significantly different composition and bond structure from that of the gaseous molecule from which it was formed. There are, however, differences of opinion about the exact nature of some of the surface radicals, and surface bonding, formed in particular systems.

The factor which controls the total number of atoms, radicals or molecules which may be chemisorbed at a given metal surface is probably the number of metal atoms which comprise that surface, since, in many systems, these numbers are equal within the limits of experimental determination. This correspondence shows that on metals the chemisorption process is not limited by the total number of empty electron energy levels in the band structure of the bulk crystal. Chemisorption on metals, therefore, results from linkage of the adsorbed radicals to available orbitals of the surface metal atoms.

Semi-conducting oxides. Chemisorption through linkage of adsorbed species to all available surface atoms is not a satisfactory model for adsorption on semi-conducting oxides. To describe the characteristic behaviour of these solids we will consider chemisorption reactions on particular solids: zinc oxide containing excess metal, which is an *n*-type semi-conductor, and nickel oxide, which is a *p*-type semi-conductor.

In the zinc oxide crystal the valence band is full, the empty conduction band is at a comparatively high energy level and the number of impurity levels, which provide the current-carrying electrons, is smaller than the number of surface atoms. When oxygen is chemisorbed at the surfaces of the solid, it is found that there is a decrease in the electrical conductivity. This is due to the removal of the defect electrons on the formation of surface oxygen ions (O^{2-}), through the chemisorption reaction of the gas. The total volume of oxygen which may be chemisorbed is, however, very much less than a monolayer, due to increasing difficulty in the removal of electrons from impurity or defect levels at progressively greater depths below the surface. Chemisorption is thus the removal of electrons from impurity levels near but not necessarily at the surface. It seems probable that such reactions may be accompanied by changes in the position of bands (on the energy scale) in the surface regions of the solid. Hydrogen chemisorbed on a sample of the same original oxide, however, forms surface hydroxide radicals. Each chemisorbed hydrogen atom neutralizes one negative charge on a surface O^{2-} ion so releasing an electron, which is accommodated in the conduction band. This energy band is very largely unoccupied before hydrogen chemisorption and it is capable of accepting all the electrons which may be donated from the surface chemisorption process. In agreement with the requirements of this theoretical model, it has been found that a monolayer of hydrogen may be adsorbed on zinc oxide and its formation is accompanied by an increase in electrical conduction.

The converse behaviour pattern is observed for nickel oxide. The volume of oxygen which may be taken up by this solid is close to a monolayer and the chemisorption process is accompanied by an increase in conduction. During oxygen adsorption electrons are removed from the conduction band by positive hole formation; a sufficient number of electrons may be taken from the full band to enable monolayer coverage to be reached. This is accompanied by an increase in the number of current-carrying entities. When hydrogen is chemisorbed on this oxide, however, the electrons which are transferred to the solid must be accommodated in impurity levels at, or close to, the surface in the positive holes in the conduction band. The volume of the gas which may be adsorbed is less than a monolayer and adsorption is accompanied by a reduction in conductivity.

Chemisorption on such solids is, therefore, most readily explained in terms of band theory and the extent of reaction may depend on the concentration of impurity levels contained within a volume extending an appreciable distance below the solid surface.

Surface-adsorbed molecule bond. In the examples considered above, the chemisorption of hydrogen and of hydrocarbons on nickel metal occurred through linkage of the adsorbed radical to the surface by a largely *covalent* bond, though this may possess some ionic character. Similarly, hydrogen adsorbed on a semi-conductor is retained at the surface by a bond that is largely covalent. Chemisorption of oxygen on these oxides, however, is believed to occur with the formation of surface ions, and, therefore, the bonding must be considered to be largely *ionic*. Other systems are known in which the chemisorption bond must be regarded as almost completely ionic. For example, the alkali metals, sodium and potassium, chemisorbed on tungsten become positively charged and exist as Na^+ and K^+ when the surface is incompletely covered and the ions are not forced to remain in close proximity to each other on adjacent surface sites. *Co-ordinate linkages* between adsorbed species and solid surfaces are also known. A number of organic sulphides, arsenic and nitrogen compounds, are known to be strongly chemisorbed on metal surfaces through the donation of a lone pair of electrons (from the S, As or N atom respectively) to the metal. Such chemisorbed species may only be removed from the surface under relatively extreme reaction conditions and such species may prevent the chemisorption of other molecules so that they behave as poisons in catalytic reactions. *Van der Waals forces* result in physical adsorption of gaseous molecules, as has been discussed previously.

Mobility of chemisorbed species. A molecule chemisorbed on a solid is not necessarily located at an immobile position on the surface. In many systems adsorbed radicals may migrate over the solid at temperatures below that at which desorption becomes significant. Probably the most direct experimental demonstration of such surface migration has been through experiments using the field emission microscope. Small amounts of gases to be chemisorbed (H_2 or O_2) were admitted unsymmetrically at low temperature to the cleaned emission tip so that chemisorption occurred on one side of the tip only. On subsequent gentle heating of the tip it was found that the adsorbed species migrated across the metal surface at rates which varied with (i) coverage or concentration of surface species, and (ii) the exposed crystallographic plane of the metal surface. Careful quantitative studies have enabled activation energies for surface migration to be measured. An alternative approach to investigation of surface mobility, for those metals which cannot be directly studied in the electron microscope, has been to measure the entropy change which accompanies adsorption. Information about surface mobility can be obtained from such measurements through the determination of the number of degrees of freedom which have been lost when the molecule is chemisorbed.

3. SOLID CATALYSTS

When two or more substances are brought in contact with an active surface a new product compound may be formed by reactions between the two (or more) reactant compounds. From this it follows that solids may behave as catalysts for chemical changes. Much of the research concerned with reactions of more than one gas with a solid has been concerned with determining the steps by which such solid-catalysed chemical changes can occur. A *catalyst* may be defined as a substance which accelerates the rate of attainment of equilibrium in a chemical system without itself being chemically changed at the end of the process. The catalyst reduces the time necessary to complete the reaction but it does not alter the relative proportions of reactant and products in the resultant equilibrium mixture.

It has been mentioned in the preceding section that the structure and bonding of a molecule may be altered on chemisorption by reactions through which dissociated radicals may be formed on the solid surfaces. Such adsorbed radicals often differ in chemical reactivity from the original gaseous molecule. The presence of dissociated species on the active surface may facilitate chemical reactions of the gases with which they are in contact without the surface undergoing a permanent change in the process. Catalytic activity may, therefore, be shown by surfaces active in chemisorption; the demonstration of catalytic properties has been cited as a diagnostic test for chemisorption. Two general types of effect may contribute towards the ability of a solid surface to facilitate a reaction, compared with the rate at which the same changes occur in the homogeneous phase. These are:

(*i*) *Alternative path mechanism.* On chemisorption, a reactant molecule may form a surface radical having a structure which, due to energy requirements, cannot be formed in significant quantities in the homogeneous phase. If a surface-catalysed chemical reaction can proceed through such a surface-stabilized intermediate, although the homogeneous reaction necessitates the formation of a higher energy intermediate, then reaction may be catalysed by the solid surface. The catalytic activity of a solid reacting in this way results from a relatively lower energy barrier to the heterogeneous reaction than to the homogeneous reaction.

(*ii*) *Surface reactant concentration.* Species chemisorbed on a surface may be crowded relatively closer together than molecules in the gaseous phase, thus increasing the probability of effective collisions between the reactants. The catalytic activity here results from an effective increase in the reactant concentrations.

Catalytic reactions often obey the Arrhenius equation:

$$k = A\mathrm{e}^{-E/RT}$$

The above effects ascribe catalytic activity, increase in the specific rate constant (k): (i) to a decrease in E, and/or (ii) an increase in A respectively, compared with the homogeneous reaction. It follows that, if chemical changes occurring at the phase interface are facilitated by the influences described above, chemisorption of at least one reactant is a necessary step in the catalytic process. For reactions which involve two reactant molecules, two general types of mechanism are possible: (i) both reactants are chemisorbed and reaction occurs during the residence time of both on the surface, and the products formed are subsequently

desorbed. This is known as the Langmuir-Hinshelwood mechanism
(ii) The alternative process is through the direct interaction of one of
the reactant molecules from the gaseous (or liquid) phase with a radical
previously formed from the second reactant and bonded to the surface.
Initial adsorption of one homogeneous phase reactant is not necessary.
This is the Eley-Rideal mechanism. The unambiguous distinction
between these alternative mechanisms for a particular reaction, on the
basis of experimental evidence, is a matter of considerable difficulty
and no general agreement has yet been reached as to which operates in
many of the most fully studied catalytic reactions.

Industrial catalysts
The acceleration of reaction rates by the use of a catalyst is clearly of
great industrial importance and ever-increasing numbers of synthesized
materials are prepared in ever-increasing quantities by techniques
which employ catalysts at some point in the manufacturing processes.
There is, however, no theoretical approach which allows general predictions of the relationship between the chemical composition of solids
and the reactions for which they may be expected to show catalytic
activity. The investigation of solids, in order to recognize those which
show useful catalytic properties was, at first, largely empirical. But in
recent years scientific principles have been applied in more systematic
searches. Considerable effort is being expended in many countries to
discover new catalytic synthetic routes, and to increase the efficiency of
application of those already known. Research techniques range from
the almost haphazard testing of every conceivable solid for its catalytic
activity in a particular reaction to the determination of the mechanism
of a specific reaction of interest on a possible solid followed by preparation of new solids having properties which the mechanistic studies have
indicated to be desirable.

Ideally an industrial catalyst should be a cheap substance which
possesses considerable activity for the reaction in which it is to be used.
It should have a long active life and be available as a preparation having
mechanical properties which enable it to be retained in the catalyst bed.
It should not produce unwanted by-products. In commercial operation
it is necessary to consider the most efficient economic balance between
the above and other more specific factors when deciding in which
catalyst, for a particular chemical process, capital should be invested.
The final choice represents a balance between economic and chemical
factors so that a pure product may be formed at low cost.

The lifetime of an industrial catalyst is probably one of the most important economic considerations. Trace impurities in the reactant may be strongly chemisorbed on active surfaces and will reduce or eliminate their desirable properties. The influence of such substances may be reduced through purification of the reactant before admission to the catalyst or by selecting a reactant source which contains a low impurity level. Alternatively, it may be more convenient to use a catalyst which has a somewhat lower initial activity than the best catalyst available, but which does not deactivate so readily. The decision between these possibilities is based on calculations to determine which course gives the greatest product yield with lowest overall investment and cost.

Careful treatment may increase the effective life of a catalyst. But, as time passes, the activity of the catalyst progressively declines through poisoning and, what is often more important, through changes in the physical properties of the catalyst particles. The industrial oxidation of ammonia is catalysed by a bed of woven fine platinum wires and, during use, the metal surface is progressively roughened until a point is reached where physical deterioration results in disintegration of the bed which must then be renewed. Another catalyst, which progressively deteriorates with use, is platinum supported on acidified alumina. Here the metal particles lose activity with time-of-use due to changes in the oxide support and progressive sintering through aggregation of the small particles of dispersed metal. In both catalyst preparations a point is reached where the catalyst must be removed from the plant and the valuable component(s) extracted, purified and manufactured into a new batch of catalyst. In certain processes the powder catalyst may be removed from the catalyst chamber and chemically treated within the plant before being returned to the reaction vessel by being transported in a gas stream. This is known as a *fluidized bed* process of catalyst regeneration or reactivation.

In the design of industrial catalytic processes it is important to provide a maximum area of contact between the active surface and the reactants. At the same time, it is convenient to use the catalyst in the form of pellets which constitute a bed through which the reactant gases are passed. This is necessary since, in contrast to a fine powder, such coherent assemblages of crystallites will not be readily carried out of the reactant chamber by the reactant gases forced to flow through it. These two requirements are, to some extent, in conflict, as will be seen if the stages of a catalytic change occurring on a solid are considered. We may divide the catalytic reaction of particular molecules into the following steps:

(1) Diffusion of reactant molecules to the active surface.
(2) Chemisorption of the reactant(s).
(3) Surface reaction.
(4) Desorption of product(s).
(5) Diffusion of products away from the surface.

Any one of these steps may exert a controlling influence on the reaction rate. In the selection of size of catalyst pellets to be used in a particular reaction, it must be remembered that small pellets may not remain in the catalyst chamber when a powerful blast of reactant gases is forced through it. However, there is a definite pellet size above which the material at the catalyst particle centre will not contribute effectively to reaction rate. This results from the factors, shown as steps (1) and (5) above, which restrict the movements of reactants to, and products from, the internal surfaces along the channels of each pellet. Much research has been directed towards the preparation of solids having suitable textures (size of crystallites, porosity, etc.) which allow maximum ease of diffusion to internal surfaces of the pellet while still retaining desirable mechanical properties (pellet size, resistance to disintegration during use, etc.). For many individual catalysts a satisfactory compromise between these somewhat conflicting requirements must be reached.

Some examples of industrial catalysts and catalytic processes are considered in the following reaction mechanism section.

Mechanisms of catalytic reactions

Throughout most of the above account of catalyst applications in industrial manufacturing processes, the existence of a suitable active solid was assumed, and attention was directed to those factors which influence the selection of optimum economic operating conditions. However, it is obvious that before a large-scale process can be designed it is necessary to establish which solid is the most suitable active catalyst available. To enable such a selection to be made, mechanistic studies of the steps by which chemical changes occur on solid surfaces have been undertaken. The information obtained in this way has, for many systems, resulted in the development of more active and/or more stable (i.e. longer life) forms of existing catalysts. Furthermore, new catalytic processes may be discovered. When considering industrial manufacturing processes the diffusion of reactants to the active surface was mentioned as exerting an influence on reaction rate; under these circumstances this may be regarded as a rate-determining factor. However, in fundamental studies of surface reactions, conditions are more usually selected to focus attention on the rate-determining properties of steps (2), (3) and (4) of the above scheme. Mechanistic studies are often undertaken on a small scale using a sample in the form of powder, wire or film. Diffusion processes, however, are only significant if (i) reaction is particularly fast, (ii) an appreciable part of the active solid surface is situated in narrow pores (~50 Å diameter) along which the reactants and products may diffuse only with difficulty, or (iii) one or more of the reactants is in the liquid phase. This topic is again dealt with below (p. 154).

Knowledge of the detailed steps in surface rate processes, and of the factors which determine the energy barriers to reaction, enables theories of catalytic action to be formulated. Such theories may then be useful in predicting behaviour in hitherto untested systems so that new and improved catalytic processes may be discovered. Results of mechanistic studies and theories of catalytic action will be described below, but first it will be useful to digress and consider three factors relevant in discussions of catalytic processes:

(*i*) *Relevance of chemisorption data.* In principle, if the rates and energetics of steps (2), (3) and (4) (in the above scheme) for each of the species involved in a given reaction on a particular solid together with the relative influence of reactants on each other are known, it should be possible to predict the catalytic activity of that solid. Furthermore, such data should enable predictions of the most efficient conditions for the particular catalytic reaction to be made. Thus, measurements of rate and extent of chemisorption and desorption reactions on solids have been used as an experimental approach to the investigation of catalytic behaviour. In this way, much valuable information has been obtained concerning the nature of surface processes. Examples will be cited below, but at least three main difficulties restrict the usefulness of this approach: (i) An adsorbed species, resulting from the reaction of a reactant molecule with a surface, which occupies the greater fraction of that solid surface, is not necessarily the active intermediate in a catalytic reaction. A fast surface reaction, involving labile surface radicals which comprise 1%, or less, of the adsorbed phase may result in the reaction of a very much greater number of molecules than the number resulting from a slower (or negligible rate) process which involves the remaining 99% of the adsorbed phase. It has been suggested that particularly labile, reactive adsorbed radicals, which provide the intermediates in catalytic processes, may be present at points of surface imperfection or discontinuity. (ii) Chemisorption measurements are usually concerned with reactions of gases with unsaturated surfaces possessing less than a monolayer of chemisorbed gas. During a catalytic process the adsorbed surface phase may be at, or close to, equilibrium with excess gaseous reactant. The residual valence forces at such surfaces may be regarded as saturated. Concentration and reactivity of surface species may differ under the two conditions. (iii) In many systems determination, from experimental measurements, of the mutual influences and reactivity of the different adsorbed species derived from more than one gaseous reactant from experimental measurements is a matter of considerable difficulty.

(*ii*) *Quantitative measurement of reaction rate.* To make comparison of the effectiveness of different catalysts for a particular reaction or for different reactants on a single catalyst, it is necessary to define a parameter which provides a measure of the catalytic activity. The rate constants for numerous catalytic reactions have been found to obey the Arrhenius equation over appreciable temperature intervals:

$$k = A\mathrm{e}^{-E/RT}$$

where the symbols have their usual meanings.

The activity of the catalyst may reside in its ability to reduce the energy barrier to reaction (E) compared with that occurring in the homogeneous phase, and thus E may be a measure of activity. Alternatively, there may be an increase of reactant concentration at the solid surface compared with that in the homogeneous reactant, and thus the reaction is accelerated through a relatively high frequency factor (A). However, it has been found that in many series of catalytic processes, where different reactions occur on a particular surface or in which a particular reaction occurs on different surfaces, there is a linear relationship between log A and E. This effect, known as the *compensation law*, shows that in such a reaction series, the reaction-rate increase resulting from a small value of E in a particular process is largely offset by a corresponding decrease in A. Thus, in making comparisons between catalytic activity, A and E may be useful. But it is often of more direct usefulness to determine the temperature (T) at which the rate constant (k) for the different reactions reaches a specified value; the reaction for which (T) has the lowest value may then be regarded as the most active catalytic process.

(*iii*) *The nature of surface reactions.* If the solid is to participate in a reaction, i.e. exhibit catalytic activity, chemisorption of at least one of the reactants is a necessary step in that chemical process. Furthermore, it is reasonable to suppose that if negligible distortion of the bonding within the chemisorbed species occurs on attachment to the solid, then the solid will not exhibit pronounced catalytic activity. At the other extreme, if radicals are very strongly chemisorbed to form particularly stable surface species, the reactivity of adsorbed molecules may be expected to be low and again the surface will not behave as an active catalyst. From such considerations it may be predicted that, on the most active catalysts for a particular reaction, chemisorption of a reactant results in some reduction in the strength of those bonds, within the original molecule, which undergo alteration in the catalysed chemical change. Chemisorption at the surface thus facilitates the formation of an adsorbed product species, for which the energy required for desorption is not prohibitively high. From this it follows that maximum catalytic activity necessitates the formation of adsorbed intermediates in which some bond distortion has occurred, as compared with the reactant, but there is a balance between the energy required for the adsorption and the subsequent desorption steps.

Mechanisms of some typical surface-catalysed reactions
Having discussed these general points, it is now relevant to consider some selected examples of methods used in, and characteristic results obtained from, fundamental studies designed to establish catalyst properties and reaction mechanisms.

(i) Decomposition of formic acid vapour catalysed by metals
These reactions have been selected for study by several workers since they represent a comparatively simple system for the characterization of the properties of processes occurring on solid surfaces, because reaction involves the chemisorption of a single reactant molecule. Comparative measurements of formic acid decomposition-rate on different metals have enabled correlations to be made between the catalytic activity of the solids and the kinetics of the adsorption and desorption processes. Quantitative measurements of Arrhenius parameters for these decomposition reactions, using different metals, and by different workers for reaction over the same metal, have been found to obey the compensation law mentioned above. Thus the temperature at which reaction reaches a specified rate may be used to provide the most satisfactory index of catalytic activity for comparisons between different systems.

Experimental measurements for formic acid vapour decomposition catalysed by nickel metal have shown: (i) Reaction rate is largely independent of vapour pressure of reactant. From this it is concluded that rapid reactant chemisorption occurs, so that during reaction a complete monolayer of reactant species is maintained on the surface. (ii) The measured activation energy for the catalytic reaction (23 kcal mole^{-1}) is close to that found for the thermal decomposition of crystals of nickel formate. (iii) The surface species formed in greatest yield, following chemisorption of formic acid on nickel, results in the appearance of infrared absorption bands very similar to those characteristic of the formate ion in nickel formate. (iv) The rate of reactant chemisorption is fast compared with the rate of product desorption.

These observations all indicate that the catalytic reaction proceeds through the formation of a relatively stable surface formate as the reaction intermediate and the rate of the catalytic reaction is controlled by the rate of decomposition of this surface radical.

The decomposition of formic acid catalysed by gold probably also proceeds through surface formate formation. On this metal the rate of reaction is approximately first order in reactant pressure, and kinetic studies have shown that the reaction has a considerable negative entropy of activation. From these, and other measurements, workers in the field have concluded that here the adsorption step, dependent on gas pressure and accompanied by loss of translational degrees of freedom of the reactant, is rate controlling. Once formed, the chemisorbed products of the decomposition reaction are relatively readily desorbed.

Comparative studies of this decomposition process on a number of other metal catalysts, in addition to the two mentioned above, where the temperature at which a selected reaction rate is reached is used as a measure of catalyst activity, show that neither nickel nor gold is a particularly active catalyst for formic acid decomposition. The former metal has a high heat of formate formation, with consequent stability of the adsorbed species, while the latter metal has a low heat of chemisorption so that adsorption is the difficult step. Those metals for which the heat of formate formation is believed to be intermediate in value, Pt, Pd, Ir and Ru, are found to be the most active metals in this catalytic reaction. These results provide experimental justification of the thesis discussed in the 'nature of surface reactions' section (p. 144), that maximum catalytic activity necessitates a balance between the energy requirements of both the adsorption and the desorption steps.

(ii) Reactions of hydrocarbons with hydrogen on metals

Research has shown that, in general, those metals which are active catalysts for the hydrogenation, dehydrogenation, cracking and exchange (*vide infra*) reactions of hydrocarbons are those which dissociatively chemisorb hydrogen. Dissociative chemisorption of hydrogen on nickel has been discussed above. Many fundamental investigations of metal catalysed reactions of hydrocarbons have used gaseous deuterium in place of hydrogen in the reactant mixture. From quantitative examination of the distribution of the deuterium atoms in the products it is possible to obtain information about the reactions which have occurred during the period of chemisorption at the surface. It is sometimes assumed that in the presence of excess deuterium, whenever a bond between a carbon atom and the metal surface is formed, this will, on breaking, yield a deuterium atom in the product. In some of the early work (1937) in this field, H. S. Taylor and his co-workers showed that on a supported nickel catalyst the C–H bonds in simple hydrocarbon molecules were broken more easily than the C–C bonds. Subsequent work by Kemball has shown that during the time that a dissociatively chemisorbed hydrocarbon radical is retained on the surface of one of several different metals, several constituent hydrogen atoms may be replaced by deuterium atoms. Catalytic reactions resulting in replacement of hydrogen atoms by deuterium atoms are known as *exchange reactions*. Some general observations on reactions of this type are given below:

(a) Methane exchange. Research on metal catalysed methane exchange reactions has shown that deuterium may enter the hydrocarbon through two different mechanisms. One reaction results in the exchange of a single hydrogen atom from each methane molecule chemisorbed; this stepwise exchange process may be represented by the following scheme:

$$CH_4 \text{ (gas)} \rightarrow CH_3 + H \text{ (adsorbed)}$$

Chemisorption

$$D_2 \text{ (gas)} \rightarrow 2D \qquad \text{(adsorbed)}$$

Desorption $\quad CH_3 + D \rightarrow CH_3D \qquad \text{(gas)}$

The alternative rate process is the multiple exchange reaction which yields CH_2D_2, CHD_3 and CD_4 from a single residence of a methane molecule on the catalyst, and is believed to proceed through the formation of CH_2 or more highly dissociated intermediate species on the metal surface. The rates of both exchange reactions increase with increase in methane pressure and decrease with increase in deuterium pressure. Furthermore, as might be expected, the latter effect is more pronounced in the multiple exchange process, where increasing surface deuterium concentration must oppose the formation of the more highly dissociated surface species. In the series of metals Ni, W, Pt and Pd, the dependency of reaction rates on deuterium pressure decreases showing that the relative strength of adsorption of this reactant decreases while the relative strength of methane adsorption increases.

(b) *Ethane exchange.* When a deuterium-ethane mixture is brought into contact with an active metal surface a proportion of all the possible deuteroethane isomers may be produced during the early stages of reaction. The 'early stages of reaction' implies the period during which there has been insufficient time for a significant number of molecules to have undergone two (or more) successive chemisorption processes. The early appearance of more highly exchanged species is attributed to successive formation of mono- and diadsorbed species at the catalytic active surface; this process may be represented by the scheme:

$$C_2H_6(gas) \searrow \quad CH_3{-}CH_2 \underset{(a)}{\rightleftharpoons} CH_2{-}CH_2 \underset{(b)}{\rightleftharpoons} CH_2{-}CH_3 \nearrow \quad C_2H_6(gas)$$

Each step in these processes involves removal of a hydrogen atom or addition of a deuterium atom; these last have been omitted, and a single symbol (H) used to increase clarity. The use of a relatively large proportion of deuterium gas in the reactant mixture results in the maintenance of a high surface concentration of deuterium atoms, compared with hydrogen atoms which are formed by the exchange process. Thus reaction results in addition of deuterium to the hydrocarbon residue with high probability compared with that for hydrogen addition. Successive repetitions of reversible mono-diadsorbed species formation on the surface, i.e. reactions (a) and (b) in the above scheme, may result in complete exchange of all the hydrogen in the molecules, since all hydrogen atoms are equivalent and may be dissociated with equal probability. On those metals (for example, Pd, Rh, Co) for which the monoadsorbed $\rightleftharpoons$ diadsorbed reaction (a) or (b) occurs more readily than desorption, the highly deuterated products predominate. However, on those metals (W, Mo and Ta) where desorption is rapid compared with exchange mono- and dideuterethanes C_2H_5D and $C_2H_4D_2$ are formed in greatest yield in the exchange products. On platinum, chromium and (within certain temperature ranges) nickel, it would appear that there are contributions by two different exchange processes, one of each of the types mentioned, to the final deuteroethane product-distribution.

(c) *Ethylene exchange.* Ethylene is deuterated on films of iron or of nickel at −100°C. It has been shown, however, that dissociative chemisorption on the active metal surface does not necessarily result in hydrogenation of the double bond since deuteroethylenes have been recognized in the gas phase during the deuteration reaction. Furthermore, such experiments have shown that in the saturation reaction of the hydrocarbon, deuteration is not simply the addition of two deuterium atoms to the double bonds since reaction products contain all seven deuteroethanes, C_2H_6—C_2D_6. Simple addition of deuterium would be expected to yield $C_2D_4D_2$ predominantly. Similarly the deuteration of cyclohexene on metal films yields a number of deuterocyclohexane isomers; $C_6H_{10}D_2$ is not the only product.

(d) *Cracking reactions.* Cracking is the term used to describe rupture, often through hydrogenolysis, of the constituent C–C bonds of hydrocarbons, to yield different, often lower molecular weight products. The term is sometimes applied to comparable reactions of other molecules.

It has been mentioned previously that hydrocarbon chemisorption on a clean nickel surface is accompanied by dissociation. When such chemisorbed species are hydrogenated in the absence of gaseous hydrocarbon, it is found that product methane formation occurs by a reaction having a very low ($<$ $\sim$2 kcal mole^{-1}) activation energy and the reaction rate is directly proportional to gaseous hydrogen pressure. This reaction is the hydrogenation of adsorbed species. These kinetic characteristics are very similar to those of methane formation by reaction of hydrogen with nickel carbide. This characteristic behaviour of these reactions is very different to the catalytic cracking process which occurs on nickel in contact with hydrogen-hydrocarbon mixtures. Here the activation energy for cracking of several different hydrocarbons has been found to be $\sim$40 kcal mole^{-1} and reaction rate was strongly opposed by increasing gaseous hydrogen pressure (Rate $\alpha P_{H_2}^{-2}$). These results show that the kinetics of methane evolution from species chemisorbed on the surface (which may have been dissociated to surface carbide) differ significantly from the behaviour observed when reaction results from a process in which there is competition for the surface by both reactants. It has not yet been established whether nickel carbide is a necessary intermediate for hydrocarbon cracking reactions on nickel.

(e) *Metals other than nickel.* Nickel has probably received more attention in fundamental studies of catalysed hydrocarbon cracking reactions than most of the other transition metals, but comparable behaviour is shown by several other metallic elements. Platinum and tungsten are active in cracking hydrocarbons; also these and several other elements show considerable activity in exchange reactions. Quantitative differences, both in catalytic activity and in product distributions, have been found from measurements for a particular chemical change over different metal surfaces. Such differences have been attributed, amongst other reasons to the following differences between the metallic phases: crystal structure, numbers of electrons in the metallic d-band, ionization potential of the atoms and heat of adsorption of reactants.

The examples of reactions which have been studied in detail have been selected to indicate some of the reasons for difficulties in experimental data interpretation, the complexity of surface chemical processes and the present position in mechanism elucidation. From the data now available it must be concluded that there is no obvious property of a metal which controls its catalytic activity. Some of the reasons for this become apparent when it is remembered that the variation of chemisorption heat with coverage has not yet been fully explained theoretically; thus the energy of reactant chemisorption is not known. We have seen that maximum activity involves bond distortion in the chemisorbed reactant, hence the most active surfaces of the solid will be those giving appropriate modification of the bonds in the reactant molecule when this reaches the chemisorbed state. Different reactants occupy different areas of the active surface, which, itself may only represent a proportion of the total surface area of the catalyst. Thus, it is not known what effective concentrations of radicals, derived from the constituents of a binary reactant mixture, are present on the active regions of particular catalysts.

(iii) *The ammonia synthesis reaction*
This is an important industrial catalytic process, on which several detailed fundamental investigations have been undertaken. The catalyst used for large-scale ammonia manufacture, iron supported on alumina with potassium and calcium oxides present, is a more complex mixture of phases than those considered hitherto. The present monograph is concerned with the role of the solid phase in such reactions, and since

the catalyst phase is not completely understood a detailed account of this well-studied reaction will not be given here.

There is at present some disagreement as to the details of the mechanism of nitrogen hydrogenation. It was considered in the 1940's that the slow step was nitrogen chemisorption on the iron surface, from which it was concluded that the reaction rate was dependent on the availability of chemisorbed nitrogen. However, more recently it has been suggested that reactions between partially dissociated species, $\overset{\diagup}{N}H$ or $\overset{|}{N}H_2$ and hydrogen at the surface might be rate-controlling. No general agreement has as yet been reached in deciding which surface reaction controls the rate of the chemical change.

(iv) The Fischer-Tropsch reaction

This reaction is mentioned as an example of a metal-catalysed surface polymerization process. Carbon monoxide and hydrogen react at (usually) an iron surface to yield product hydrocarbons. The yields of different product compounds decrease with increasing chain length and larger proportions of branched hydrocarbons are found in the higher molecular weight compounds. The reaction $(CO + H_2)$ on the surface probably involves the formation of a radical which may be regarded as dissociatively chemisorbed methanol. Two such species may subsequently combine, with elimination of water, to yield an adsorbed ethanolic species which may undergo a further water elimination process through combination with a further adsorbed methanol radical. Hydrogenation of such dissociated species may then result in desorption of a product paraffin molecule. Detailed mechanisms of reaction at the surface have been proposed, which provide a satisfactory theoretical explanation of the relative proportions of different hydrocarbons in the products. In the present context it is interesting (and perhaps puzzling) to note that the incorporation of carbon into the iron lattice, to form iron carbide, does not destroy the activity of the solid, since iron carbide is an active Fischer-Tropsch catalyst. Nickel and cobalt also catalyse reactions of this type, but the activity of both metals is reduced or eliminated on carbide formation.

(v) Reaction catalysed by oxide semi-conductors

It has been shown that the activity of metal oxides for the catalytic decomposition of nitrous oxide is controlled by the defect structure of solid semi-conductors. The initial step in this catalytic reaction is the transfer of an electron from the solid to the chemisorbed species with rupture of the nitrogen–oxygen bond to yield a nitrogen molecule and a singly charged negative oxygen ion. Pairs of such ions subsequently combine to yield molecular oxygen and return the electrons to the solid phase. Results have shown that p-type semi-conductors, e.g. Cu_2O, NiO, are the most active catalysts. The adsorption step on such oxides occurs with transfer of electrons from the solid at $\sim 20°C$ but desorption of these species does not occur at an appreciable rate until $\sim 200°C$. The ease with which the electron transfer process occurs thus facilitates reaction. n-type semi-conductors, however, do not readily transfer electrons to such adsorbed species, hence such oxides, ZnO, CdO, are relatively poor catalysts. This characteristic behaviour represents a parallel to that described for oxygen adsorption on such oxides in that nickel oxide chemisorbs a monolayer of oxygen, while the volume taken up by zinc oxide is small. The catalytic activity of some insulating oxides, e.g. CaO and Al_2O_3, has been found to be intermediate between those of p-type and n-type semi-conductors.

(vi) Silica-alumina catalysts.
Silica and alumina mixed phases, formed by low temperature calcination of the mixed hydroxides, have been found to be particularly active catalysts for reactions of olefins. Such surface processes may yield a wide spectrum of products, including hydrogen, methane, alkanes and olefins (both straight and branched chains), and aromatic hydrocarbons. The catalytic activity is attributed to the presence of surface acidic sites which may be of two types:
    (i) A Lewis acid. This is a surface hydrogen atom of a hydroxyl group attached to a silicon atom which is, in turn, bonded through oxygen to neighbouring cations in the solid, or
    (ii) A Brønsted acid. This is a site at which the negative charge, associated with an aluminium atom bonded through oxygen to four neighbouring silicon atoms, is balanced by a hydrogen ion located at the solid surface.
    The surface of the solids containing these groups exhibit acidic properties. For example, the total number of such groups may be estimated by titration.
    Olefins may react with such acidic sites to yield carbonium ions by a reaction of the type:

$$R—CH=CH_2 + H^+ \text{ (surface)} \rightarrow R—CH^+—CH_3 \text{ (adsorbed)}$$

L

This adsorbed ion may then react with a further olefin molecule and by successive reactions a polymer may be formed on the surface. There is evidence that such a polymer, directly bonded to the surface, may be formed at a relatively low temperature ($\sim$80°C) but the reaction products are not dissociated from the surface at significant rates until higher temperatures (sometimes $\sim$350°C) are reached. It is believed that the rearrangements and breakdown reactions of this complex determine the rate of product formation. The catalytic activity of such solids, therefore, resides in the acidic properties which they possess and thus the ability to form the surface carbonium ion and polymer. The complex mixture of reaction products obtained from the decomposition of such surface radicals, shows that numerous reactions, including cracking, isomerization, aromatization and double bond shifts, can occur. For example, it has been found that cyclopentene cracking on silica-alumina catalysts yielded products from reactions of the types mentioned above, e.g. alkanes, alkenes (straight and branched chains) and several aromatic compounds, including benzene, toluene, naphthalene, anthracene. The cracking of cyclopentane was significantly slower and, from the results, this was attributed to difficulty in the initial step involving carbonium ion formation from the saturated hydrocarbon.

Platforming catalysts. This title is the contracted expression used to describe the catalyst used in the 'platinum reforming reaction' which is widely used in large-scale reactions in the petroleum industry. This catalytic process is used to enrich the proportion of those hydrocarbons in a petroleum mixture which have desirable properties for use in the internal combustion engine, i.e. highly branched and aromatic hydrocarbons, at the expense of the straight chain hydrocarbons in the mixture. The catalyst contains silica-alumina acidic cracking functional groups together with a metal, usually platinum, which is an efficient catalyst for hydrogenation-dehydrogenation reactions. The function of the metal is to facilitate the formation of aromatic compounds and olefins. The latter compounds may be isomerized, through reactions at the acidic sites of the oxide under reaction conditions (temperature, pressure) which are selected to favour the formation of the desired products from the particular reaction feed-stock used. By the use of low reaction temperatures, the production of low molecular weight products, ethane, propane, etc., is minimized.

The chemical changes mentioned in the preceding section form a small number of representative examples of chemical processes which occur at the solid-gas interface. The present book, however, is concerned with the solid phase and the properties of solid surfaces; catalysis was here derived from consideration of chemisorption of two compounds on one surface. The above account has been written from this particular (partisan) point of view and must not, therefore, be regarded as a general treatise on catalysis, the general study of which must be concerned with more than just the chemistry of solid surfaces.

Chemisorption bonds in catalysts

Considering now the linkage formed between the adsorbed molecule and the surface during catalytic reactions, we have seen that there are several different types of bond with the active solids. Chemisorption on metals often involves the formation of largely covalent bonds, which may possess some ionic character, and such chemisorbed species may be present during the catalytic hydrogenation of hydrocarbons on nickel. Retention of a reaction product at the catalyst surface through ionic bonding has been mentioned for catalytic processes involving semi-conducting oxides. Physical adsorption does not usually result in surface catalytic processes since such bonding results in little distortion of the molecule, though it may influence reaction rates through increasing reactant concentration in the vicinity of a solid surface. For example, in a surface reaction which occurs through the Eley-Rideal mechanism, one reactant may be concentrated near the reactant surface, physically adsorbed, while the second is chemisorbed. Bonding of a molecule to a metal surface by a co-ordinate linkage may result in chemisorption which is sufficiently strong to prevent access of reactant molecules to that surface. Such bonding does not always result in dissociation of the strongly chemisorbed species, however, since a strain may not be imposed on the bonding of the adsorbed molecule. Thus, such surface species do not participate in surface reactions. When a surface has been completely covered by such an inert layer it may not catalyse reactions for which the solid normally exhibits activity; the chemisorbed material is known as a poison. Many sulphides (mercaptans, hydrogen sulphide) which may form donor linkages to a metal surface, normally act as poisons for exchange reactions. The carbon-sulphur bond in such molecules may be broken by hydrogenation over a catalyst for which the molecule does not act as a poison; for example, molybdenum sulphide or tungsten sulphide. Sulphur-containing molecules, which behave as poisons on metal surfaces, are removed from crude oil by hydrogenation over a sulphide catalyst before the reactant feed-stock is brought in contact with the platforming catalyst.

It will be noticed that in the above accounts of fundamental catalytic studies particular attention has been directed towards the recognition of reaction rate-determining step. In principle, the more that is known about the chemistry of this process the more accurately it is possible to define, and possibly prepare, a substance which gives greatest ease of formation and decomposition of the appropriate adsorbed intermediate. Thus it may be possible to find a catalyst of maximum activity. It is not advantageous to accelerate those reaction steps which already occur quickly compared with the slowest.

Catalysis in liquids

Catalytic reactions involving liquid phase molecules show many closely similar characteristics to those for gaseous reactants. The chemisorbed intermediates, in catalytic process of both types, are strongly attracted to the solid surface, and, when bonded to the solid, have been effectively removed from the homogeneous phase from which they were obtained. One factor, for which due experimental allowance must be made, is that reactions for which there is one (or more) liquid phase reactant may be rate controlled by the relatively slow diffusion processes involving molecules in the liquid phase, as compared with those in the gaseous phase. When making kinetic measurements for such systems, sufficiently close contact between the reactants must be maintained to overcome this effect, if surface processes are to be rate-limiting. This applies more particularly at the upper end of the temperature scale studied, where reaction rate is a maximum.

One criterion of adequate mixing, which was used in a study of the nickel catalysed hydrogenation of liquid benzene, was the quantitative examination of the variation in the shape of the Arrhenius plot with degree of agitation of the reaction vessel. The rate constants measured for slower, low temperature reactions were largely independent of the degree of reactant agitation, showing diffusion effects to be insignificant. At higher temperatures, and faster rate of product formation at the reaction interface, however, the rate constants measured increased in value with increasing agitation rate. The degree of agitation (by shaking) was increased until a linear Arrhenius plot was obtained, indicating that diffusion was no longer the rate-controlling step over the temperature range studied. The conditions so determined were then used in subsequent kinetic measurements.

Representative examples of kinetic studies involving liquid phase catalysed reactions are given below, it must, however, be emphasized that somewhat comparable behaviour has also been observed for reactions involving gaseous reactants. Surface catalytic processes are largely independent of the phase from which the chemisorbed species was derived, since the heat of chemisorption is usually large compared with the heat of vaporization of a liquid.

Adsorption of products. If a substance, which is chemisorbed on the active surface of a catalyst, is present in a reaction mixture, the rate of a particular chemical process may be reduced as result of competition between additive and reactants for the surface. A dynamic equilibrium between solution and the two adsorbed species may be established. The rate of the catalytic process may then be expressed:

$$\frac{dc_1}{dt} = k\frac{b_1c_1}{b_1c_1 + b_2c_2}$$

where b_1 and c_1 are the adsorption coefficient and reactant concentration respectively and b_2, c_2 are the corresponding quantities for the additive. If the additive is an unreactive impurity the activity of the solid will be reduced by a factor dependent on the b_1/b_2 ratio and its temperature variation. Poisons represent an extreme case of such adsorption for which $b_2 \gg b_1$, thus effectively eliminating the catalyst activity. The above equation may be regarded as Langmuir-type adsorption of the two molecular species. If, however, the 'additive' is a product of the catalytic process the reaction kinetics may be more complex since c_2 is dependent on c_1 and time. An example of a system, which has been shown to behave in this way, is the nickel catalysed hydrogenation of phenol, which occurs in two steps:

$$C_6H_5OH \xrightarrow{2H_2} C_6H_{10}O \xrightarrow{H_2} C_6H_{11}OH$$

During the reaction the phenol concentration progressively decreases, that of the intermediate, cyclohexanone, increases at first, reaches a maximum value and subsequently decreases as it is hydrogenated to cyclohexanol. The rate of cyclohexanol formation is initally slow and accelerates, reaching an approximately zero order value, which is maintained over an appreciable fraction of reaction before finally decelerating as the reactant is consumed. This reaction is complex compared with the two limiting types of successive reactions which may occur:

(i) Complete hydrogenation in a single step. Benzene is catalytically hydrogenated on nickel to cyclohexane in a single process and no significant amount of desorption of potential intermediates, cyclohexadiene or cyclohexene, is observed.

(ii) Two distinct steps in hydrogenation. Naphthalene is hydrogenated to tetralin in a single step at low temperature and reaction ceases. Complete hydrogenation to decalin does not occur except after a further reaction which occurs at a higher temperature.

4. THE SOLID-LIQUID INTERFACE

Adsorption at solid liquid interfaces. When the surfaces of a solid are covered by a liquid, chemisorption of molecules from the liquid phase may occur if the solid surface possesses unsaturated character and if sorbate-sorbent bonds are formed; these are normal criteria for chemisorption. Hydrocarbon chemisorption was seen to occur, as intermediate species, in the liquid phase hydrogenation of organic compounds mentioned above. At the other extreme, a solid may not be wetted by a liquid at the interface. This occurs in systems for which the forces of attraction between molecules within the liquid phase are strong and specific chemisorption bonds between molecules of the two phases are not formed. This is observed, for example, at the mercury-glass and the water-solid paraffin wax interfaces.

When a solution is brought into contact with a solid which it does wet, both solvent and solute molecules may be attracted towards the phase interface. Chemisorption of one or other species may occur, but studies of this phenomenon are difficult, except in particular situations, for example, where a catalytic reaction involving a surface intermediate occurs. However, in a large number of systems, reversible adsorption equilibrium for both types of molecules is established which is controlled by the relative abilities of the two species to reduce the interfacial surface energy. Thus there may be preferential concentration of one or other compound in the vicinity of the surface, a tendency opposed by the random molecular motions in the solution, so that there may be an increase or a decrease in the concentration of that species in the homogeneous phase compared with that of a completely homogeneous solution. Many examples of solute adsorption have been shown to obey Freundlich equation. This may be written in the form:

$$\log V = \log k + (1/n) \log C$$

where V is the weight adsorbed from solution at concentration C, and k and n are constants. The weight of solute adsorbed from successive equal increments of solution concentration decreases with increasing solution strength. Examples of systems which obey the Freundlich equation include the adsorption on charcoal of bromine and of phenol from aqueous solution and of benzoic acid from benzene solution. Several regularities in behaviour have been observed for different, but comparable, systems. For example, the amount of fatty acids adsorbed on charcoal increases as the homologous series is ascended.

Adsorption equilibrium results from the tendency of the solute and solvent to concentrate at the interface and it is possible that in certain systems there may be a change between which of the possible species is concentrated there, with change in solution concentration. For example, it has been observed that ethyl alcohol is adsorbed at the charcoal-solution interface when it is present as a dilute solution in benzene. However, when the proportion of alcohol is increased, benzene is preferentially attracted to the interface.

An important and widely useful application of adsorption from solution is through *chromatography*. A solution, containing a mixture of solutes, the components of which it is desired to separate, is poured through a column filled with a high area solid; sometimes alumina powder is used. The column is then washed through (*eluted*) with a suitable solvent until the separated constituents of the original solute are obtained in separated aliquots of the effluent. That constituent of the solution which is most strongly adsorbed at the solid-liquid interface, will be washed through the column comparatively slowly while the less strongly adsorbed molecules will equilibrate to give a greater concentration in the solution phase, the flow of which is maintained in a constant direction. This material will, therefore, be washed out from the end of the column most readily. This effect is represented diagrammatically in Fig. 35. This method has been used to separate the chemially very similar lanthanide ions, the actinide ions and the different carotenes.

Similar principles are used in *gas-solid chromatography*. The gas mixture to be separated is passed, in a carrier gas stream, through a column of particles of high surface area solid. Those molecules which are most strongly physically adsorbed at the solid surface are retained in the column longer, i.e. move downwards more slowly than those less strongly adsorbed. The emergence of different components of the mixture from the column may be detected from changes in the physical properties (e.g. thermal conductivity) of the effluent gases. *Gas-liquid chromatography* makes use of the different partition coefficients of gases in a mixture between the gaseous phase and solution in a non-volatile liquid supported on a solid that is virtually inert, on passage of the mixture (in a stream of carrier gas) through a column of the solid-liquid mixture.

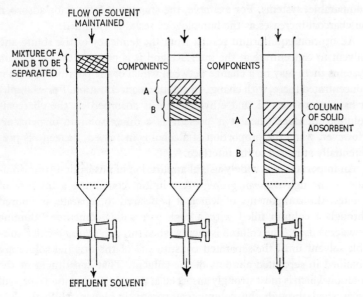

FIG. 35. Diagrammatic representation of chromatography. The three figures represent successively later stages in the process.

As liquid is passed through the column of active solid (e.g. alumina) the components of the mixture (A and B) travel downwards at different rates so that B emerges first, and later A, the more strongly adsorbed component, may be eluted if the flow of liquid through the column is maintained.

Adsorption of ions from solution. For completeness, three main subjects in this field will be mentioned briefly, since all involve the properties of solid surfaces. But detailed descriptions of the phenomena are outside the scope of this book. These topics are the adsorption of ions at (i) the surfaces of solid particles of lyophobic colloids, (ii) liquid-solid interfaces, and (iii) electrodes.

Lyophobic colloids. Small crystals of insoluble ionic salts in a solution containing excess constituent ions tend to grow through deposition of successive lattice layers at the surface. When a single ionic constituent is in excess and the other present in low concentration, the tendency to extend the lattice is limited to surface adsorption of those dissolved ions present in excess. This results in the accumulation of a charge at the crystallite surfaces. The presence of such a charge opposes aggregation of particles through mutual repulsion on the approach of a pair of crystallites, so that reduction of total surface energy by particle growth does not occur and the dispersed system achieves stability. For example, during the titration of sodium chloride with silver nitrate, the first-formed particles of silver chloride are stabilized in the dispersed colloid phase due to a negative charge on each particle resulting from adsorbed chloride ions in lattice extension positions. At this stage, chloride ions are present in the solution. However, when excess silver has been added the particles become positively charged since the tendency for lattice extension operates through cation adsorption because a negligible quantity of chloride ions are now present in solution (Fig. 36).

Ions which are not a constituent of the lattice may be adsorbed by an ionic (or largely ionic) bond if they are capable of forming a sparingly soluble, or, alternatively, a weakly ionized compound with ions of opposite charge in the lattice; this generalization is known as the *Fajans-Paneth rule*. For example, radium ions may be accommodated at the surface of barium sulphate particles, since Ra^{++} may be accommodated at a lattice extension position which would be occupied by Ba^{++} ions. An existing lattice may thus tend to extend through adsorption of ions having comparable chemical properties to its own constituents. Radium ions are not, however, accommodated on the surface of silver chloride since radium forms a soluble and ionized chloride.

Adsorption of a weakly ionized dyestuff may be used to determine the endpoint of a titration in which colloidal particles are precipitated. We have seen that initally silver chloride acquires a negative charge in the presence of excess chloride ions. The weakly ionized negative ion of the dye fluorescin, in solution, is not adsorbed on this surface. However, in the presence of a very slight excess of the silver ion the solid surface becomes positively charged and the fluorescin readily forms the slightly ionized silver complex on the surface, which confers a pink-red tinge on the precipitate. This change of colour may be used to detect the equivalence point of the titration.

The Zeta potential. When a current flows through an ionic solution in a capillary tube, the solution tends to move in a particular direction. This is known as electro-osmosis and is attributed to the existence of a

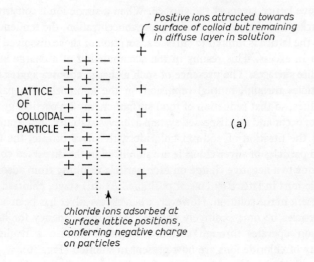

Positive ions attracted towards
surface of colloid but remaining
in diffuse layer in solution

LATTICE
OF
COLLOIDAL
PARTICLE

(a)

Chloride ions adsorbed at
surface lattice positions,
conferring negative charge
on particles

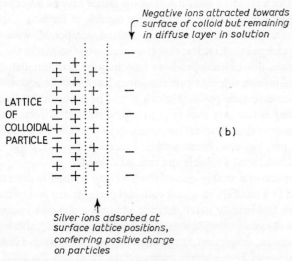

Negative ions attracted towards
surface of colloid but remaining
in diffuse layer in solution

LATTICE
OF
COLLOIDAL
PARTICLE

(b)

Silver ions adsorbed at
surface lattice positions,
conferring positive charge
on particles

FIG. 36. Representation of charge distribution at surfaces of colloidal silver chloride. Silver chloride in solution containing excess (a) chloride ions and (b) silver ions. (c) Colloidal particles do not readily coalesce since charged surfaces repel. The negative surfaces approach in this diagram, positive ions are present in the diffuse layer.

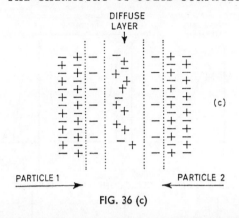

FIG. 36 (c)

potential, the zeta (ζ) potential, across the solid-liquid junction. Helmholtz considered that a sharp potential boundary existed at the interface (Fig. 37). Gouy and Chapman considered only a diffuse potential boundary. These simple models have been subsequently developed by Stern to include both sharp and diffuse layers of ions in this region. Two situations may be considered: (i) a strongly held immobile layer of ions of one particular sign and the charge thus present inducing a second diffuse layer (or ionic atmosphere) of opposite sign in the vicinity (Fig. 37), or (ii) a strongly bonded layer of ions of one sign at the surface and further, more diffuse adsorption (ionic atmosphere) of ions of the *same* sign, to yield a diffuse layer near the surface. The region which defines the zeta potential is indicated in Fig. 37.

The sign and magnitude of the zeta potential result from equilibrium of the ions between the boundary layer and the solution. A glass-water interface may acquire a negative charge due to the ionization of surface silicic acid, or, alternatively, adsorption of hydroxyl ions from solution. Ions in a solution may also exert an influence on the magnitude of this potential since it has been shown that a glass surface in contact with dilute solutions of salts of the following metals, with monovalent anions, had negative zeta potentials decreasing in the sequence K^+, Ba^{++}, La^{3+}, while that of a Th^{4+} solution was positive. The increasing facility for cation adsorption with increasing positive charge thus demonstrates a connexion between zeta potential and the relatively greater ability of multivalent ions to flocculate colloids. Both effects result from the tendency for multivalent ions to increase in concentration at the solid/liquid interface.

Electrode processes. Reactions at electrodes are often the reactions of

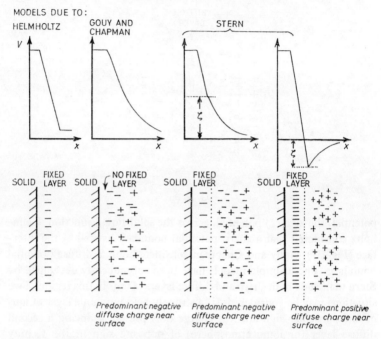

FIG. 37. Diagrammatic representation of theories of ion distributions at solid surfaces. Two types of distribution are considered (i) fixed layer at surface, and (ii) diffuse layer in vicinity of surface. x represents the distance from the surface.

ions with charged solid surfaces, in which one step is the donation or removal of an electron by the solid. The overall reaction mechanism of chemical processes which occur at such boundaries may be governed by the five-stage scheme given above for catalytic process, with the added provisions that (i) reaction occurs at a liquid/solid interface, (ii) an ion is involved at some stage, and (iii) during the process an electron transfer step occurs. A detailed account of electrode reactions is considered to be outside the scope of the present volume.

CHAPTER FIVE

Reactions of Solids

Kinetic studies of those chemical processes which occur in the homo-geneous phase have shown that reaction rate is often directly propor-tional to the reactant molecule(s) concentration raised to a power (the reaction order). When, for example, reaction rate is directly proportional to the number of reactant molecules available, the reaction is said to be first order. It should be stressed, however, that many exceptions to this generalization are known, i.e. where homogeneous reactions are complex, occur through a chain reaction, etc. Most heterogeneous reactions, which include the reactions of solids, do not, in general, obey those kinetic laws in which rate is dependent on a power of reactant concentration. As an exception to this generalization, the first-order equation has been found to fit the results in certain particular circumstances, some of which will be mentioned below. More usually, however, reactions in-volving solids occur at a reactant-product interface, and such behaviour results in characteristic kinetic properties. The rate of product formation in processes which occur through an interface reaction may be expected to be dependent on:

(i) The variation in the surface area, or interfacial area, at which the reaction of the solid occurs during progress of the chemical process resulting from (a) generation of new areas of reactant I/reactant II or reactant/product interface at places on the solid where reaction has not previously occurred (*nucleation*) and (b) changes in the geometry of the reaction interface(s) during progress of this interface through the lattice of the unreacted solid (*growth of product nuclei*, or, more simply, *growth* step).

An alternative description of these processes may be given. Reactions of solids often occur at the area of contact of two solid phases; thus before the chemical change takes place it is necessary to generate this interface. This process is termed nucleation. For a reaction involving a single solid, nucleation may sometimes occur rapidly over all surfaces, or at the points of initial contact between the constituents of a mixture of

163

solids. However, for a number of reactions of solids, the initial generation of small product crystallites may be a difficult process, which can only occur at a limited number of surface sites. Once such a product crystallite, embedded in the reactant matrix, has been formed the chemical change may proceed with greater facility at the reactant-product interface. For many such processes, the reaction rate is directly proportional to the total interfacial contact area in the system, and this, for any growing nucleus, changes progressively as reaction proceeds.

(ii) Rate of progress of the interface through the reactant. As reaction progresses, a layer of unreactive, or inert, products may be deposited which tend to reduce, or even prevent further chemical change due to reduction in area of reactant-reactant or reactant-product contact.

Before proceeding to a systematic account of reactions in the solid phase, two general points may be made:

(i) The reactivity of a solid substance is often dependent on the history of the particular crystal sample being investigated. This contrasts with the behaviour of liquids and gases since it is only solid particles which retain scars of handling or preparation which may influence their subsequent reactivity. Damaged external surfaces, superficial lattice imperfections, scratches, etc., are often chemically more reactive than more perfect crystal face areas. It has been mentioned that the chemical activity of such sites may be the factor which determines the catalytic activity of solid surfaces. Variations in reactivity between different crystals of a particular salt, which result from differences between grain boundary structures, parallel the somewhat comparable behaviour which has been mentioned for the low-temperature electrical conductivity observed for different salt samples. This has also been attributed to differences in microstructure of different salt preparations. It is believed that chemical changes of solids may occur most readily in the most highly deformed, or defective, regions of the lattice. Thus the reactivity of a particular sample depends on the total concentration of such sites.

(ii) The rate at which a chemical process involving a solid occurs is often controlled by the surface area of that solid, since reactions are frequently initiated at surfaces and these are the regions of contact between a pair of reactants. Reaction kinetics of a process may thus be influenced by the average crystallite size and the particle size distribution about this value.

It is important, therefore, when reporting and discussing kinetic results for solid-phase reactions, to specify the form of the sample (single crystal, crushed powder, etc.) and any special treatments (grinding, sieving, recrystallization, etc.) to which it has been subjected.

Derivation of general mathematical expressions which relate the variation in product yield, resulting from the growth of nuclei, with time, for the reactions of solids, have resulted in relatively complicated equations. Fortunately, however, considerable simplifications are possible for many particular systems, and these have enabled kinetic measurements to be made for many reactions which occur in the solid phase. Much of the research carried out in this field, to the present time, has been concerned with those systems most amenable to experimental measurement and to kinetic interpretation. These include thermal decomposition reactions which yield a gaseous product when a pure solid is heated, and the reaction of a single solid with a gas. An account of experimental results and kinetic data obtained from such studies is given in the systematic consideration of solid-phase reactions below. Outlines of some results from more complex systems are also mentioned.

1. REACTIONS OF A SINGLE SOLID

On heating, a solid may undergo physical and/or chemical changes, which include sintering, melting and thermal decomposition. Sintering results from crystal growth at the contact area between touching crystals (probably at the expense of one of them) so that the crystallites become bonded together and the average crystallite size may increase. Sintering of metals occurs somewhat below the melting point and this occurs as the result of mobility of some of the lattice components, probably originally located in the surface regions. These constituents tend to migrate across surfaces into positions such that the total surface area, and, therefore, the surface energy, of the powder sample is reduced.

At higher temperatures, the constituents of the lattice units become mobile and melting occurs; the ordered lattice array is replaced by the long-range disorder of the liquid state. The melting point of a crystal is sharp because the movement of a relatively small number of molecules (atoms or ions), due to thermal energy, from the stable lattice positions in the more perfectly crystalline regions results in the perturbation of a large number of lattice units in the vicinity. Each of the constituents of these perturbed units has itself reached a position in which the thermal energy approaches that necessary to overcome the bonding forces of the crystal. Therefore, the movement of a small number of particles reduces the order in the lattice, so reducing the cohesive forces of the solid as a whole, and liquefaction of that region of crystallite follows. This contrasts with the melting of a glass where the constituent bonds differ in strength and softening occurs over an appreciable temperature range.

Thermal decomposition reactions

On heating certain solids, chemical reaction between the lattice constituent units may occur below the melting point. The study of such reactions is probably the most fully explored field of reactions which involve solids only, and much attention has been devoted to kinetic studies of reactions of the following general type:

$$A \text{ (solid)} \rightarrow B \text{ (solid)} + C \text{ (gas)}.$$

These reactions are experimentally simple since the extent of reaction, usually denoted by α, the fractional decomposition, can be directly measured from the product gas pressure evolved or the reactant weight loss.

Kinetic studies of reactions through measurement, at suitable time intervals, of the gaseous product pressure evolved in a constant volume apparatus may be made using an apparatus similar to that shown in Fig. 34. The following modifications in technique may be made: (i) Initially the apparatus and the sample must be thoroughly evacuated for at least two hours to remove adsorbed gas from the glass apparatus walls and from the reactant solid surfaces. To do this a two-stage mercury diffusion pump, backed by a rotary pump, may be used; this combination is capable of giving vacua of the order of 10^{-6} mm Hg. During pumping, the glass walls of the apparatus may be warmed to facilitate the removal of adsorbed gases. While the initial evacuation (outgassing) is proceeding, the sample must be maintained at a temperature significantly below the value at which appreciable decomposition may be detected. After isolating the evacuated constant-volume reaction vessel and gauges from the pumps by closing a tap (or a mercury cut-off) the sample is heated to reaction temperature as rapidly as possible. This can be achieved in several different ways. A furnace may be raised so that it surrounds the glass reaction vessel; this, however, involves considerable thermal disturbance. It is more convenient for many systems to design the reaction vessel so that the sample, contained in a small glass tube, can be held in a cool part of the apparatus during outgassing and may then be lowered on a wire, using a glass winch, into the reaction zone already maintained at the constant, measured, reaction temperature. Alternatively, a single reactant crystal may be dropped from a rotatable glass spoon into the heated vessel, after completion of the outgassing period. (ii) It is not possible to measure the production of condensable products using the McLeod gauge. It is, therefore, usual to insert a U-shaped trap in the apparatus between the heated reaction vessel and the gauge. This bend is immersed to a level, maintained constant, of refrigerant (liquid nitrogen, $-195°C$, or solid carbon dioxide/acetone $\sim -80°C$) to remove volatile and/or corrosive reactants. Traces of strongly bonded impurity water evolved initially on heating anhydrous reactant crystals would obscure the onset of reaction and cause an error in subsequent readings, particularly during the early stages of reaction, if they were not removed by condensation at the chilled glass surfaces.

Comparable studies have been made using the alternative experimental arrangement in which the loss in reactant weight at suitable time intervals can be measured in an apparatus of the type represented in Fig. 34(b). Many variations of these experimental approaches have been designed to measure the α-time relationship for the decomposition of particular salts at a constant temperature.

The α-time relationships for some typical solid phase thermal decomposition reactions are shown in Fig. 38. The reaction shown in Fig. 38(a) is *deceleratory* throughout, i.e. the rate progressively decreases as the reactant is consumed. In Fig. 38(b) there is a short initial *acceleratory period*, during which reaction rate increases, and thereafter reaction rate is deceleratory. The reaction depicted in Fig. 38(c) shows a more pronounced acceleratory period which is followed by a deceleratory period. Fig. 38(d) shows a complex reaction consisting of two stages: (i) an initial deceleratory reaction, giving a small total product yield; probably from a reaction limited to the surfaces of the reactant particles. This process is followed by (ii) a sigmoid shaped α-time curve similar to that shown in Fig. 38(c).

Chemical rate processes which give sigmoid shaped α-time plots (Fig. 38c) usually result from reactions which occur at a reactant-product interface. This interface is initially established at a limited number of points on the surface of the reactant crystal (nuclei) by the formation of micro-crystals of product. Reaction thereafter proceeds within the strained contact area of the reactant-product interface. During the initial formation of nuclei the area of such interface is small so that reaction is very slow in the period immediately following reactant heating. For many solids there may be a significant time-interval, the *induction period*, between the time that reactant reached reaction temperature and the detection of significant product formation. During this

M

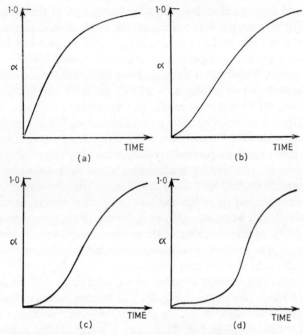

FIG. 38. Typical fractional decomposition α-time plots for solid phase thermal decomposition reactions.

(a) Deceleratory throughout, (b) short initial acceleratory reaction, (c) pronounced initial acceleratory reaction, and (d) short initial deceleratory reaction followed by sigmoid shaped curve (i.e. as c).

interval (see Fig. 39) *germ*, i.e. small, nuclei of solid product are being established at a limited number of points on the reactant surfaces.

It has been shown experimentally for several solids that, once nuclei have been established, there is a constant rate of advance of reaction interface through the solid for reaction at constant temperature. From the representation shown in Fig. 39, it may be seen that the growth of such nuclei results in an increase in the area of product nuclei-reactant surface contact. There is thus an increase in the rate of product formation and the reaction is acceleratory. A diagrammatic representation is shown in Fig. 39 (a) and (b). On continued growth of such nuclei a point is reached where reaction interfaces from different nuclei begin to overlap – at these junctions the reaction interface is eliminated. At first, the effect of such overlap is to reduce the rate of interface expansion (thus product formation) and the rate of acceleration is decreased.

Subsequently, this factor progressively increases in importance so that thereafter the reaction rate becomes deceleratory. When the point has been reached where those regions of the solid which comprised the ori-

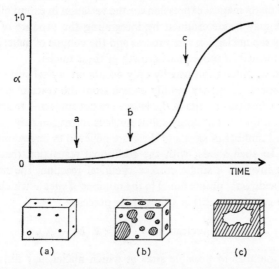

FIG. 39. Interpretation of sigmoid α-time curve in terms of nucleation and growth of product phase on a single crystal of reactant.

Appearance of crystal at various points on the α-time plot: (a) At the start of the reaction a small number of nuclei are formed at random positions on the crystal surface. The area of reactant-product interface is small and reaction is, therefore, slow.

(b) At a later stage of reaction, some nuclei have grown to a significant size and other nuclei are being formed on the surfaces of the crystal. Reaction rate is greater than that found in (a) since the reactant-product interfacial area has increased with the progress of the reaction.

(c) Section of the crystal later in the reaction. Nuclei have overlapped so that the whole surface has undergone decomposition and further nucleation cannot occur. The central regions of the crystal still contain undecomposed material. Further reaction results in progressive decrease in the area of the reactant-product interface, so that reaction is now deceleratory.

ginal surfaces of the reactant have been decomposed and the solid products incorporated in growing nuclei, the existing reaction interfaces may still continue growth towards the central, unreacted, regions of the crystal (Fig 39c). During this stage there is a progressive decrease in interfacial area and reaction rate becomes deceleratory thereafter, until complete decomposition of the reactant has occurred.

Kinetic characteristics of solid phase decomposition reactions

A general mathematical expression for the variation in extent of reaction with time may be determined by integrating the product of the law expressing the nucleation rate process and the volume of material which has been formed in subsequent growth of these nuclei.

Nucleation. Nucleation usually only occurs on crystal surfaces, from which product gases may readily escape from the reactant and where particular constituent units of the lattice are not subjected to spherically symmetrical forces. For many solids nucleus formation may only occur at a limited number of sites and these are believed to be regions of local disorder. In such solids, with the additional restriction that nucleus formation involves a single surface chemical reaction, the nucleation rate may be directly proportional to the number of sites at which nucleus formation can occur; this is a first order process:

$$\text{rate of nucleation} = \frac{\mathrm{d}N}{\mathrm{d}t} = k\,(N_i - N).$$

N_i is the number of possible sites at which nuclei may form and N nuclei are present at time t. This equation may be rewritten:

$$\frac{\mathrm{d}N}{\mathrm{d}t} = k\,N_i\,\mathrm{e}^{-kt}.$$

From this it may be seen that for reaction in solids where k is small, the rate of nucleus formation is approximately constant during the initial periods of reaction $(\mathrm{d}N/\mathrm{d}t \simeq k\,N_i)$. For systems in which k is large, all possible nuclei are formed rapidly at the beginning of reaction and further nucleation does not occur.

The above equation, and the approximations derived from it, was obtained assuming that a single chemical reaction could result in stable nucleus formation. If more than a single step is required, however, the variation in number of nuclei with time is given by an expression of the type: $N = k't^\beta$. For example, it has been experimentally observed that, for the thermal decomposition of barium azide crystals, $N = k't^3$.

Growth. Growth of a nucleus is the movement of the reactant-product interface in a direction normal to its surface due to the thermal decomposition reaction occurring in the strained region of contact between the adjoining phases. Growth rate has been shown to be constant for reactions in particular salts where the rate of interfacial progression through the reactant can be directly measured and the growth rate increases with increase in reaction temperature.

In the illustration used to explain the sigmoid curve, given in Fig. 39, it was assumed that nuclei grow in three dimensions. This has been observed during the decomposition of several substances but is not a general conclusion, however, since experimental observations for other compounds have shown that the growth of nuclei in other particular substances may be confined to particular lattice planes. The growth of such a nucleus may yield semicircular lamina of product, following growth from a particular point on the crystal surface (two-dimensional growth). It is also possible to envisage growth of nuclei confined to a single line or group of lines of crystal constituents where growth may not spread to adjoining lines and is therefore confined to one dimension. It is usual to use the symbol λ to represent the number of dimensions in which nuclei grow.

The general expression for the rate of a solid phase decomposition in which nucleation rate obeys a power law and nuclei grow in λ dimensions has been shown to be

$$\alpha = k_1 t^{(\beta + \lambda)} = k_1 t^n.$$

This expression applies in the early stages of reaction before appreciable overlap of nuclei occurs. Obedience to this expression has been observed, at low values of α, for the thermal decomposition of silver oxide (where $n = 3$) and of barium azide (where $n = \sim 6$).

The characteristics of a thermal decomposition reaction, proceeding through nucleation and growth steps, have been studied in greater detail for the reaction of barium azide than for most other reactants. This reaction may be expressed:

$$BaN_6 \rightarrow Ba \text{ (metal)} + 3N_2.$$

Kinetic measurements for a single large crystal reactant have shown that the equation $\alpha = k_1 t^n$ is obeyed, where $n = 6$, $\beta = \lambda = 3$. The same thermal decomposition reaction for a sample of salt which has been crushed to a very fine powder, an assemblage of very small crystallites, has been shown to obey first-order kinetics; the reason for this difference will be discussed in a subsequent section. Such α-time measurements represent the total reaction for all the nucleation and growth processes in the whole reactant assemblage of crystals. These conclusions may be supplemented and, to some extent, confirmed by direct observation on the formation and growth of nuclei since this salt yields solid particles of product metal which may be directly observed during reaction, using a reactant heater which possesses a transparent window through which the sample may be seen with a microscope. Quantitative measurements have shown (i) nucleation obeys the power law: $N = kt^3$ (i.e. $\beta = 3$). (ii) Three-dimensional nuclei are formed (i.e. $\lambda = 3$), and (iii) the rate of reaction interface progression through unreacted material is constant at constant temperature.

From the above account it may be seen that α-time measurements may be used to obtain information about the values of β and λ for a particular reaction. When a set of such values $(\alpha - t)$ is to be fitted to an equation of the form $\alpha = kt^n$ there may be uncertainty concerning the moment at which $t = 0$, due to thermal disturbances following the introduction of the reactant to the heated zone. Furthermore, for many substances, there is evidence that very small nuclei of product, each of which consists of a small number of molecules (or atoms) and are relatively unstable, grow at a rate slower than that subsequently attained when product crystallite size has been increased. It has been shown that quantitative allowance for both effects may be made in the kinetic expression by modification of the point on the time scale at which the zero is taken. Making a time correction, t_1, to the measured time, t, equations of the power law form may be expressed

$$\alpha = k_1 (t - t_1)^n.$$

The value t_1 may be determined for a particular set of measurements by making log α against log $(t - t_1)$ plots using different values of t_1 until the best straight line fit is obtained for the results. The value of n may be found from the slope of this plot.

The above expression holds well in the initial stages of many decomposition rate processes, but further equations connecting α and t have been developed in which allowance for the effect of overlap of growing nuclei has been included. As nuclei grow, the overall rate of reaction may be reduced through (i) cessation of reaction at those areas of contact formed by coalescence of the reaction interfaces where growth of two adjoining nuclei have resulted in a common boundary, and (ii) removal of potential nucleus-forming sites on the surface through incorporation of such regions into the growth of existing nuclei. The mathematical analysis of the change in area of reaction interface (directly proportional to reaction rate) with time, for a process involving nucleation and growth in which quantative allowance is made for the two effects mentioned above, results in complex equations. These may be simplified, however, for particular salts by making appropriate reasonable assumptions. Such calculations have shown that a reaction of this type may be expressed by the general equation

$$- \log (1 - \alpha) = (kt)^n.$$

This equation is often termed the Avrami-Erofeyev equation, after workers who developed equations of this form.

The methods by which this equation may be used to obtain information from experimental data and some of the conclusions which may be reached as result of such analysis are conveniently illustrated by reference to a particular reaction, the thermal decomposition of ammonium perchlorate. This reaction has attracted interest since, in the temperature range 200–300°C, reaction proceeds by a nucleation and growth process (such nuclei can be directly observed) to yield a product material which, surprisingly, has a chemical composition virtually identical with that of the reactant before decomposition. In this reaction $\sim 30\%$ of the reactant (by weight) is decomposed and it has been shown that the surface area of the product salt is very much greater than that of the reactant. This is interpreted as indicating that the low temperature decomposition reaction is confined to the intergranular and adjacent material of the reactant. These are the disordered regions between the more perfect parts of the lattice which, when removed, give a product consisting of large numbers of small crystallites with channels running between them. Decomposition of the latter does not occur in this temperature range.

Another characteristic of this reaction is that the rate increases between 200 and 240°C. The variation in rate constant with temperature obeys the Arrhenius equation, but at 240°C a crystallographic transformation occurs from the orthorhombic lattice to the cubic high temperature form stable $> 240°C$. Due to this transformation the reaction rate at 242°C is slower than that at 238°C and, $> 242°C$, reaction rate again increases. The crystallographic transformation may result in considerable rearrangement of the lattice constituents in the inter-granular material, thus increasing the stability of the salt, and decomposition occurs somewhat less readily.

Decomposition of ammonium perchlorate yields a large number of different products, including oxygen, nitrogen, oxides of nitrogen, chlorine, oxides of chlorine and water. But it has been shown that the permanent gas product yield remains constant during the low temperature reaction. Reaction rate may, therefore, be measured by determination of the gas pressure evolved at known time intervals in a constant volume system, using a McLeod gauge separated from the reaction vessel by a $-195°C$ trap. Measurements of decomposition kinetics for samples of the salt in the form of whole crystals, powder and compacted pellet have been made and will be discussed here.

Direct observation has shown that decomposition of large single crystals of ammonium perchlorate occurs through formation of product nuclei, which grow as reaction proceeds. It may be expected, therefore, that the Avrami-Erofeyev equation may express the α-time variation and, from the slopes of $\log \log (1/1 - \alpha)$ against $\log t$ plots, it has been shown that at low extents of reaction, $\alpha < 0.2$, $n = 4$. Thus reaction may be regarded as single-stage nucleation ($\beta = 1$) with three dimensional growth ($\lambda = 3$, supported by direct observation); $n = \beta + \lambda = 4$ during the acceleratory period. After completion of the initial reaction and when nuclei overlap ($0.2 < \alpha < 0.9$) $n = 3$. It is seen that complete decomposition of the original crystal surface precludes further nucleation (thus $\beta = 0$) and the solid is decomposed by the three-dimensional growth of existing nuclei ($\lambda = 3$). This equation is applicable to results during the deceleratory reaction since allowance for overlap of nuclei has been made in the derivation of the equation through use of the logarithmic term. The plot of $\log \log (1 - \alpha)$ against $\log t$ does not allow accurate determinations of the rate constants, but once the value of n has been found, more accurate functions may be used. Results showed that plots of $\{\log[1/(1 - \alpha)]\}^{1/4}$ against t for $\alpha < 0.2$ and $\{\log[1/(1 - \alpha)]\}^{1/3}$ against t for $0.2 < \alpha < 0.9$ gave good straight lines for the experimental data. Such functions give the zero time correction, t_1, as an intercept on the time axis. These observations show that the reaction gives satisfactory obedience to the Avrami-Erofeyev equation. Rate constants may be found from the slopes of the $[\log 1/(1 - \alpha)]^{1/n}$ against time plots, and values obtained over a suitable temperature interval enable activation energies for decomposition to be measured by use of the Arrhenius equation.

The same decomposition reaction for a sample consisting of a crushed powder reactant (in place of the single crystal) obeys the Avrami-Erofeyev equation with $n = 4$ up to $\alpha \simeq 0.7$. The surface area/volume ratio for the assemblage of reactant crystallites is higher than that for a single crystal and a nucleation process must occur on each crystallite surface before that particle is decomposed. Reaction is, therefore, closely comparable to that of the initial stages of whole crystal decomposition except that the effect of surface nucleation extends to a much greater fraction of the decomposition, i.e. up to $\alpha = 0.7$ and $\beta = 1$ and $\lambda = 3$.

When the reactant salt is in the form of a pellet made by compression of powder it is found that $n = 3$ over the greater part of the reaction. Nucleation is completed rapidly on initial heating of the sample on these surfaces which have been subjected to mechanical working during compaction. Rapid initial nucleation is followed by three-dimensional growth and thus $n = 3$ for $0.05 < \alpha < 0.75$ and $\beta = 0$, $\lambda = 3$.

Decomposition of the same salt at temperatures above the 240°C crystallographic transformation occurs in a mosaic in which the dislocation structure has undergone considerable rearrangement. Kinetic measurements have shown that the decomposition of all three forms of salt, crystal, powder and pellet obey the Avrami-Erofeyev equation for which $n = 2$ over a large fraction of the reaction. Plots of $\{\log[1/(1 - \alpha)]\}^{1/2}$ against time for the data obtained gave good straight lines. From this evidence it has been concluded that the physical differences between the different forms of reactant were largely removed during the crystal lattice change. The value $n = 2$ is interpreted as showing that $\beta = \lambda = 1$, or a single nucleation step was followed by growth effectively limited to one dimension. Decomposition of each nucleated micro-crystallite may result in nucleation of a single adjoining crystallite, on average.

Incomplete low temperature decomposition of ammonium perchlorate is attributed to reaction occurring in the intergranular material only. It has been suggested that exciton formation in these regions is the rate-determining step:

$$NH_4^+ + ClO_4^- \rightarrow NH_4 + ClO_4$$

to form surface radicals. Reaction between these species may be expected to yield several products by a complex reaction mechanism. Several of the products observed have been listed above. Experimental measurements have shown that at temperatures $>350°C$ decomposition of the residue from low temperature reaction occurs by a process obeying different kinetic equations and having a higher activation energy than the low temperature decomposition.

These reactions of ammonium perchlorate represent more complex behaviour than those found for many other inorganic salts in which a crystallographic transformation does not occur in the middle of the decomposition temperature range and which may be less sensitive to the sample preparation method. The results cited above do show, however, that crystal structure and physical form of reactant sample may influence the course of the decomposition process. Reports in the literature show that the kinetic behaviour observed for the decomposition of salts other than ammonium perchlorate also obeys the Avrami-Erofeyev equation. Particular examples include nickel formate, nickel oxalate and sodium azide.

The Prout-Tompkins equation. In 1944 Prout and Tompkins showed that the kinetics of potassium permanganate thermal decomposition fitted the equation

$$\log\left(\frac{\alpha}{1 - \alpha}\right) = kt + C$$

an expression which is often referred to as the Prout-Tompkins equation. To provide a theoretical interpretation of this observation, these workers suggested that reaction proceeded in the solid by a somewhat similar mechanism to the chain-branching radical processes which had been described for gas-phase reactions. The model applied to the solid-state reaction proposed that nucleation formed an active species which could then, after reaction, yield two (or more) active species which could, in turn, react to increase the number of active centres as reaction progressed. However, the effect of such chain-branching was offset by the possibility of elimination of active radicals by direct combination, the probability of such radical number reduction increasing with their concentration. Characterization of the exact nature of the species involved in this chain process is a matter of some difficulty, and subsequent research has suggested it may be associated with cracking of the crystallites of reactant as decomposition proceeds. It has been concluded, however, that the direct transfer of energy from one active radical to a reactant is not a tenable mechanism since if such energy were not to be converted to thermal energy it would be necessary for it to be transferred to a new reactant very much more rapidly than the interval which (from kinetic measurements) is known to exist between successive steps in the chain.

While details of the theoretical basis of this equation in terms of a reaction mechanism are not fully understood, it must be emphasized that it has been usefully applied in studies of many decomposition reactions which yield sigmoid α-time curves. Qualitatively the reason may be seen by consideration of the differential form of the equation:

$$\frac{d\alpha}{dt} = k'\alpha(1 - \alpha).$$

Reaction rate is proportional to the fraction of the solid which *has* decomposed, α (this factor is dominant early in the reaction, during the acceleratory period) and to that fraction which *has not* decomposed

$(1 - \alpha)$, more significant in the latter stages of reaction. The equation shows acceleratory and deceleratory periods, comparable to the behaviour described for nucleation and growth processes.

Salts for which α-time measurements have been found to fit the Prout-Tompkins equation include nickel formate, silver oxalate and ammonium perchlorate. Plots of $\log[\alpha/(1 - \alpha)]$ against time for many salts show a discontinuity in the median region with two linear regions,

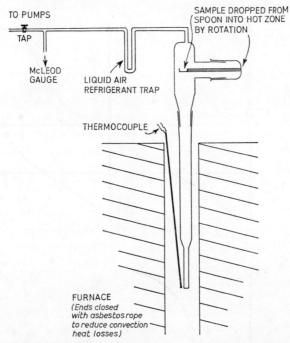

TO PUMPS

TAP

McLEOD GAUGE

LIQUID AIR REFRIGERANT TRAP

SAMPLE DROPPED FROM SPOON INTO HOT ZONE BY ROTATION

THERMOCOUPLE

FURNACE
(Ends closed with asbestos rope to reduce convection heat losses)

FIG. 40. Simple apparatus which may be used to measure the kinetics of the solid phase thermal decomposition of potassium permanganate crystals.

slopes k'_1 and k'_2, on either side showing that different rate constants apply during acceleratory and deceleratory periods. Results for ammonium perchlorate show an appreciably curved median region; for this salt the Avrami-Erofeyev equation must be regarded as providing a more satisfactory description of the kinetic behaviour.

The thermal decomposition of potassium permanganate may be used as an introductory experiment for students to the kinetic measurements of solid phase reactions. α-time plots are sigmoid in shape and results give a good fit to the Prout-Tompkins equation. A simple vacuum apparatus, which may be used, is shown in Fig. 40. Fig. 41 shows the typical sigmoid and Prout-Tompkins plots which may be found. The exact shape of the α-t plot depends on the history, size, degree of scratching, etc., to which the samples have been subjected, and some variation between the kinetic behaviour of different crystal preparations may be expected. When making the Prout-Tompkins plot it must be

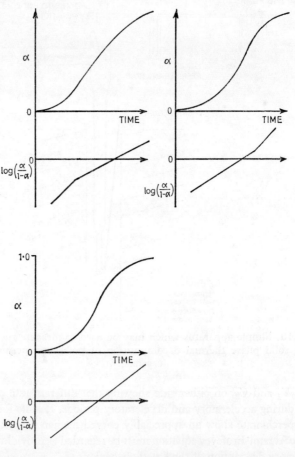

FIG. 41. The shape of the sigmoid curve for the thermal decomposition of potassium permanganate depends on temperature and individual crystal properties. The above curves show types of behaviour which are found, together with appropriate Prout-Tompkins plots.

remembered that the equation does not provide a good fit at the limits, but two satisfactory linear regions may usually be found within the approximate range $0.05 < \alpha < 0.9$.

Deceleratory Equations

In the solid-phase decomposition reactions considered above, attention has been directed towards those substances for which an initial acceleratory period is observed. Such behaviour is not characteristic of all solid phase decompositions, see Fig. 38(a). Two equations which have been found to hold for those reactions which are deceleratory throughout are the 'contracting cube' equation and the first-order equation; the latter is sometimes referred to as the unimolecular decay law.

(i) *Contracting cube equation.* If the initial nucleation step occurs rapidly over all surfaces for a single cube of reactant and the interface established progresses thereafter in the direction of the centre of the crystal, reaction is deceleratory throughout since the reaction interface progressively decreases. This may be seen by reference to Fig. 42.

If the edges of the initial cube are of length x and after reaction for time t are $(x - 2k't)$ it follows that

$$\alpha = \frac{x^3 - (x - 2tk')^3}{x^3}$$

or

$$(1 - \alpha)^{1/3} = 1 - 2k't/x$$

or, as the contracting cube equation is more usually written,

$$1 - (1 - \alpha)^{1/3} = kt.$$

The same formula may be shown to apply for the kinetics of a reaction proceeding through comparable contraction of a sphere. The thermal decomposition of the following salts have been shown to obey this kinetic equation (or slight modifications of it): calcium carbonate, ammonium perchlorate (high temperature, $> \sim 350°C$ decomposition) and copper sulphate pentahydrate (dehydration reaction).

(ii) *First-order equation (unimolecular decay law).* The decomposition of some solids, when prepared in the form of a fine crushed powder sample, obeys the first-order equation. Reaction of each individual crystal results from the formation of a single nucleus on the surface of that particular particle. Thus the decomposition rate is controlled by the nucleation process and since each individual particle in the assemblage may be nucleated with equal probability, the rate of decomposition

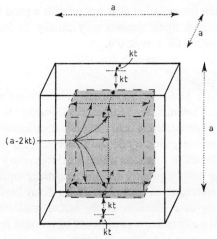

FIG. 42. Diagram to illustrate the derivation of the 'contracting cube' equation, see text.

obeys first-order kinetics:

$$-\log(1 - \alpha) = kt.$$

Obedience of decomposition kinetic behaviour to this equation has been observed for the reaction of several carbonates and the azides of barium, calcium and lead (the β form).

Effect of crystallite size on reaction kinetics

When theoretically deriving kinetic formulae for decomposition of samples consisting of an assemblage of crystallites with different sizes, it is difficult to make quantitative allowance for the distribution in particle size. In two of the examples given in this chapter, the effect of reactant crystal size has been considered. These examples are: (i) the decomposition of a single, or a small number of large single ammonium perchlorate crystals where reaction occurred in two stages (a) nucleation and growth, and (b) the overlap of nuclei and progression towards the centre of the crystal. Kinetic behaviour differed from that observed for a powdered reactant; (ii) obedience of the decomposition of finely powdered barium azide samples to first-order kinetics in contrast to nucleation and growth behaviour characteristic of large single crystals.

Between these (somewhat limiting) examples of kinetic behaviour there are situations where sample particle size distribution may influence the kinetic characteristics of the decomposition reaction. No general quantitative formula for the influence of particle size on reaction kinetics has yet been established, but two examples may be used to illustrate the types of effect which are possible. (i) Consider a reaction which proceeds by the contracting cube mechanism in an assemblage of cube shaped particles having edge lengths within the limits a_1 and a_2 ($a_1 > a_2$). It will be remembered that the formula was derived from consideration of a reaction occurring in a single cubic particle. The reaction interface progresses away from the original crystallite surfaces at equal rates in all particles and reaction will be completed in all these cubes of edge a_2 before complete decomposition in cubes with edge a_1. The model on which the equation was derived is, therefore, not strictly applicable and it can be seen that kinetic behaviour must be dependent on crystallite size distribution in the reactant. (ii) Kinetics of nucleation and growth processes may also be influenced by crystallite sizes. Nucleation is favoured by an increase in reactant surface area, so that, at first, reaction rate is increased by a reduction in particle size. After a certain crystallite size has been reached, however, further reduction limits the volume of the single salt particle decomposed, following nucleation on that particular crystallite. In accordance with this theoretical prediction it has been shown that, as the average particle size is decreased, the maximum slope of the α-time plot for low temperature ammonium perchlorate decomposition first increases to a maximum value and thereafter decreases.

The above account of the kinetic analysis of reactions in the solid phase has been concerned with the theoretical derivation of kinetic formulae from consideration of the variation in the area of reaction interface during its progression through the solid. This may be regarded as a problem in solid geometry, in which suitable approximations to exact general formulae are necessary to enable comparisons to be made between kinetic measurements and the kinetic predictions determined from a theoretical model. It must be emphasized that agreement between data and formula does not *necessarily* mean that the particular model applies, and, whenever possible, supplementary information should be obtained to confirm conclusions reached from kinetic data. Such additional information may include direct microscopic observation of nuclear growth, reaction confined to certain crystal faces, etc. It has been mentioned above that the α-time data for ammonium perchlorate fits both the Avrami-Erofeyev and the Prout-Tompkins equations, but supplementary observations indicate that the former provides the more satisfactory description of the reaction.

Initial deceleratory reaction

The thermal decomposition of lithium aluminium hydride, of nickel oxalate, and of aged mercury fulminate give α-time plots of the form shown in Fig. 38(d). For such solids, in which this type of two-stage reaction is observed, the initial rate process is usually limited to decomposition of a small reactant fraction (often $\sim 1\%$) and it is deceleratory throughout. Such a reaction has been attributed to (i) the decomposition of unstable regions of the crystals at surface dislocations, edges of crystals and at grain boundaries, and (ii) evolution of decomposition products formed by changes during storage but in which the products are retained at the surface until the reactant is heated. After the initial desorption process has been completed, subsequent decomposition of the solid proceeds by a rate process having the characteristics (the sigmoid shaped α-time plot) of nucleation and growth reactions.

Arrhenius parameters

Turning our attention now to the consideration of reaction interface progress through the solid, it is seen that the rate of this process is expressed by two parameters; (i) the Arrhenius pre-exponential factor, νC, which represents a concentration term at the interface, and (ii) the activation energy, E, which represents the energy barrier to reaction. Both terms are included in the Polanyi-Wigner equation for rate of interface progression, which is

$$\text{reaction rate} = \nu C \, e^{-E/RT}$$

Arrhenius pre-exponential factor: This factor contains both ν, the vibration frequency in the reaction co-ordinate and C which is a measure of the reactant molecule concentration in unit area of interface. The magnitude of ν is expected to be of the order 10^{12}–10^{13} sec^{-1}. Experimentally measured values from kinetic data for the dehydration reactions of copper sulphate and potassium alum have been found to agree with this value, within a factor of 10. This is considered to be satisfactory agreement considering (i) the accuracy with which $\log_{10} A$, the term which includes ν, may be determined is often no better than ± 0.5, (ii) it is difficult to establish an accurate independent estimate of the vibration frequency, ν, for molecules or ions at the solid-solid interface.

In contrast to these examples, for which there is satisfactory agreement between theoretical and observed values, there are several salts for which the ν values are greater, by several orders of magnitude, than those which may be reasonably ascribed to a vibration frequency. Theories suggesting the formation of intermediate products or phases, have been proposed to account for this apparent disagreement but there is not, as yet, general agreement as to the validity of such arguments.

Arrhenius activation energy

Several endothermic decomposition reactions, for example, the removal of water from a hydrate, occur with a reaction activation energy approximately equal to the salt dissociation energy. This has been observed for the dehydration of copper sulphate pentahydrate. The energy barrier to reaction, other than the energy necessary for dissociation, is small so that the rate process may be compared to a liquid evaporation and the dissociation energy measured from the variation in equilibrium product pressure in contact with the solid at different temperatures. The activation energy for the decomposition reaction may be found under conditions where the product is continually removed, thus preventing establishment of gas-solid equilibrium. Some reactions of carbonates also show this characteristic behaviour, two examples being the thermal decomposition of silver carbonate and of calcite.

An energy barrier, the magnitude of which determines the stability of the substance, must be overcome before an exothermic decomposition reaction can occur. The factors which determine the height of this barrier have not been established for all such processes, but, since many reactions for which information is available are reactions of ionic solids, an electron transfer process must occur. It has been suggested for decomposition of a number of particular solids that electron transfer may be the initial step in the chemical processes. For example, it has been argued that the activation energy for the low temperature ammonium perchlorate decomposition reaction is the energy necessary for exciton formation:

$$NH_4^+ \quad ClO_4^- \longrightarrow NH_4 \quad ClO_4.$$

The radicals so formed may decompose subsequently. It will be remembered that a single nucleation step ($\beta = 1$) is required for this reaction and subsequent growth of product nuclei is believed to occur through the same intermediate step in the strained reactant-solid product interface.

The most completely studied reaction for which $\beta > 1$ is the thermal decomposition of barium azide. From detailed examination of the energy of nucleation and subsequent growth, it has been concluded that

N

nucleation involves the formation of two F-centres by the decomposition reaction:

$$Ba^{2+} + 2N_3^- \rightarrow Ba + 3N_2$$

the metal being retained in the salt by F-centre generation. The subsequent aggregation of two individual F-centres may yield a stable product nucleus. The detailed steps which occur at the reaction interface during its progression through the reactant have not been fully established.

Photolysis of solids

Radiation may be absorbed by a solid with reversible movements of electrons between the trapping levels of the band structure. An example is exciton formation with subsequent dissipation of this energy as heat. Irreversible transitions may also occur where chemical changes in the solid follow the absorption of radiant energy. Numerous investigations in this field have been concerned with furthering understanding of the photographic processes, but research has also been reported for the decomposition of ionic salts during exposure to radiant energy of various wavelengths from visible to X-radiation.

Photographic processes. The study of photolytic processes in the silver halides has attracted particular attention since the irreversible changes which result from light absorption are used as the basis of photography. The light sensitive area, used as a photographic emulsion is a homogeneous assemblage of small crystallites of halide dispersed on a suitable carrier, transparent to the radiation to be detected. Emulsion preparation and dispersion on the film are carried out in the absence of light. On short exposure of the halide crystallites to illumination, irreversible changes occur in the solid lattice which generate potential nucleus-forming sites where metallic silver crystallites may grow when the halide is subsequently reduced by immersion in a suitable solution (development). The film is washed. The unreduced silver, present in those crystallites in which no nucleus was formed during the exposure to light, is then removed by dissolving in a sodium thiosulphate solution (fixing). The film image is not now damaged on exposure to daylight. After a thorough final washing, the resulting negative provides a record (over the area of the emulsion) of the illumination intensity to which it was exposed prior to development. Those regions which were most highly illuminated possess a high density of crystals bearing nuclei, and, therefore, after development, a large number of silver crystallites; such areas are opaque. Those areas which were not so strongly illuminated remain somewhat more transparent in the developed negative. The developed film represents a negative image of the illumination intensity. Repetition of this process, through exposure to a light source of an emulsion supported on paper masked by the negative, enables a positive print of the original illumination pattern to be obtained.

The irreversible changes which occur during a short exposure to light, conditions used in normal photographic work, represent a nucleation process, and subsequent growth of silver particles, during the development process, is largely confined to those regions where nuclei are present. However, it has been shown that under strong illumination of dry silver halide crystals, silver metal separates and elemental halogen is released. Also, on illumination of a strained silver halide crystal a network of metallic crystallites may be precipitated at those regions of the solid where the silver may be accommodated with the minimum strain energy, i.e. in the grain boundary regions. Photographic representations of the dislocation network and grain boundary structures in silver halide crystals have been obtained in this way.

Photolysis of inorganic solids, azides and oxalates. On exposing barium azide or potassium azide in vacuum to suitable wavelength radiation, decomposition of the salt occurs to yield gaseous nitrogen and product metal crystals. The reaction rate, while the salt is exposed to such radiation, shows some initial variation but thereafter attains a constant value which is very largely independent of product yield and of whether or not the reaction has been interrupted. Common characteristic features observed in the photolytic decomposition of those three salts which have been most completely studied (barium azide, potassium azide and silver oxalate) are: (i) reaction rate is proportional to the square of the illumination intensity (rate $= kI^2$), (ii) quantum yields are low (~ 0.01), (iii) reaction activation energies are low (2–5 kcal mole^{-1}), and (iv) reaction continues for a short time after the radiation source has been removed. Since photoconductivity was not observed during illumination of these salts, it must be concluded that light absorption does not result in promotion of electrons to the conduction band.

Jacobs and Tompkins have developed a quantitative theory which they applied to the photolytic decomposition of potassium azide and of silver oxalate. In this theory it is assumed that the first step in reaction on quantum absorption is exciton formation. Such energetic species then migrate through the lattice and they may be trapped at imperfections. From experimental observations it was concluded that reaction follows such a trapping process at surface anion vacancies. At this trap an F-centre complex is formed in which an electron is associated both with the vacancy and also with a positive hole. When two such excitons are accommodated in a single trap, decomposition occurs to yield (i) product gas, (ii) the trap, and (iii) after successive reactions at the same original trap, a nucleus of metallic product.

Decomposition of solids under X-radiation. Decomposition reactions may also occur when solids are exposed to these more powerful radiation quanta. However, relatively few detailed studies of such reactions have been made. Those results which have been obtained indicate that when a solid is exposed to X-rays the formation of decomposition products may not be confined to reaction at external surfaces. This limitation has been stated or implied to occur in those decomposition reactions described hitherto in the present chapter.

It has been observed that, on exposure to X-rays, potassium perchlorate apparently undergoes little decomposition, as measured by the volume of product gas evolved, during an interval measured in hours, after which the crystals suddenly disrupt energically. This behaviour is attributed to progressive product accumulation within the crystal lattice, and at internal surfaces, until the breaking strain of the reactant solid remaining is exceeded by the compressive force of the products retained within it. This contrasts with the continued product removal which has been mentioned for those reactions in which product formation is confined, or very largely confined, to external reactant surfaces.

Self-heating and explosion

A number of solids, for which the isothermal reaction kinetics have been described above, explode when maintained at somewhat higher reaction temperatures. These substances include lead azide, mercury fulminate and also several perchlorates. The conditions under which low temperature isothermal decomposition reactions are studied are selected so that the rate of heat generation from an exothermic reaction is so low that the departure from isothermal conditions is sufficiently small to be neglected. This is achieved by using a small reactant mass (a few milligrams) decomposed during an interval measured in hours. Reaction may then be considered to proceed at the temperature of the surrounding vessel. Similarly the heat losses in endothermic reactions occurring at a comparable rate may be neglected; endothermic reactions will not be considered further here. In contrast to reactions considered in the present section, it was assumed that in those isothermal decomposition reactions mentioned in previous sections no significant temperature variation occurred.

As the reaction temperature of an exothermic decomposition is increased, the rate of reaction, and thus the rate of heat liberation, is also increased so that the reactant sample may be maintained at a temperature somewhat greater than its surroundings. Such temperature elevation further increases the rate of heat liberation. In any particular decomposition reaction the magnitude of this rise is determined by (i) the reaction temperature, (ii) the Arrhenius parameters of the reaction, i.e. change in reaction rate with temperature, and (iii) the heat conduction of reactant and solid products, the heat of reaction and rate of heat loss from the reactant. Self-heating may influence the apparent reaction rate through (i) temperature variation within the sample due to exothermic reaction, or (ii) explosion; both types of behaviour will be considered.

(i) A decomposing solid in isothermal surroundings may reach a temperature just greater than that of its surroundings; this temperature difference undergoes changes during the course of the reaction. Such equilibrium, or near-equilibrium conditions, may be reflected in changes in reaction kinetics in the initial stages. For example, it has been found that in certain reactions obeying the power law ($\alpha = kt^n$) the apparent value of the index n is increased, for those reactions in which there is self-heating, above that value which is observed in the temperature range where the reaction may be considered isothermal. An equation which has been applied to the heat balance for a small degree of self-heating is

$$M\frac{\mathrm{d}T}{\mathrm{d}t} = A(T_0 - T).$$

This has been applied to reactions in surroundings at temperature T_0 of a substance having mass $\times$ thermal conductivity $= M$, and A is a term giving the product of reactant surface area and the heat transfer coefficient. The function $\mathrm{d}T/\mathrm{d}t$ is dependent on the rate law obeyed by the particular reaction being considered.

(ii) At somewhat higher reaction temperature the greater rate of heat generation during decomposition may result in substantial acceleration of reaction rate. Here the establishment of equilibrium conditions representing balance between heat generated and heat lost, may not be possible and the consequent rapid rise in reaction rate causes an explosion. The form of the α-time plot in which explosion occurs characteristically shows an initial rapid acceleration of reaction rate, followed by the explosion which gives a sudden pressure rise coupled with scattering of reactant solid products from the reaction vessel and sometimes a visible glow. Such behaviour is observed during the mild combustion in exothermic decomposition reactions. Experimental methods capable of more rapid detection of pressure changes than those described above must be used for the investigation of more violent detonations.

The time interval between introduction of a solid to the heated zone and subsequent explosion is known as the *induction period*, $\varkappa$. It has been shown for many systems that $\varkappa$ is related to the isothermal reaction zone temperature by an Arrhenius-type equation:

$$\log \varkappa = A + E/RT.$$

The apparent activation energy (E) for this process may be found from an appropriate plot, but the physical parameters which determine the value of E have not been fully established.

Such explosion induction periods do not necessarily represent the interval required for rapid reaction acceleration caused by self-heating alone, since it has been shown that if lead azide is heated for a short time, removed from the heated zone and later readmitted, the total induction period is very nearly the same as that found for an induction period which has been interrupted with cooling; all measurements for reaction at constant temperature. The time required for the onset of an explosion cannot thus be attributed to self-heating in isolation from other factors. From isothermal studies, it is known that, during nucleation of lead azide, the extent of decomposition is small, hence little self-heating occurs here. The subsequent rapid autocatalytic growth of nuclei, however, leads to the observed explosion.

Several solids, when ignited, burn explosively, setting up a shock wave (which rapidly travels through the solid) within which rapid exothermic reactions occur; such solids are termed detonators. An established detonation front, in such a substance, may be transferred to and proceed in a different explosive (TNT or amatol) at speeds of several thousands of metres $\sec^{-1}$; the combustion of the second explosive occurs at a very much slower rate when it is ignited by means other than the detonation front.

Decomposition with melting.

It has been found that the decomposition of organic solids is sometimes accompanied by superficial melting or the formation of liquid products in which the reactant may be soluble. Simultaneous decomposition may thus occur in both the homogeneous and in the heterogeneous phases, and kinetic equations allowing for the occurrence of both reactions have been developed. For several solids, malonic acid is an example, it has been found that decomposition in the homogeneous phase is faster than that of the solid. Many studies of the thermal decomposition of organic solids have been particularly concerned with those substances which are used as explosives, e.g. aromatic nitro compounds.

2. GAS-SOLID REACTIONS

It has been seen that the kinetic characteristics of the decomposition reactions of single solids are often controlled by the progression of a reactant/product interface through the substance and that the kinetic laws obeyed may be found from consideration of the geometry of the changing interfacial area during the course of the reaction. Somewhat similar behaviour has been observed for many gas-solid reactions, though complicating factors often make the kinetic analysis more difficult. Three general types of reaction will be discussed in this section.

(i) Nucleation and growth of a product phase

The reduction of nickel oxide with hydrogen shows a sigmoid α-time plot, characteristic of nucleation and growth phenomena. Delmon has shown that data for the acceleratory period of reaction fitted the equation:

$$\alpha^{1/4} = kt.$$

This is one form of the power law which has been seen to be applicable to the decomposition of a single solid. Other examples of gas-solid reactions which probably proceed through the nucleation and growth of a product phase, although the kinetic behaviour is more complex, are the reactions of nickel carbide with hydrogen chloride (gas) and with hydrogen sulphide (gas).

(ii) Reaction confined to original reactant surfaces

It is possible that one component of a binary, or more complex, alloy-type solid phase may diffuse to existing crystal surfaces, and there undergo reaction with a gas resulting in its removal from the solid phase. Clearly, such a reaction may occur only in those solids where one constituent is mobile and in which no fundamental change occurs in the character of the solid when it is removed. The reaction

$$Ni_3C + 2H_2 \rightarrow 3Ni + CH_4$$

appears to satisfy these requirements. Reaction is first order in carbon content of the bulk carbide phase and results show no evidence of nucleation and growth phenomena and do not fit the contracting cube equation. It is, therefore, believed that this reaction may be confined to reactant surfaces.

(iii) Formation of a product layer over all surfaces

Many gas-solid reactions proceed at an interface which is initially established over all surfaces of the solid and thereafter penetrates the reactant particles. If the original reactant consists of a set of equal sized cubic crystallites, this may result in obedience to the contracting cube kinetic equation, as described for decomposition processes of single solids above, and reaction is deceleratory throughout. However, where the second reactant is involved, the properties of the product layer must exert some influence on the reaction kinetics. For clarity, such effects will be considered in two stages: (i) the characteristics for reaction at a planar surface where effects due to particle size and shape are neglected and, (ii) the influence of the latter factor will be considered.

Many of the more fundamental studies of interface penetration rate into the solid have been concerned with metal-oxygen or metal-halogen reactions. The laws governing interface penetration rate which have been observed may be classified into four main types, and these are considered in turn:

(i) Linear rate. The product from such a reaction does not provide an effective barrier to further chemical change and rate is independent of product layer thickness. (Fig. 43a). Zero order kinetics are obeyed. Such behaviour is observed for alkali and alkaline earth metal oxidation for which the product oxide volume is less than that of the original metal. Cracks are developed in the product layer which permit continued access of gas to the metal surface and the weight of product (W) is directly proportional to the time during which the metal was exposed to a constant gaseous reactant pressure:

$$W = kt.$$

(ii) Protective film formation. Such reactions provide a direct contrast to those which obey the linear law. A metal may react with a gas to form a coherent, strongly adherent product layer through which the reactants may not pass and further reaction is prevented. The reaction ceases when such a barrier layer has been formed over all the available solid surfaces, Fig. 43(b). At higher temperatures some mobility of one or other reactant in the product layer may become possible and further reaction may be observed.

Chromium and aluminium form strongly adherent product oxide layers which prevent bulk oxidation of the metal. On exposure of a clean aluminium or chromium surface a volume of gas is taken up but reaction rate rapidly decreases due to the barrier layer formation (Fig. 43b).

(iii) *The parabolic rate law.* If an adherent solid product layer, formed over the surfaces of the solid, is penetrated by one of the reactant species,

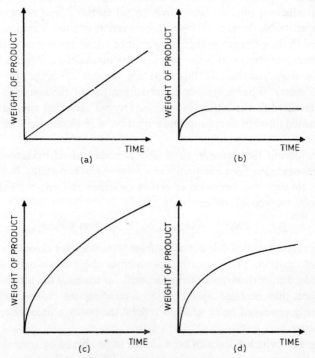

FIG. 43. Characteristic curve shapes showing variation in weight of product with time for gas-solid reactions.

the reaction interface may continue to move into the bulk of the solid while the reactant gas remains in contact with the solid product. The rate of interface movement decreases progressively as reaction proceeds (Fig. 43c), due to increasing difficulty in penetrating the barrier layer of progressively increasing thickness. Several chemical processes, which occur by a mechanism of this type, obey the parabolic rate law:

$$\frac{dz}{dt} = \frac{k}{z}$$

which may be integrated:

$$\Delta z = \frac{2kt}{\Delta z} + Z$$

where z is the thickness of the oxide layer at time t and Z is a constant. The nickel-oxygen reaction, for example, obeys this equation, for the oxidation of nickel metal strips linear Δz against $t/\Delta z$ plots have been obtained.

The adherent product layer covering all surfaces does not provide an impenetrable barrier to contact between reactants. Reaction may proceed in the presence of such a layer since one of the reactant species may enter and move within the product lattice as a defect. Product compounds from reactions of this type are capable of deviations from stoichiometry. Thus a species derived from one of the reactants may migrate through the lattice as an ion. Overall electrical neutrality is maintained through an appropriate migration of an electron or a positive hole.

Considering the example cited above, nickel metal oxidation, the product oxide has been mentioned as a p-type semi-conductor. Reaction occurs through the formation of cation vacancies and positive holes at the oxide/oxygen interface:

$$\tfrac{1}{2}O_2 + 2Ni^{2+} \rightarrow O^= + 2Ni^{3+} + \text{cation vacancy.}$$

This process results from deviation from stoichiometry through excess anion formation. The vacancies generated at the gaseous oxide interface may diffuse throughout the solid, and, on reaching the metal-oxide interface, may be filled by nickel ion formation, the electrons simultaneously produced being used to reduce the positive hole content of the lattice.

The parabolic law has also been shown to be obeyed by several other gas-solid reactions including the oxidation of titanium, of copper and of zirconium, and the reactions of halogens with silver. This law is, however, only applicable when the product layer is relatively thick since a strong electrical field may be developed in the vicinity of the solid reactant/solid product interface. The influence of such a field may extend through a thin product layer, exerting an effect on the movement of electrons and ions which is reflected in deviations from the parabolic law. At greater extent of reaction such a field extends through only a fraction of the product layer thickness and its influence on overall reaction kinetics is relatively smaller. Equations for reaction rate during the interval during which thin layers are present have been developed from investigations of the initial stages of gas-solid reactions, especially the reactions of metals.

(*iv*) *Other rate laws.* Not all gas-solid reactions obey one of the three types of kinetic behaviour discussed above; a number of different complicating factors may arise, two of which are described below.

Multiple phase formation. Oxidation of iron may yield three different solid product phases (FeO, Fe_3O_4, Fe_2O_3). It seems probable that in such systems the migration rate of each of the reaction interfaces conforms to the general principles mentioned above. However, the overall kinetic behaviour observed for a system in which three different chemical reactions may occur, each with a characteristic ease of reactant entity migration, is very much more complex than that found for oxidation to a single product. Fundamental kinetic studies of such reactions are consequently more difficult to interpret.

Another type of deviation from the above kinetic laws results from behaviour intermediate in character between the well-defined processes described above. For example, at temperatures above 350°C zinc oxidation obeys the parabolic law indicating coherent product layer formation. However, the low temperature ($< \sim 225°C$) oxidation of zinc under appropriate conditions has been shown to obey the logarithmic law (Fig. 43*d*). The latter behaviour may result from product layer cracking, a process which tends to facilitate contact between reactants.

Powder reactants

The formulae discussed in the previous section have been concerned with reactions at planar surface and we must now consider the influence of reactant particle size and shape on reaction rate. From a model similar to those made for the 'contracting cube' equation, described on p. 179, and with the additional assumption that a gas-solid reaction may be controlled by rate of gas diffusion through a product layer, Jander derived the equation:

$$[1 - (1 - \alpha)^{1/3}]^2 = kt.$$

This is a 'parabolic law' type reaction of a gas with powder particles, and is a modification of the 'contracting cube' equation.

The derivation of this equation has been criticized by Carter on the following grounds:

(i) The ratio of surface area of partially oxidized crystallites to area of reaction interface progressively changes during reaction and allowance for this has not been made in the Jander treatment.

(ii) The reactant atomic volume and the product molecular volume are not equal (let this ratio $= 1/z$). Accordingly Carter developed the formula:

$$[1 + (z - 1)\alpha]^{2/3} + (z - 1)(1 - \alpha)^{2/3} = z + 2(1 - z)kt/r_0{}^2$$

to include both these influences and he showed that this equation fitted data for oxidation of homogeneous nickel spheres having initial radius r_0 up to a value of α which closely approached 1·00.

Other equations have been reported in the literature; the above example was selected to show the increasing complexity of kinetic equations which results from a more detailed quantitative treatment of the effects which influence reaction rates.

3. LIQUID-SOLID REACTIONS

As a close parallel to surface catalytic processes involving liquid reactants, the course of many solid phase reactions is not strongly influenced by whether the homogeneous reactant is in the liquid or the gaseous state. Low boiling point gaseous reactants may form a physically adsorbed reactant layer at the solid surface. This closely approximates to a thin layer of liquid reactant. However, since, in general, diffusion processes may limit the rate at which a solute may reach a solid surface with which it reacts, such reactions involving the liquid phase may be diffusion-controlled. An example of a solution-solid reaction is the growth or dissolution of crystals and the necessity for equal access of homogeneous solution to all crystal surfaces to obtain well formed crystals has been emphasized. Adequate maintenance of solution homogeneity in the vicinity of the solid must be ensured if meaningful measurements of growth or dissolution rates are to be made.

The principles which control rates of those reactions which occur through interface progression and kinetics of gas-solid reactions have been discussed in preceding sections. The topic mentioned in the present section is included for completeness sake, together with the statement that diffusion phenomena may exert an influence on reaction kinetics.

Reactions which occur during rock crystallization processes in the earth, under pressure, may proceed at a solution/solid interface. Many geologists believe that, even at relatively high temperatures under conditions where the pressure is also high, a thin layer of aqueous solution may be present at the surfaces of the silicate minerals which comprise the reactant assemblage. Nuclei of a new product phase, more stable than the phases present under the high temperature and pressure conditions which obtain during metamorphism, may be formed in the liquid or at the surface of an existing phase. These may grow through reaction of ions from the thin solution layer. The ions thus removed from solution are then replaced by dissolution of less stable phases in the reactant assemblage. It has been found difficult to establish whether or not geochemical recrystallizations occur by such a mechanism. Growth of new phases do occur in rocks and many geologists consider the model outlined above to be a more probable mechanism to the possible alternative mechanism in which ionic reactions proceed as result of migrations within solid lattices.

4. SOLID-SOLID REACTIONS

All those reactions proceeding in the bulk, or restricted to solid surfaces, which have been considered hitherto, involved at least one homogeneous reactant which possessed the property of facile migration to cover all surfaces of the solid reactant. Gases or adsorbed molecules showed lateral surface mobility and may, therefore, migrate to the active chemical reaction interface. Thus at least one reactant in each system could vary its distribution with respect to the geometry of the second, rigid, reactant. However, when chemical reactions occur which involve two solids, and liquefaction does not occur, the progress of chemical change is a complex process which depends on the area and defect structure of the contact areas between the reactant solids *and* the products. Product formation at the interface tends to reduce ease of contact between reactants, and, as with the adherent produce oxide layers described above, reduce reaction rate. The progress of such chemical changes is strongly influenced by two factors: (i) the contact interfacial area. In general, the reaction rate is not dependent on the absolute reactant mass (as it often is in homogeneous reactions) but is controlled by the area of interfacial contact. Two large single crystals touching at a small area may yield, after a fixed time at constant temperature, a smaller total amount of product than that obtained from a smaller mass of compacted fine powder reactant mixture where the contact area is greater. (ii) The ease of diffusion of reactants through a product layer depends upon temperature, defect structure of product layer(s), which act as a barrier between the reactants, grain boundary concentration (to which reactant migration at low temperatures may be confined), presence of impurities and effectiveness of phase boundary contacts. Some of these factors are dependent on the history of the particular solid sample since crystal microstructure may be changed by strain, thermal sintering, etc. Thus reaction rates for a particular chemical change may vary considerably between different reactant samples, which have been subjected to different pretreatments.

In the elucidation of the mechanism of any reaction, the identification of intermediate species is an important object of study. For many solid-solid reactions of interest this is a particularly difficult task since the product phases formed may have different properties from those prepared by different chemical methods due to different concentrations of defects and different crystallite structures. Furthermore, reactant solids are not always pure but many form solid solutions with a product phase. Due to the difficulty in obtaining satisfactory data for reactions of this type, comparatively few detailed mechanistic studies of solid-solid reactions have been undertaken. A systematic account of these somewhat ill-defined systems will not, therefore, be attempted here. But selected examples of those reactions which have been studied will be included to illustrate some of the points mentioned in this general account and to show the type of information which has been obtained from research in this field. The examples are not intended to consider all aspects of solid-solid reactions but rather to illustrate some of the underlying principles.

(*i*) *Solid catalyst for the thermal decomposition of a solid.* Several solid phase thermal decomposition reactions have been shown to be catalysed by transition metal oxides. For example, manganese dioxide changes the mechanism of ammonium perchlorate decomposition through reduction or elimination of the induction period and, for mixtures of loose powder, complete decomposition of the salt may occur at temperatures where reaction only proceeds to $\sim 30\%$ in the absence of additive. Preliminary kinetic measurements, using mixed powder reactants ($NH_4ClO_4 + MnO_2$), gave α-time values which varied between different experiments at a constant temperature, since the solid reactant-catalyst interfacial area was sensitive to the degree of mixing and varied during disintegration which occurred during reaction. Reproducible reaction rates were obtained, however, using compressed (~ 5 tons in^{-2}) pellets containing a large proportion (90%) of oxide, which adhered to form a rigid oxide matrix. This oxide matrix did not disintegrate during reactions; the salt particles were embedded within it.

It was found that the decomposition reaction obeyed the 'contracting area' formula:

$$1 - (1 - \alpha)^{1/2} = kt.$$

This equation is derived from a model similar to that used for the 'contracting cube' except that it is assumed that the contact *area* (salt-catalyst) decreases progressively during reaction. Decomposition occurs at the salt-oxide interface, the latter phase being immobile during reaction. After salt-oxide contact has been effectively reduced to a negligible value, possibly by deactivation of the oxide surface, the remainder of the salt decomposes ($\sim$30% reaction) by the uncatalysed process. This contrasts with complete decomposition observed for powder reactants where mixing of reactant phases is possible.

The activation energy measured for the oxide catalysed reaction was close to 32 kcal mole^{-1}, the value associated with exciton formation in the pure salt. It is concluded that reaction occurs by exciton formation in the pure salt followed by transference of the electron across the salt-oxide contact to a manganese ion which undergoes reduction

$$Mn^{4+} + e^- \longrightarrow Mn^{3+}.$$

The trapped electron is subsequently returned to an ammonium ion but such exciton stabilization, through metal ion reduction, facilitates thermal decomposition. Increasing decomposition reduces interfacial contact between salt and catalyst so that the catalytic process eventually ceases. It is also possible that reaction products may poison or alter the oxide surface irreversibly.

Ferric oxide and other transition metal oxides have also been shown to catalyse ammonium perchlorate decomposition.

(*ii*) *Solid phase oxidation of carbon.* In the above reaction the rate of decomposition was not opposed by the formation of a barrier between the reactants. Such an effect is, however, observed during the solid phase oxidation of carbon by potassium perchlorate where accumulation of product potassium chloride reduces reaction rate. This reaction may be represented:

$$KClO_4 + 2C \rightarrow KCl + 2CO_2$$

and since it occurs $\sim$350°C, which is appreciably lower than the decomposition temperature of potassium perchlorate ($\sim$500°C), carbon must facilitate the decomposition of, or removal of oxygen from, the perchlorate ion. Gaseous oxygen does not appear to be a reaction intermediate and was not reported as a reaction product.

Patai and Hoffmann have made a detailed study of this reaction and emphasize that the rate of chemical processes in a mixture of solids is markedly dependent on the interfacial contact area between the reactants. This area is influenced by the sample history since it may be changed by compaction, wetting, grinding and ageing of the mixture. Strict control of reactant treatment was, therefore, necessary to obtain reproducible kinetic results. From such kinetic data these workers propose an empirical equation which fits their results:

$$\mathrm{d}x/\mathrm{d}t = k(a - x)^{2/3}/x^{1/3}.$$

The reaction is believed to take place at the salt-carbon contact areas, the extent of which varies during reaction. Since carbon particles were smaller than those of salt, this component may be taken as being in excess and the concentration term, a, was that of the initial potassium perchlorate concentration relative to that of carbon. The $(a - x)^{2/3}$ term was included as a measure of the oxidizing salt surface area and the $x^{1/3}$ term associated with the reduction of contact area between reactants resulting from product formation.

(*iii*) *Solid compound formation.* Both above reactions yield gaseous products. When solid products only are formed, studies of the reaction become experimentally very difficult. Often semi-quantitative measurement of product yield from the intensity of X-ray diffraction lines is the most satisfactory method whereby measurement of a particular phase formation can be studied. This method gives low accuracy, particularly for those substances which are formed, with highly defective lattices, i.e. are poorly crystallized, from solid phase reactions.

Several reactions of the type:

$$A + B \rightarrow AB$$

have been studied. Such a reaction can only proceed through the ability of an ion (or molecule) of reactant to migrate through the AB phase. Mobility of a single reactant, say, A, is sufficient and reaction rate depends on (i) the mobility of A in the AB lattice bulk, or (ii) facile diffusion of A, and possibly also B, in the grain boundaries and defective regions of AB. In such reactions, mechanism (ii) is often a very significant contributory process. Tammann has shown that as a general rule defects become mobile close to $0.52 \times$ (melting point of the solid °K). Where solid-solid reactions occur through defect migrations the reactivity of a particular solid often shows a marked increase close to the Tammann temperature of one of the reactant phases.

An example of a reaction of the above type is:

$$2AgI + HgI_2 \rightarrow Ag_2HgI_4.$$

Both silver and mercuric ions are mobile in the product complex salt, and reaction may proceed at both reactant product interfaces. Another example of a reaction of this type is:

$$PbO + PbSiO_3 \rightarrow Pb_2SiO_4$$

where it seems probable that PbO is the migrating entity.

When two solid phases result from reaction, the rate is controlled by the slower diffusion process. Two examples of such reactions are:

$$BaO + PbCl_2 \rightarrow BaCl_2 + PbO$$
$$Cu + AgCl \rightarrow CuCl + Ag.$$

Detailed kinetic measurements for such systems are experimentally very difficult, and research is mainly directed towards establishing the solid phases formed and the species which are able to migrate through them at reaction temperature.

Bibliography

The following books are recommended for further reading; these give more detailed accounts of the topics considered in the present monograph.

CHAPTER ONE

C. A. COULSON, *Valence*, Oxford University Press (2nd ed.), Chapters XI and XII.
R. C. EVANS, *Crystal Chemistry*, Cambridge University Press.

CHAPTER TWO

W. E. ADDISON, *Structural Principles in Inorganic Compounds*, Longmans.
H. E. BUCKLEY, *Crystal Growth*, Wiley.
C. W. BUNN, *Chemical Crystallography*, Oxford University Press.
R. C. EVANS, as above.
J. R. PARTINGTON, *An Advanced Treatise on Physical Chemistry*, Vol. 3: *The Properties of Solids*, Longmans.
F. C. PHILLIPS, *An Introduction to Crystallography*, Longmans.

CHAPTER THREE

W. E. GARNER (Editor), *Chemistry of the Solid State*, Butterworths.
A. L. G. REES, *Chemistry of the Defect Solid State* (Monographs on Chemical Subjects), Methuen.

CHAPTER FOUR

G. C. BOND, *Catalysis by Metals*, Academic Press.
W. E. GARNER, as above.
D. O. HAYWARD and B. M. W. TRAPNELL, *Chemisorption* (2nd ed.), Butterworths.

CHAPTER FIVE

W. E. GARNER, as above.
A. L. G. REES, as above.

Some of the specific reactions mentioned in the text are discussed more fully in the literature references given below.

CHAPTER FOUR

F. COUSSEMANT and J. C. JUNGERS, *Bull. Soc. Chim. Belg.*, **59,** 295 (1950) 'Kinetics of phenol hydrogenation on nickel'.

J. FAHRENFORT, L. L. VAN REYEN and W. M. H. SACHTLER, *Heterogeneous Catalysis*, Ed. de Boer. Amsterdam Symposium, 1960, Elsevier. 'Decomposition of formic acid on metals.'

L. J. E. HOFER, R. B. ANDERSON, and others. *J. Amer. Chem. Soc.*, U.S. Bureau of Mines Reports and other journals. Fischer-Tropsch reactions and chemistry of transition metal carbides.

C. KEMBALL, *Bull. Soc. Chim. Belg.*, **67,** 373 (1958) *Advances in Catalysis*, **11,** 223 (1959) 'Exchange reactions'.

C. KEMBALL, and J. J. ROONEY, *Proc. Royal Society A* **257,** 132 (1960) and **263,** 567 (1961). 'Cracking reactions on silica-alumina catalysts.'

P. W. SELWOOD, *Adsorption and Collective Paramagnetism*, Academic Press. 'Chemisorption on nickel.'

H. S. TAYLOR, and others. Several papers in *J. Amer. Chem. Soc.* 1936–7 and later on metal catalysed hydrocarbon hydrogenolysis.

CHAPTER FIVE

Experimental methods suitable for undergraduate measurements of the kinetics of the potassium permanganate thermal decomposition reaction have been described in *J. Chem. Education* **37** (1960), by A. K. GALWEY, p. 98 and by E. G. PROUT and P. J. HERLEY, p. 643.

Studies of the thermal decomposition of ammonium perchlorate have been reported by L. L. BIRCUMSHAW and B. H. NEWMAN, *Proc. Royal Society* **A227,** 115, 228 (1954–5), and A. K. GALWEY and P. W. M. JACOBS, *ibid.* **254,** 455 (1960), *J. Chem. Soc.* 837 (1959), *Trans. Faraday Soc.* **55,** 1165 (1959). The solid phase oxidation of carbon by potassium perchlorate is reported by E. HOFFMAN and S. PATAI, in *J. Amer. Chem. Soc.* **72,** 5098 (1950) and *J. Chem. Soc.* 1797 (1955).

Index

Index

Where possible the word *solid* has been omitted from the entry.

Acceleratory reaction, 167–9, 172
activated adsorption, 130
activation energy, Arrhenius, 138, 143, 182–4, 188
adsorption, 33, 113, 118–37, 166
  activated, 130
  heat of, 118
  ions from solution, 158–62
  isobars, 131
  isotherms, 121–6
  measurement of, 120–2
  physical, 113
  rate of, 118–19
  at solid-liquid interface, 156–62
  temperature and, 119
  volume, 119
aged crystals, 182, 198
allotropes, 31
angles between crystal faces, 36–7
  measurement, 37
annealing, 95
area of solid surfaces, 112, 124–6, 197
Arrhenius activation energy, 138, 143, 182–4, 188
  equation, 138, 143, 182–4, 187–8
  pre-exponential factor, 143, 182
Avrami-Erofeyev equation, 173–7, 181
axis of symmetry, 38

Band, conduction, 86–9, 135
  energy, 26–7, Chap. 3, 91
    and intermetallic compounds, 110
  theory, 26–7, Chap. 3
  valence, 86–9, 135
bond, chemisorption, 132–7, 144–8, 153–4

co-ordinate, 136–7, 153
covalent, 11–12, 14–15, 20, 24, 67, 74, 133, 136, 153
  energy calculation, 17–18
  hydrogen, 28–9
  ionic, 15–19, 58–65, 67, 71, 78, 136, 153
  metallic, 16, 22, 24–8, Chap. 3
  van der Waals, 6, 12, 20, 70, 75, 98, 113, 137
Born-Haber cycle, 21
Bragg equation for X-ray diffraction, 49–50
Bravis lattice, 48
Brunauer, Emmett and Teller adsorption isotherm, 124–6
Burgers vector, 92–3

Carter equation, 194
catalyst, poison, 137, 153
  industrial, 139–41
  solid, 137–56
catalytic reactions, 139–56
  ammonia synthesis, 149–50
  cracking, 148–9
  exchange, 146–8
  Fischer-Tropsch, 150
  formic acid decomposition, 144–145
  hydrocarbons on metals, 146–9
  industrial, 139–41
  in liquids, 154–6
  mechanisms, 138–56
  on semi-conductors, 150–1
  solid-solid, 196–7
  steps in, 141
cell, unit, 45–8
centre of symmetry, 38
chain reaction, 176

charge on colloidal particles, 158–161

chemisorption, 113, 126–37, 142–143
  bond, 132–7, 144–8, 153–4
  heats of, 131–2
  kinetics of, 130–1
  on metals, 127–9
  on semi-conductors, 135–6
  surface mobility and, 137

chromatography, 157–8

classification of solids, 4–5

clay minerals, 71–2

cleavage planes, 31

climb, 94–5

charge on colloidal particles, 158–61

coefficient of expansion, X-ray measurement, 56

colour centre, 102

compensation law, 143

conducting solid, 9, 14, 16, 22, 83, 86–9, 135

constant shape of crystals, 30

contracting area formula, 196
  cube formula, 179, 190, 193, 197

co-ordinate bond, 136, 153

co-ordination number, 60–3

covalent bond, 11–12, 14–15, 20, 24, 67, 74, 133, 136, 153
  crystal, 5, 9–16, 67–81, 90

cracking reactions, catalytic, 148–9, 151–2

cracking of solid product phase, 193

crystals, angles between faces, 36–37
  constancy of shape, 30
  covalent, 5, 9–16, 67–81, 90
  edges, 83
  entropy and defects, 97
  growth, 33–6, 94
  index of faces, 43–5
  ionic, 5, 15–22, 30, 32, 58, 68, 90, 104, 113, 158–9
  lattice, caesium chloride, 62
    diamond, 10
    fluorite, 63–4
    graphite, 12–14
    metallic, 22–4

metals, 22–3
molecular, 5–9, 17, 90
nickel oxide, 53–4
rutile, 63–4
silicates, 66–73
sodium chloride, 18, 46–7, 57
metallic, 5, 16, 22–8, 91, 113, 126–9, 132
orientation, measurement by X-rays, 55–6
size determination, using X-rays, 55–6, 117
systems, 39–41

crystallite size, effect on reaction rate, 180

crystallization, water of, 65–6

cubic crystals, 41

Deceleratory reactions, 130–1, 167–169, 179–82, 191–4

decomposition reactions, 166–89
  with melting, 188–9

defect, lattice, 83, 92, 95–8
  and crystal entropy, 97
  Frenkel, 96–8
  Schottky, 95–7, 99, 104

defective regions of lattice, 83, 92, 95–8, 164, 173, 185

dendrites, 33

density of solids, pore investigation, 117

detonation, 188

diffraction. See X-rays

diffusion, 98–9, 141, 192, 194–5
  in liquids, 154

dipole, 6

dislocation, 83, 91–5
  edge, 92–3
  screw, 93–4
  properties of, 93–5

dispersion forces. See van der Waals bonding

Edge dislocation, 92–3

electrical conduction in solids, 9, 14, 16, 22, 83, 86–9, 98–100, 102–4

electrode processes, 161–2

electron-atom ratio, intermetallic compounds, 109
'electron gas', 25, 84
electron microscope, 114–15
Eley-Rideal mechanism of catalytic reactions, 139, 153
Elovich equation, 131
enantiomorphism, 38–9
energy bands, 26–7, Chap. 3
energy band measurement, 91
epitaxial growth, 34
etch pits, 39
evaporated metal films, 128
exchange reactions, catalytic, 146–8
exciton, 91, 183–4
explosion, 186–8

F-centre, 101–2, 184, 186
face, unit, 41, 45
Fajans-Paneth rule, 159
Fermi level, 86
field emission microscope, 116, 128
    and surface mobility, 137
field ion microscope, 117
first order kinetics, 171, 179–80
flashed filaments, 127–8
fluidized bed, 140
Frenkel defect, 96–8
Freundlich adsorption isotherm, 124, 156

Gas-solid reactions, 189–94
    chromatography, 157
gaseous state, 3
germ nuclei, 168
glass, 3, 80–1, 166
glide, 94
Goldschmidt co-ordination number, 60–3
goniometer, 37
grain boundaries, 92, 99, 112, 164, 185, 195
growth, crystal, 33–6
    epitaxial, 34
    product nuclei, 163, 165, 168–75, 179, 184, 189, 194

Habit, 31
Hall effect, 105–6
heat of adsorption, 118, 131–2
    of sublimation, 7–8
hexagonal lattice, 41
hour-glass effect, 33
Hume-Rothery rule, 109
hydrogen bond, 28–9

Infrared spectra of adsorbed species, 119, 134
imperfect regions in crystal lattices, 83, 92, 95–8, 164, 173, 185
impurities in crystals, 83, 101, 104–106, 128, 195
index, crystal face, 41–5, 49
    planes, 51–4
induction effect, 6
    period, 167, 188
industrial catalysts, 139–41, 149, 152
initial deceleratory reaction, 182
insulating solid, 86–9
interface, reactant-product, 163, 169–71, 179, 184, 189, 194
interferometer, multiple beam, 115
intermetallic compounds, 109–10
interstitial positions, 96–8
    compounds, 107–9
inversion symmetry, 38
ions, relative numbers, 17, 63
    sizes, 17, 60–3
ionic bond, 15–19, 58–65, 67, 71, 78, 136, 153
    crystals, 5, 15–22, 30, 32, 58, 68, 90, 104, 113, 158–9
    radius, 58–60
    radius ratio, 60–3
    shape, 17, 58–60
isomorphism, 66
isobar, adsorption, 131
isotherm, adsorption B.E.T., 124–6
    Freundlich, 124, 156
    Langmuir, 123–4
    Temkin, 123

Jander equation, 193

Kinetics, solid phase reactions, Chap. 5
  first order, 171, 179–80
  of photolysis, 185–6

Langmuir-Hinshelwood reaction mechanism, 138–9
Langmuir isotherm, 123–4
lattice. See also Crystal lattice
  Bravis, 48
  definition, 4
  energy, 19–20
  imperfections, 83, 92, 95–8, 164, 173, 185
  impurities, 83, 101, 104–6, 128, 195
  parameter measurement (X-rays), 52–5
  planes, 45–50, 171
  structure determination, 50–4
lattice structures, cubic, hexagonal, orthorhombic, monoclinic, tetragonal, triclinic, trigonal, 41
lattice vibrations, 4, 20, 83, 182
Laüe, X-ray method, 56
layer of adsorbed ions, 158, 161–2
level, Fermi, 86
linear rate of reaction, 190
liquid, 3–4
  catalysis in, 154
  crystal, 3, 79
  diffusion in, 154
  -gas chromatography, 157–8
  -solid interface, 156–62, 194–5
lyophobic colloids, 158–9

Madelung constant, 19–20
magnification of crystal surfaces, 114–17
melting, 8, 11, 21
  decomposition and, 188
metallic bond, 16, 22, 24–8
  crystals, 5, 16, 22–8, 91, 113, 126–9, 132
microscopes, 114–16, 128

Miller indices, 44–5, 49
minerals, clay, 71–2
molecular crystals, 5–9, 17, 90
molecular orbital theory (applied to solids), 25–6, 88–91
monoclinic lattice, 41

n-type semi-conductivity, 102–3, 105–6
non-stoichiometry, 101–4
nucleation, 163, 169–71, 173–5, 179, 183–4, 189, 194
nuclei, germ, 168
  growth of, 163, 165, 168, 170–5, 179, 184, 189, 194
  overlap of, 172–3
number of nearest neighbours in lattice, 8, 11, 17, 22, 24, 60–5

Optical microscope, 114
order–disorder transition, 107
organic polymers, 74–8
  linear, 75–7
  three-dimensional, 77–8
  natural, 78
orientation of crystals, 55–6
orthorhombic lattice, 41
outgas, 125, 166

p-type semi-conductors, 103–6
parabolic rate law, 191–3
period, induction, 167, 188
photoconductivity, 90, 185
photographic process, 184–5
photolysis, 184–6
physical adsorption, 113, 118–20, 124–6
physical properties of solids, 8–25
  covalent crystals, 11, 14–15
  ionic crystals, 15, 20–2
  metals, 22
  molecular crystals, 8
piezoelectricity, 39
plane, cleavage, 31
  lattice, 45–50, 171
  of symmetry, 38

planar surfaces of crystals, 30
platforming catalysts, 152
point groups, 48
poisons, catalyst, 137, 153
Polanyi-Wigner equation, 182
polymers. See Organic polymers
pores in solids, 117, 125-6
porosimeter, pressure, 117
positive hole, 103-4, 186
powder reactants, 193
power law, 172, 187, 189
precursor states, 130
probability, sticking, 130
product-reactant interface, 163, 169-71, 179, 184, 189, 194
product solid, cracking of, 190, 193
product adsorption, in catalytic reaction, 155
protective film, 190
Prout-Tompkins equation, 176-9, 181
pyroelectricity, 39

Qualitative analysis by X-rays, 54-5

Radius, ionic, 58-60
radius ratio, ionic, 60-3
rational indices, law of, 41-5
reactant-product interface, 163, 169-71, 179, 184, 189, 194
reaction, chain, 176
  catalytic, 144-53
reaction rate, acceleratory, 167-9, 172
  deceleratory, 130-1, 167-9, 179-182, 191-4
reaction rate, initial deceleratory, 182
  linear, 190
  parabolic, 191-3
reactive solid surfaces, 126-9
reactivity of solids, 164-5
  solid surfaces, 119-21, 126-37
reference axes for crystals, 39-45
rhombic lattice, 41
rule, 8-N, 15, 27
  Hume-Rothery, 109

Schottky defect, 95-7, 99, 104
screw dislocation, 93-4
self-heating, 186-8
semi-conductors, 88-9, 102-6, 192
  as catalysts, 150-1
  chemisorption on, 135-6
  n-type, 102-3, 105-6
  p-type, 103-6
'semi-solid' states of matter, 78-81
shape, crystals, 30
  ionic, 17, 58-60
silicates, principles of classification, 15, 67-8
silicates, clays, 71-2
  chain, 69-70
  ionic, 68, 70
  sheet, 69-71
  three-dimensional, 72-3
sintering, 165
solid-gas, chromatography, 157
  interface, adsorption at, 118-37
  reactions, 189-94
solid-liquid interface, adsorption at, 156-62
  reactions, 194-5
solid-solid reactions, 195-9
solid solutions, 66, 106-10
space lattice, 48
specific heat of solids, 84
spherical ions, 58-60
states of matter, 3-4
states, precursor, 130
sticking probability, 130
structure of solid substances, 58-78
superlattice, 107
surfaces of solids, Chap. 4
  area, 112, 124-6, 164
  energy, 113-14
surface, examination of, 113-17
  nucleation, 170
  reactivity, 119-21, 126-37
  step, 114
symmetry, axis of, 38
  centre of, 38
  inversion, 38
  plane of, 38
  and point groups, 48

Tammann temperature, 198
tetragonal lattice, 41
topography of surfaces, 114
transition, order – disorder, 107
transport numbers in solids, 98–9
triclinic lattice, 41
trigonal lattice, 41

Ultramarine, 73
ultra-violet absorption, 91,102
unit cell, 45–8
  face, 41, 45

Valence bond theory applied to
  solids, 27–8, 89–91
  band, 86–9
van der Waals forces, 6, 12, 20, 70,
  75, 98, 113, 118, 137
vector, Burgers, 92–3
vibrations, lattice, 4, 20, 83, 182
vitreous state, 3, 80–1

Water of crystallization, 65–6

X-rays and Bragg equation, 49–50
  complex molecule investigation,
    57
  crystal size determination, 55–6,
    117
  decomposition of solids, 183,
    186
  diffraction by crystals, 49–57,
    85
  glass, 79
  Laüe method, 56
  liquid crystals, 79
  orientation of crystal determina-
    tion, 55–6
  qualitative analysis, 54–5
  scattering, 20, 55–7

Zeolites, 75
zeta potential, 159–62